WAFFEN-SS 1

Right: What the well-dressed Waffen-SS Panzergrenadier wore while digging on the Eastern Front in April 1944. He has a camouflaged helmet cover, camouflaged battledress, belt with M36 buckle, two triple sets of Model 1911 rifle ammunition pouches, from which two *Eiergranaten 39* hand grenades are suspended, and an S84/98 bayonet at his side. *All photographs in this book — unless specifically credited otherwise — are provided from the Brian L. Davis collection*

WAFFEN-SS 1

Michael Sharpe and
Brian L. Davis

CHARTWELL
BOOKS, INC.

This edition published by 2007 by

CHARTWELL BOOKS, INC.
A Division of
BOOK SALES, INC.
114 Northfield Avenue
Edison, New Jersey 08837

ISBN 10: 0-7858-2323-9
ISBN 13: 978-0-7858-2323-0

© 2007 Compendium Publishing Ltd, 43 Frith
Street, London, W1D 4SA
Previously published in the Spearhead series

Cataloging-in-Publication data is available from
the Library of Congress

Printed in China through Printworks Int. Ltd

Acknowledgements
All photographs in the Leibstandarte section of this
book came from the collection of Brian L. Davis,
with the exception of those on pages 67 inset (Wade
Krawczyk), 67 main (Peter Amodio); 70 and 71 inset
(Peter V. Lukacs WW2 Militaria AB); 71 main (Wade
Krawczyk); 74 (Wade Krawczyk); 75 (Peter V. Lukacs
WW2 Militaria AB); 78 and 79 (Wade Krawczyk).
    All black and white photos in the Das Reich
section of this book were provided by Brian L. Davis,
while the colour reenactment photos were provided
by WW2 Living History Group, SS/Pz. Gren. Regt. 3
Deutschland, 9/Kompanie, New England, USA.

Right: A reenactor showing off the uniform of a
Leibstandarte Panzergrenadier in front of a Russian
T-34 tank. *Peter Amodio*

CONTENTS

LEIBSTANDARTE
Hitler's Elite Bodyguard

ORIGINS & HISTORY

The 1st SS-Panzer Division *Leibstandarte*-SS Adolf Hitler was the first armed SS formation and, by most measures, the most capable. Based from the early 1930s at Lichterfelde Kaserne (barracks), Berlin, its troops were the standard-bearers of the fledgling SS, although initially they were referred to contemptuously by army regulars as the 'asphalt soldiers' for their obsessive spit and polish drill and purely ceremonial duties. After the campaigns in Poland and France, contempt gave way to genuine respect as *Leibstandarte* earned its reputation as a combat unit, which lived, as one *Leibstandarte* captain later reflected, for the 'sheer beauty of the fighting'.

EARLY HISTORY

The history of the *Leibstandarte* is inextricably tied to that of the Waffen-SS, the military wing of the *Schutzstaffel* (SS). Its early origins, therefore, lay in the men who provided protection for the leaders of the fledgling *Nationalsozialistische Deutsche Arbeiterpartei* — the National Socialist German Workers' Party, or Nazis — in the often violent political scene of Germany of the 1920s and 1930s . These bodyguards were first drawn from the party's Sports and Gymnastics Section, which later grew into the Sturmabteilung (SA) under the leadership of Ernst Röhm.

The year 1923 saw the formation of the *Stabswache* (Headquarters Guard), a rather grandiose title for what was, in reality, just two men acting as bodyguards to Hitler. The creation of this unit, the first such body dedicated to the personal protection of the Führer, was motivated by Hitler's growing mistrust of the SA, the ranks of which were filled with former Freikorps volunteers and members of the Brigade Ehrhardt, a right-wing organisation whose eponymous leader was openly contemptuous of Hitler. Hitler's fears were soon confirmed when Ehrhardt withdrew his men from the SA, and the Stabswache was disbanded. Realising that he needed to exercise greater control over the SA, Hitler appointed his trusted comrade Göring to lead it, but despite Göring's success in restructuring the unit

Below: The newly formed '*Stosstrupp* Hitler', the Adolf Hitler Shock Troop, leaving for the German Day (*Deutscher Tag*) held in Bayreuth on 2 September 1923. These early German Day gatherings were the precursors of the huge Nuremberg *Parteitagen* (Party Days), the largest of which was that held on 5–12 September 1938.

the gulf between the SA and party leadership continued to grow. Subsequently, the *Stosstrupp* (Shock Troop) Adolf Hitler was formed from men whose personal loyalty to Hitler was beyond question. Among its members was Josef 'Sepp' Dietrich, the most famous of *Leibstandarte* commanders, and Rudolf Hess, who rose to be Deputy Leader of the Nazi Party.

In November, along with the numerically superior SA, the *Stosstrupp* participated in the failed Munich Beer Hall Putsch, the NSDAP's ill-conceived and semi-farcical attempt to wrest control of Germany by coup d-état. At least 12 *Stosstrupp* members were shot down and killed around the Nazi leaders as they marched at the head of an army of rebels. While Hitler languished in Landsberg prison for his part in the coup, the various factions of the now-outlawed and leaderless party became divided. The SA, also banned by law, was reorganised by Ernst Röhm into the *Frontbann*, and by the time that Hitler was released, it boasted some 30,000 members. Such visible growth in Röhm's power concerned Hitler greatly, and he was soon in dispute with the Röhm and the *Frontbann*, members of which had begun to openly criticise Hitler's leadership.

Above: Berlin, 30 January 1938. To mark the fifth anniversary of the National Socialists coming to power, a parade was held in front of the Reich Chancellery in the Wilhelmstrasse, Berlin. Here a contingent of the *Leibstandarte*-SS marches past Hitler, who is accompanied by — from left to right — Rudolf Hess, Deputy Leader; Sepp Dietrich, commander of the LSSAH; and Reichsführer-SS Heinrich Himmler.

CREATION OF THE SS

Hitler reacted by removing Röhm in April 1925 and that same month created the SS as a kind of praetorian guard. Initially this was comprised of only eight men, all of whom had demonstrated unswerving loyalty to Hitler. SS units, each of ten sober, healthy men with untainted criminal records, were subsequently raised in other districts, but as a gesture to the still-powerful SA they were placed under its control. The SA resented the elitism of the SS and in turn the SS was embittered by the offhand treatment it received at the hands of its SA overlords. It was also frustrated by the

Above: The *Leibstandarte*-SS Adolf Hitler marches through the streets of Nuremberg led by its commanding officer, Sepp Dietrich, during the 1935 *Reichsparteitag*.

ORGANISATION OF LEIBSTANDARTE-SS ADOLF HITLER REGIMENT AS OF OCTOBER 1934

Stab (HQ) with Sig Pl and Band
3 x *Sturmbanne* (mot)
   each of 3 x *Stürme* (mot),
   1 x Sig Pl and 1 x MG-*Stürme*
   (mot)
1 x MC *Sturm*
1 x Mortar *Sturm* (mot)
1 x Recce Pl

Note: *Sturmbann*—Storm Battalion—is the name given to SA units in the early years of Nazism. The word *Sturmbann* would disappear in unit terms but continue to be used in SS ranks such as *Sturmbannführer* (see list on page 4).

restrictions on its numbers, while the SA, which was willing to accept almost any man, continued to expand. Control of the SS passed through the hands of two leaders in quick succession, neither of them able to stand up to the bullying of the SA. Morale among the membership declined, and with the arrival of the a new leader, Heinrich Himmler, in 1929, the SS seemed condemned to a history of mediocrity.

Few had reckoned on the relentless ambition and drive that Himmler would bring to the role of leader of the SS. His meek appearance and mild manner were interpreted as weaknesses by his party peers, but his participation in the abortive Munich putsch, fanatical devotion to the cause and loyalty to Hitler were well known. Thus this one-time chicken farmer, industrial chemist and homeopathy enthusiast became leader of the SS, and set about turning it into a unit that would rival and eventually supplant the SA as the military wing of the Nazi party.

The SS that Himmler took over had barely 280 members. He determined to expand it according to his own politico-eugenic theories, which had imbued in him a belief in the racial superiority of the Germanic race, and a desire to foster a nation of racially pure supermen, with the SS at its head. He persuaded Hitler to allow him to introduce tough membership rules, by which new members had to prove their family lineage extending back for three generations. Undesirables were ejected and discipline tightened. SS numbers grew slowly, reaching 1,000 by the end of 1929, as more and more recruits began to favour the disciplined elite status of the SS over the rowdy, loutish and drunken SA. At the end of 1930, SS membership stood at 3,000, and Himmler had successfully wrested control of the unit from the SA.

The SA had become a major problem for Hitler by this time. It had grown out of control, while the party itself had split into rival factions. The inevitable confrontation broke out in mid-1930, when the SA deputy commander demanded that Hitler reduce party interference in SA affairs. Hitler refused, brought back Ernst Röhm to replace the SA commander, Ernst von Salomon, and demanded that SA members swear an oath of allegiance to him. They refused, and by the new year the air was again thick with rumours of a plot against the leader, but when the SA attempted to take over the party in April 1931 the rank and file remained loyal to Hitler and the rebellion melted away.

SS strength rose dramatically that year, and on the eve of the elections that swept Hitler to power he could count on some 30,000 men. In March 1933, a select band of these were chosen by Oberstgruppenführer Sepp Dietrich to form the SS-*Stabswache* Berlin, the progenitor of the *Leibstandarte*, a Praetorian guard responsible for protecting Hitler.

Dietrich, a fellow Bavarian and trusted party comrade of Hitler's, created the *Stabswache* with 120 hand-picked men who were paragons of the SS ideal: 25 years old, 1.8 metres tall, and with no criminal record. On 17 March, the first unit muster was held at the Alexander Kaserne in Friedrichstrasse. In April it transferred to Lichterfelde Kaserne, Berlin, where it was retitled SS-*Sonderkommando* Berlin and a 12-man guard under Wilhelm Mohnke was posted to the Reich Chancellery. Its first published appearance as an honour guard for the Führer came during an SA rally at the Berlin Sports Palace on 8 April. The following month a special training unit, SS-*Sonderkommando* Zossen, was raised from three companies of troops to support the bodyguard unit. Initially, the duties of the SS-*Sonderkommando* Berlin were almost purely ceremonial. It mounted a 24-hour guard outside the Reich Chancellery and the Führer's residence in the Wilhelmstrasse. A very select group, known as the *Führerbegleitkommando* (Führer escort commando) served as Hitler's personal staff — waiters, valets, drivers and the like. Whenever he appeared in public in his famous open Mercedes, he was flanked by *Leibstandarte* troops.

A further name change came in July, when SS-*Stabswache* Berlin was renamed SS-*Sonderkommando* Jüterbog. During that summer a detachment of the FBK under Theodor 'Teddy' Wisch stood guard for the first time at Hitler's summer retreat near Berchtesgaden.

The final act of this period of reorganisation came in September 1933, when SS-*Sonderkommando* Jüterbog and SS-*Sonderkommando* Zossen combined as the Adolf Hitler *Standarte*. At Hitler's suggestion this was changed to *Leibstandarte* Adolf Hitler, a name redolent of the old Imperial Bavarian Life Guards. The name was enshrined at the September *Parteitag* rally, for which the *Leibstandarte*, turned out in the striking jet-black SS uniform, provided the honour guard. Another significant event was the official swearing in of the men at a ceremony on 9 November to mark the tenth anniversary of the Beer Hall Putsch. It was held at the Feldherrnhalle War Memorial, in Munich's Odeonplatz. The highlights of the ceremony, full of pomp and pageantry, were a recantation by torchlight of the SS oath of allegiance to the Führer by some 835 LAH members, and the presentation of the first regimental colours.

Such spectacles, and the presence of its troops outside the Chancellery, Berlin's three airports, various ministries (including SS headquarters), as well as the private homes of the Führer and Reichsführer-SS Heinrich Himmler, had helped the *Leibstandarte* Adolf Hitler (the 'SS' was inserted later) quickly to gain for itself a very public profile. Its role would soon extend, however, into the darker corners of the Nazi regime.

Above: Adolf Hitler, chancellor since 30 January 1933, addresses a political meeting held in the Berlin Sports Palace on 8 April of that year. This photograph shows the meeting being guarded by full-time armed and steel-helmeted members of the newly formed SS-*Stabswache* Berlin. Six months later, by then named the SS-*Sonderkommando* Jüterbog, the unit was once more retitled, this time at the 1933 Nuremberg *Parteitag* Rally, becoming the Adolf Hitler *Standarte*.

NIGHT OF THE LONG KNIVES

The threat posed by the half-million SA members to Hitler's dominance emerged again in early 1934. Its leadership and many of the rank and file had become disillusioned with the Nazi party, which they felt had become too much a part of the establishment that the socialist-orientated SA sought to overthrow. When Röhm expressed these reservations in a speech in February 1934 and demanded a greater role for the SA in Germany's future, Hitler moved quickly.

On 30 June, the so-called 'Night of the Long Knives', Hitler, Dietrich and a six-man LAH escort travelled to Bad Wiesee, where a conference of senior SA officers was to take place, with. They arrested Ernst Röhm and other SA leaders, taking them to Stadelheim prison where they were executed by an LAH firing squad. In Berlin, LAH units were even more active, arresting more SA men and other political enemies whom the Nazis wanted eliminated. It is difficult to be precise about the number killed by firing squad: the figure was well over 100. The decapitated SA was disarmed and the power of the organisation faded rapidly. SS fortunes, by contrast, were very much in the ascendant.

READY FOR WAR

Below: Reichsführer der SS Heinrich Himmler (1900–45) was a ruthless, fanatical Nazi whom Hitler made head of the SS on 6 January 1929. When he took command the SS numbered 300 men: by 1933 its membership was 50,000. In 1939 Hitler made him Reichs Commissar for the Consolidation of German Nationhood — and Himmler responded by finding ever more means of exterminating 'racial degenerates'. He became Minister of the Interior on 25 August 1943. On 21 July 1944 he took control of the Volkssturm but in the final days of the Reich his influence with Hitler faltered, particularly after his attempt to capitulate to the Allies using Swedish diplomatist Count Bernadotte as an intermediary. Captured by British troops northeast of Bremen, he committed suicide on 23 May 1945.

In the mid-1930s the military forces of the Third Reich were expanded to ready them for Hitler's campaigns of conquest. Under this expansion both the army and the SS dramatically increased their strength, and by September 1939 the German armed forces were certainly the most disciplined, highly trained and best equipped in the world.

From the outset Himmler had desired a separate armed force for the SS, and he pushed and won approval for the creation of separate paramilitary units under the jurisdiction of the SS. Of course, there already existed two armed units — the *Leibstandarte* was one; the other were the *Totenkopfverbände* (Death's Head units) that guarded the concentration camps — the first three, set up in 1933 were Dachau, Buchenwald and Sachsenhausen — purpose-built to detain those accused of political and ideological crimes against the Reich. With the downfall of the SA in 1934 the SS took over camp administration. The *Totenkopfverbände* were subsequently reorganised by Theodor Eicke and would go on to form the core of the *Totenkopf* division.

However, Himmler had greater ambitions for the men that he had preached in 1931 would be the 'Gods of the new Germany'. On 16 March 1935, Hitler announced the formation of the SS-*Verfügungstruppen* (special purpose troops). The SS-VT was created by amalgamating established SS-*Politische Bereitschaften* (political readiness squads) into three regiments each with engineer and signals battalions. These formed the core of what became in 1940 the Waffen-SS, or armed SS. For administrative purposes, the *Leibstandarte* was considered to be part of this body, and although it was often preoccupied with ceremonial duties, received much of its early military training from SS-VT troops.

The SS-VT was distinct from other arms of the SS, although the two organisations mingled. It was expected to be a military organisation completely obedient and loyal to its master, Adolf Hitler, but its purpose was never entirely clear, since national defence was already in the hands of the Wehrmacht. Himmler and Hitler never came up with a satisfactory answer, usually referring to the SS-VT as a *Weltanschauliche Truppen* or 'political soldiers' that served Hitler directly as 'the spearhead of National Socialism'. In reality, its purpose was to carry out whatever task Hitler and Himmler demanded; its existence became Himmler's justification for the continued growth of the SS.

In mid-1934 the *Leibstandarte* added SS to its official name, the abbreviation changing to LSSAH. Correspondingly its duties were expanded and the unit was reorganised along military lines. Between October and December 1934, it re-equipped as a motorised unit and by the end of November it consisted of three battalions, a motorcycle company, a mortar company, an armoured car platoon and a signals platoon. In addition it maintained a band. At the time of the reoccupation

of the Saarland in February 1935, the *Leibstandarte* had a strength of around 2,500 men, or a quarter of the SS total. On Hitler's triumphant motorised parade into Saarbrücken, LSSAH provided the escort, much to the chagrin of the Wehrmacht, and on 1 March it was again in the spotlight at the head of the forces reoccupying the Rhineland.

Hostilities between the conservative, rigidly class-conscious regular army — *das Heer* — and the upstart armed SS formations reached a new height in 1935, and although Hitler was quick to play down the independent military role of the SS for fear of ostracising the army, the antagonism continued. Within the confines of the SS, *Leibstandarte* commander Sepp Dietrich's personal relationship with Himmler, who could intimidate most of his subordinates, was also less than cordial, and the two were frequently at odds.

The Waffen-SS and the Wehrmacht differed in many, many respects — political motivation, allegiance and structure among them. Less obviously, SS men were from predominantly rural backgrounds and had received less schooling than their Wehrmacht counterparts, although they had to conform to higher physical standards. *Leibstandarte* entry requirements were particularly stringent; in fact, before regulations were relaxed men were routinely rejected for having just a single tooth filled! Rapid expansion of the army to 35 divisions after 1936 forced the army to lower certain conditions of recruitment, and in turn it limited the number of conscripts it would allow to join the SS.

Hitler's territorial ambitions had been far from satisfied by the reoccupation of former German territories in 1935, and he viewed it as the birthright of the German people to expand further, occupying 'Lebensraum' populated by 'lesser' races. Such expansion clearly required a strong military force, which Hitler began slowly building since 1933. The expansion of all branches of the military, in flagrant disregard for the Versailles Treaty that outlawed any such expansion, included the SS. Under Reichsführer-

Above: Members of the SS-VT inspect the result of their musketry practice. Note the SS runes on the sides of their Model 1916 helmets. The old Model 1916 was used until the end of the war — albeit mainly by Volkssturm personnel — despite being replaced on 1 July 1935 by a lighter, redesigned issue.

Above: An SdKfz 7 halftrack is put through its paces. The SdKfz 7 was the most numerous German halftrack — 12,000 units were built between 1938 and 1944 — that was mainly used as artillery prime mover, with an eight-ton haulage capacity. Variants carried quad 20mm or single 37mm Flak guns. 1944.

SS Himmler this was growing into a vast self-contained political apparatus — the shining star of the Nazi regime — with interests that extended into economic, military and social spheres.

The SS-VT, the military wing, had emerged with great prestige from the occupation of the Saarland, but its precise role in any future conflict was somewhat muddled, and despite the undoubtedly high physical qualities of its soldiers, it lacked combat experience. The first problem stemmed from the fact that, although it had ostensibly been established as a 'permanent armed force at (Hitler's) disposal', he had also publicly stated on numerous occasions that the SS-VT would, in time of war, be attached to the regular army and fight as soldiers under its command in defence of Germany. Thus its role appeared to overlap with that of the Wehrmacht, which resented any such intrusion on its territory. Privately, Hitler expressed his feelings that it was necessary for the SS to prove itself in combat, in order to secure the confidence and respect of the population.

So to Himmler he entrusted the recruiting and training — both military and ideological — of the SS-VT, and in 1936 he appointed an experienced former Wehrmacht officer, Paul Hausser, to the Inspectorate of the SS-VT. With his subordinates Felix Steiner and Cassius Freiherr von Montigny, Hausser devised a tough and thorough training programme for the SS-VT regiments, involving weapons and unarmed combat training, and particular emphasis was placed on physical training. Exercises were frequently conducted using live ammunition. Additionally, the SS soldier was subjected to frequent lectures on Nazi politics, racial superiority and the like. The same programme was adapted to the *Leibstandarte*, which conducted its training at the grandiose Lichterfelde barracks,

Right: Hitler on a tour of inspection of the SS barracks, Christmas 1935. Hitler is seen with Dietrich inspecting the contents of a young soldier's locker.

although it already had a busy ceremonial schedule to fulfil.

One such public duty for the *Leibstandarte* was the honour guard for the 1936 Winter Olympics, a role it repeated at the Summer Olympics in Berlin. Both events were heralded as a showcase for the 'miracle' of National Socialism, but Hitler's true intentions for the Germany were at that very moment being played out behind closed doors.

He had since 1933 been courting Austrian voters and expressing his desire to unite the countries under one leader. He had already, in 1934, backed a failed coup d'état by the Austrian Nazi Party to overthrow the government. In the aftermath hundreds of Nazi were jailed, but were soon released to begin scheming once more. Hitler continued the pressure on the national government through sympathisers in the Austrian assembly, and in 1938, the final year of peace under the Third Reich, he began another phase of expansion that ultimately led to war, brief glory and, after six long years, defeat.

For the March occupation of Austria — the Anschluss — the *Leibstandarte* was under General Heinz Guderian's XVI Army Corps, and provided an escort for Hitler as he rode in triumph to the Austrian capital. Here it stayed until April under the command of 2nd Panzer Division, and then returned to Berlin.

In April Hitler ordered planning to begin for *Fall Grün* (Operation Green), the occupation of the Sudetenland, a mountainous area between Bohemia and Silesia where 3.25 million Germans were living under Czech rule. At the end of September, after manoeuvring around the British and French at Munich, Hitler was able to occupy the Sudetenland. For the operation, *Leibstandarte* was again attached to the XVIth Army Corps and it was achieved without incident. Further appeased, he bullied and cajoled the Czech government to renounce the country's independence and accept status as a German protectorate. When they agreed, Hitler moved quickly and in mid-March 1939 sent troops in to occupy the remaining Czechoslovak territories. This, too, was achieved without incident, but the increasingly active role of the SS (all three SS regiments took part in the Czech operations), and the fact that they were now wearing the same field grey uniforms as the army, did not please the OKW.

A month later there was a return to official duties when Hitler opened the 7km Tiergartenstrasse in an official ceremony honouring his 50th birthday. With *Leibstandarte* troops lining the road as the Honour Guard, the Führer drove the length of the spectacular new highway in his open Mercedes. Emboldened by the weakness he perceived in the British and French, he was already planning the next stage of conquest, into Poland, and in January had already renewed his demands for the return of Danzig.

Above: Men of the SS parade in the Luitpold Arena, Nuremberg, 13 September 1936. Following on from the militarism of the 1935 rally, the 1936 rally showed the results of rearmament — tanks, armoured cars and aircraft. The massed ranks of the SS, 250,000 party members, and 70,000 spectators watched Hitler tell the world that the Third Reich would last a thousand years. The Luitpoldhain was so named for an old Bavarian monarch, an exhibition park that was laid out in 1906.

IN ACTION

POLAND — *Fall Weiss*

For Germans of all political leanings the Republic of Poland and the Danzig Corridor that divided the territory of East Prussia from the rest of Germany were constant and bitter reminders of the humiliation meted out by the Treaty of Versailles at the end of World War I.

In January 1939, following his diplomatic successes of 1938, Hitler began to demand that the territories be fully restored to Germany. The demands were rebuffed but, encouraged by the continuing British and French posture of appeasement, on 3 April he ordered the *Oberkommando der Wehrmacht* (OKW) to formulate plans for an attack. He remained, however, fearful of antagonising the Soviets, and so forged an unlikely alliance with that country on 23 August — the Molotov-Ribbentrop Pact. This secretly divided Eastern Europe into German and Soviet spheres of influence, allowed for the attack on Poland and the splitting of the territory gained between the two countries.

Newly schooled in the tactics of Blitzkrieg, the OKH planned to use maximum surprise in the attack, codenamed *Fall Weiss* (Operation White). Some 98 Wehrmacht divisions were mobilised in preparation for the offensive, and throughout July and early August these units moved quietly to positions on both sides of Germany — to the east on the Polish border ready to invade, and to the west to take up defensive positions to meet the anticipated counter-attack by the British and French. In the north General Fedor von Bock's Fourth Army was to attack from Pomerania; the Third Army, also under command of Bock's Army Group North, would advance from East Prussia on the other arm of a giant pincer movement. In the south Generaloberst Gerd von Rundstedt's Eighth (Blaskowitz) and Tenth (von Reichenau) Armies would strike from Silesia toward Warsaw, and the Fourteenth Army (List) would move on Krakow in the south-west to cut off any Polish retreat.

Below: Accompanied by members of his military staff and his personal SS bodyguard, Hitler is cheered on by enthusiastic German soldiers during a visit he made to the front in Poland in 1939.

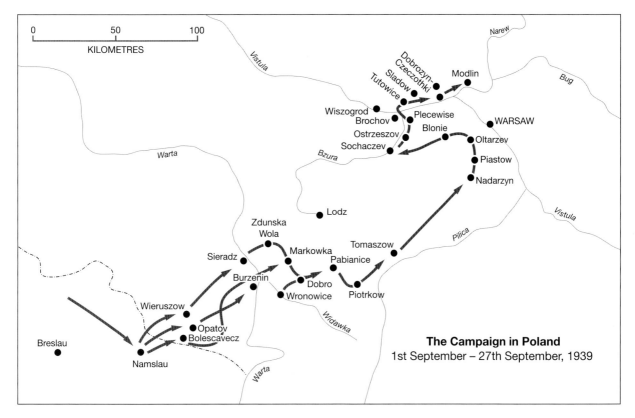

0
50
100
KILOMETRES

Narew

Vistula

Dobrozyn-
Czeczothki
Sladow
Tutowice
Modlin
Wiszogrod
Plecewise
Brochov
Blonie
WARSAW
Ostrzeszov
Oltarzev
Sochaczev
Piastow
Nadarzyn
Bug
Warta
Bzura
Vistula
Lodz
Zdunska
Wola
Tomaszow
Pilica
Sieradz
Markowka
Pabianice
Burzenin
Dobro
Wronowice
Piotrkow
Wieruszow
Widawka
Opatov
Bolescavecz
Breslau
Namslau
Warta

The Campaign in Poland
1st September – 27th September, 1939

Above: *Leibstandarte*'s part in the Polish campaign, 1–27 September 1939. In spite of criticism by regular army units, the regiment was involved in intense fighting and performed creditably.

Leibstandarte had been preparing for the campaign since June, and in August had received orders to move from Lichterfelde Barracks to an assembly area around Hundsfeld-Kunersdorf east of Berlin. The OKW remained highly sceptical of SS abilities away from the parade ground, yet had little option but to acquiesce to Hitler's wishes that the SS be included in the attack. *Leibstandarte*, therefore, was attached to XIII Corps, part of Johannes Blaskowitz's Eighth Army in Army Group South, tasked with defending the left flank of Walther von Reichenau's Tenth Army, which was to drive east in a two-pronged movement to cut off the Polish forces west of Warsaw. During the initial advance the *Leibstandarte*, being a fully motorised unit, was to come under the control of 17th Infantry Division and was tasked with reconnaissance forward and the defence of the slower moving army units.

For the attack on Poland *Leibstandarte*'s main units comprised three motorised infantry battalions, transported in trucks; a motorcycle company; an engineer platoon; and a section of armoured reconnaissance vehicles. This unit was under the command of Kurt Meyer, who renamed it 'Panzer Meyer' before the assault on Poland. (The nickname would stick and he would be 'Panzer' Meyer henceforth.) It is worth noting that many of the officers commanding *Leibstandarte* units during this campaign would go on to become respected commanders later in the war.

Shortly before 01:00hrs on 1 September some 37 German divisions began to move from their start points toward the German–Polish border. By dawn the *Leibstandarte*, advancing south of Breslau, was crossing at River Prosna at Gola, over a bridge lightly defended by the Polish 10th Infantry Division. The Polish Army, with a potential strength of 1,800,000 men, was not an insignificant force, yet most of its weaponry was of World War I vintage and the Polish General Staff had dispersed this force along the whole frontier, rather than concentrate it at the most gravely threatened points.

Above: Men of a Waffen-SS assault troop advancing against an enemy position. The original caption implies that this is during action in Poland, although it's more likely to be during training for Fall Weiss. It gives a good view of the sort of equipment carried into battle — including bayonet, entrenching tool and a spare machine gun barrel within the tubular container.

From Gola the advance into Poland was rapid; Boleslavecz fell quickly, and despite spirited counter-attacks by the Polish 10th, 17th and 25th Infantry Divisions, and the mounted troops of the Wielpolska and Wolwyska Cavalry Brigades, *Leibstandarte* had almost achieved all its objectives by the afternoon of the first day. Advancing through Opatov along the Prosna River, finally, by the evening of 1st, the bulk of the regiment was across the river and preparing to advance on Wieuroszov, where it was to link up with the 17th Division. This was accomplished, and early the next morning troops of the *Leibstandarte* advanced towards Burzenin, where it was ordered to assault across the Warta River. Fierce resistance brought a frustrating delay and casualties.

On 7 September elements of Tenth Army advanced north-east to within 30 miles of Warsaw, in the first move of a double pincer envelopment, and succeeded in cutting off Polish forces before they could retreat behind the Vistula. The Eighth Army succeeded in taking Lodz, 75 miles south-east of Warsaw, that same day. *Leibstandarte* moved next on the transport hub of Pabianice, 10 miles south-west of Lodz near the Pilica River. The 1st Battalion was to isolate Pabianice from the north, while the 2nd Battalion would move south and the 3rd Battalion would remain in reserve with the artillery along the highway. The army lent a little support; a company from 17th Infantry Division and some armour (PzKpfw IIFs) from 23rd Panzer Regiment . To the north, 1st Battalion encountered no great opposition and secured its objectives quickly. To the south, however, the 2nd Battalion had to capture and hold a second highway running into Lodz, but well-sited dug-outs and stubborn defence slowed the advance, as Polish reinforcements were thrown into the battle. In the face of fierce counter-attacks from woods south of the scene of action, at one point the *Leibstandarte* seemed threatened with encirclement and was only saved by the timely intervention of Infantry Regiment 55.

Early on the 8th Pabianice fell, but for all its efforts the *Leibstandarte* was severely criticised by Generalmajor Loch, commander of the 17th Division, for forcing the diversion of 55th Infantry Regiment at a crucial juncture. He demanded its withdrawal to the reserve, and although his demand was not met, the unit was subsequently quietly transferred to Reinhardt's 4th Panzer Division.

With the route to Warsaw now wide open, von Reichenau's Tenth Army turned its axis of advance north and advanced toward the capital from the south-west, while the Fourth Army closed from the north. Guderian's armoured corps advancing from the north-west met with Ewald von Kleist's armour moving from the south at Brest-Litovsk on the 14th, effectively cutting off any potential escape route.

On the western approaches 1st Battalion of *Leibstandarte*, now reinforced by artillery, fought bitterly to wrest Oltarzev from its stalwart defenders. However although battered, the Poles were far from beaten, and had declared Warsaw a fortress. Instead of withdrawing east to escape the pincer movement, on 10 September the Polish commander, Marshal Edward Smigdly-Rydz, ordered a retreat to south-east Poland and struck south at the Eighth Army, that was protecting the northern flanks of the Tenth Army. The Polish attack temporarily threw the Germans off balance; on the outskirts of the city counter-attacks against *Leibstandarte*, fighting alongside the 4th Panzer Division, forced it onto the defensive and wiped out the 6th Company of the 2nd Battalion. Withdrawn to the west, it was attached to the forces attempting to encircle the Polish forces on the Bzura.

Von Reichenau had positioned his Tenth Army on the Bzura River, which flows into the Vistula to the north of Warsaw, and on the 14th began a northward drive to seal off the Bzura 'pocket'. Under XVI Corps, *Leibstandarte* played a major part in this operation, which was the largest battle of the Polish campaign. Some of the heaviest fighting took place in the streets of Sochaczev, where *Leibstandarte* encountered strong resistance. The Battle of Bzura was distinguished by the great bravery of the trapped Polish forces, by now facing annihilation, but finally on the 19th the jaws closed around them. In truth, the Soviet Union had delivered the death knell when it began its invasion of Eastern Poland on the 17th.

After the defeat at Bzura, all attention now focused on beleaguered Warsaw and its surrounding garrison forts. Guarding the northern approaches, the forts of Modlin and Zacrozym were attacked by battle groups from the SS-*Standarte Deutschland*, while in the centre the *Leibstandarte*, attached to XV Corps, moved on Warsaw from the west. The reduction of the forts by German artillery, aided by Luftwaffe bombers, was completed by 25 September, and two days later the Polish commander of the city sued for peace.

On 30 September, as the remaining Polish forces were mopped up, the *Leibstandarte* was awarded a special standard in light of the heavy casualties it had suffered during the campaign. In the aftermath of the Polish campaign, army commanders were quick to criticise SS units. Indeed, casualties had been inordinately high among the three SS-VT units that had served in Poland. *Leibstandarte* alone suffered more than 400 killed, wounded or missing. This, the army believed, was proof that the SS was poorly led and trained, and reckless in the attack to boot. The SS countered that the OKW had consistently used the SS for the most dangerous tasks, and that the practice of dividing SS units among army formations (only *Leibstandarte* fought as a cohesive unit) was detrimental to their effectiveness in battle. Additionally, the OKW was incensed by reported atrocities against Polish civilians, particularly Jews, by SS men, but its attempts to bring the culprits to justice were frustrated. (It should be noted that Wehrmacht personnel were also hardly guilt-free on this score.)

Overall, through their ability to redeploy rapidly from one sector of the fighting to another, the *Leibstandarte* had proved the effectiveness of motorised units in battle. This proved of vital importance in the Russian campaign.

CZECHOSLOVAKIA

During October, with most German units massed in western Europe poised for an expected attack by the British and French, the *Leibstandarte* relieved SS-*Standarte Der Führer* on its occupation duties in Czechoslovakia and paused for rest and relaxation. November and December passed quietly, and no attack came in the west, and some of the regiment was able to enjoy a peaceful Christmas at home. On 23 December Hitler joined the 1st Company for its Christmas celebration dinner at Bad Elms, Germany, at which gifts of tobacco, cake and wine were presented to each man.

ORGANISATION OF LEIBSTANDARTE-SS ADOLF HITLER REGIMENT IN 1940

1st *Sturmbann*
2nd *Sturmbann*
    each of 3 x *Stürme*, 1 x MG *Sturm*
3rd *Sturmbann*
    3 x *Stürme*, 1 x MG *Sturm*, 1 x lt Inf Gun *Sturm*, 1 x PzJg *Sturm*, 1 x MC Sturm, 1 x hy Inf Gun *Sturm*
4th Guard Battalion
    (later *Wachtruppe* Berlin)
Artillery Regiment
    (3 batteries of 10.5cm guns)
Panzer-Späh-Zug (Armd Recce Pl)
Nachrichtenzug (Sig Pl)
Kradmeldezug (MC Messenger Pl)
Kraderkundungszug (MC Recce Pl)
Pionierzug (Pionier Pl)
Panzer–Sturm–Batterie
Musik-Zug (Band)
Leichte Infanterie Kolonne (Light infantry column that consisted of a set number of horse-drawn vehicles capable of transporting a fixed tonnage)

THE PHONEY WAR

When the campaign in Poland ended, Hitler, contrary to popular belief, did not have a clear idea of what to do next. At a 23 September conference, he raised the question of what measures should be adopted 'in case of war' with Britain and France. He decided that a siege of Britain would be made more effective if the German Navy held bases in Norway, but both the Naval staff and OKH were pessimistic about such a venture and during the October and November lull that became known as the 'Phoney War', Hitler devoted himself instead to planning the attack on Belgium and France.

In preparation for the coming offensive in the west, *Leibstandarte* began a period of intensive training at Koblenz under the command of General Heinz Guderian. This coincided with a major restructuring and expansion of the SS. Criticism of the SS performance under fire could not dissuade Hitler from ordering the creation of three new SS divisions, and the establishment of a separate recruiting office under Gottlob Berger, the *Erganzungsamt der Waffen-SS*. By recruiting ethnic Germans from occupied territories (the so-called *Volksdeutsche*), which the army was prevented by law from doing, Himmler was able to expand the SS and to avoid conflict with the army over allocation of conscripts. Thus the SS-VT, which from March 1940 officially became the Waffen-SS, was expanded to three divisions: the SS-*Verfügungs* Division (an amalgamation of the SS-*Standarten Deutschland*, *Germania* and *Der Führer* that would eventually become the 2nd SS Panzer Division *Das Reich*), the *Totenkopf* and the *Polizei*, recruited from members of the police force. In March 1940, Hitler authorized the formation of a *Leibstandarte* artillery battalion armed with 105mm guns.

By the spring, growing signs that the British and French would intervene in Norway and Denmark persuaded Hitler that he, too, must act and ordered landings for 9 April. In the run-up to the invasion, the regiment was put on standby alert, but again there was no counter-punch by the Allied armies, swollen by now to 148 divisions of French (100), British (11), Belgian (22) and Dutch (10) troops. Denmark fell in a day, and although resistance in Norway continued until June, most of the country was in German control by the middle of April.

Below: Waffen-SS troops seen during the fighting in France. The soldier on the right is firing a Luger pistol complete with shoulder stock. The Pistole 08 was of World War I vintage and in its long-barrelled version could be attached to a wooden stock that allowed it to be used as a machine-pistol. The man on left carries a 7.92mm Karabiner 98b, with its side sling and sword bayonet mounted.

INVASION OF THE LOW COUNTRIES — *Fall Gelb*

The diversion in Norway somewhat delayed preparations for the next phase of German conquest — into France and the Low Countries of Holland and Belgium, but by early May these had almost been completed. The strategic plan OKH had prepared for the coming offensive, *Fall Gelb* (Operation Yellow), was itself modelled on the old Schlieffen Plan of 1914. For the battle three army groups — A, B and C under Gerd von Rundstedt, Fedor von Bock and Wilhelm von Leeb respectively — were created. The main effort would be made by Bock and von Leeb through Belgium either side of Liège, where the Belgian Army was concentrated on a defensive line on the Albert Canal and Meuse River, to seize the strategically important fortress at Eben Emael. This was much as the Allied commanders predicted, believing that an attack in north-eastern France against the formidable defences of the Maginot Line, a belt of fortifications built in the 1930s from Switzerland to Longuyon, was highly unlikely, and equally unlikely a move through the ravined and forested Ardennes region, considered impassable to armour.

The original plan called for an attack in November 1939, but after repeated postponements because of poor weather conditions, the date was firmly set for 17 January 1940. However, over the winter, Hitler and some of his strategists began to question the plan, and acting upon the suggestions of von Rundstedt *Fall Gelb* was revised. The new plan, devised by General von Manstein with the assistance of his commanding officer von Rundstedt, was based on the same Blitzkrieg tactics — the deep strategic penetration by independently operating armoured forces, with tactical air support — that had proved so effective in Poland. Under the new plan the key tank units, including the 5th and 7th Panzer Divisions under Erwin Rommel, the Kleist Armoured Group (with XIX Corps under Guderian) and the 6th and 8th Panzer Divisions under Georg-Hans Reinhardt were transferred to von Rundstedt's group (thus reducing to three the number. of armoured divisions in Bock's group). It was to make an audacious, coordinated thrust through the Ardennes and move behind the main concentration of Allied forces to Sedan, thus bypassing the Maginot Line. From there it would race to the

Above: So swift was the German advance through France and Belgium in 1940, that the exhausted troops had to snatch precious sleep whenever they could.

Below: Lying beneath the shelter of a railway wagon these men of the Waffen-SS take aim with their MG34 7.92mm machine gun.

undefended Channel coast, before turning to complete the encirclement. After it was shown to Hitler he immediately ordered it to be adopted.

For the offensive the Germans could muster some two million troops, and were thus outnumbered by the four million of the combined French, British, Dutch and Belgian armies. In tanks the Germans and Allies were roughly equal, although German tanks were generally faster, but in aircraft they enjoyed a clear advantage. The difference in opposing forces was less a question of numbers than in the way in which they were employed, and here the Germans, in their use of new methods of warfare, showed a clear advantage.

After further delays because of the weather, the assault finally began before daylight on 9 May, with extensive air attacks on the Dutch and Belgian airfields and the seizure by paratroops of vital river crossings at Moerdijk and Rotterdam. At dawn Georg von Küchler's Eighteenth Army, including the 9th Panzer Division and *Leibstandarte*, drove into Holland, the main column striking toward the southern Netherlands to envelop the southern flank of the densely populated 'Vesting Holland' (Fortress Holland) region formed by rivers and canals around the five major Dutch cities — Amsterdam, Rotterdam, Utrecht, Leiden and Den Haag — where the 400,000-man conscripted Dutch army had concentrated. *Leibstandarte*, attached to the 227th Division of Army Group B, had been given a vital role in penetrating these defences, and securing the road and river bridges along the advance to the Ijssel River after they had been captured by airborne troops of the Fallschirmjäger — 7th Flieger Division and 22nd Luftlande Division (see *Spearhead 3 7th Flieger Division*).

By midday *Leibstandarte* was 50 miles inside Dutch territory, but at Boernbrock found its progress blocked by a blown bridge. Undaunted, the regiment crossed the canal on makeshift rafts, and pressed on. Again, despite a lightning advance to Zwolle on the Ijssel, *Leibstandarte* was unable to prevent the destruction of two vital bridges there by Dutch engineers. To the south, the 3rd Battalion found another crossing point near Zutphen, and before it halted to rest that night the regiment had covered 215km (130 miles). At this juncture, *Leibstandarte* joined the 9th Panzer Division for the

drive to Rotterdam. Although German airborne troops held the key Maas (the river the French call the Meuse is the Maas in Holland) bridge at Moerdijk, to the north of the city tenacious Dutch defence had thus far prevented them from crossing. Hitler would not countenance delays and issued an ultimatum to the Dutch — capitulate or Rotterdam would be bombed. Negotiations began, but the Luftwaffe attacked anyway and destroyed the city, later citing in its defence a breakdown in communications. On 13 May, following the air raid, *Leibstandarte* was advancing through Rotterdam and was involved in an incident which later drew heavy criticism from the army. Spotting Dutch troops loitering outside a building soldiers — apparently from *Leibstandarte* — opened fire. In fact, Dutch and German officers were negotiating the surrender in the building and the fire severely wounded celebrated airborne forces' commander Karl Student. For the army, it was proof again of the indiscipline of the SS. Undeterred, Dietrich moved on and the following day *Leibstandarte* reached the Hague.

FRANCE

In response to the attack on Holland the French Seventh Army (Giraud) had moved across northern Belgium to Breda on 11 May to help the Dutch, who had fallen back from the Maas. In Belgium, the army soon fell back on a defensive line based on the defences behind the Dyle River. Holland fell on the 14th, but although it initially appeared that the Allies had succeeded in delaying the Germans here, Rundstedt had already sprung the trap on the central front. Here, opposed by only four light cavalry divisions, the *Chasseurs Ardennais* and 10 hurriedly prepared infantry divisions, von Kleist's two panzer corps pushed through the Ardennes and across the Meuse. By 16 May, the spearhead had advanced as far as Vervins and Montcornet. In the centre von Kluge had pushed back Blanchard's First Army to Beaumont, and Küchler had advanced south as far as Antwerp. After crossing the Meuse, von Kleist's armour moved rapidly and captured on 18 May St Quentin, nearly halfway to the Channel from Sedan. The next day he reached Amiens and Doullens, barely 40 miles from the Channel coast and on 20 May Abbeville fell.

Rundstedt's lightning drive to the Channel split the French forces in two, and cut the British line of communications with their main base at Cherbourg. With the Belgians already back on the Lys River defending Ghent, and the collapse of the French Ninth Army threatening the British rear, on 22 May the British commander, Lord Gort, ordered the BEF to hold a line extending from south of Dunkirk to the

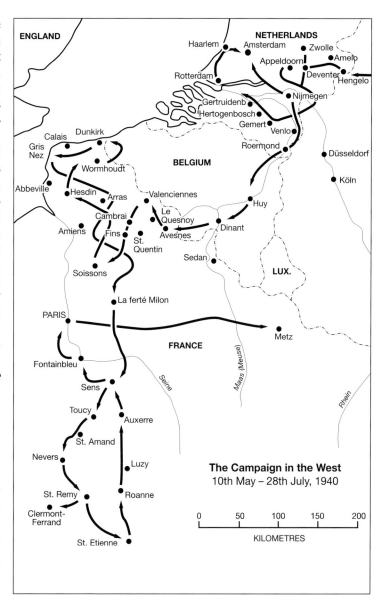

Above: Leibstandarte's part in the campaign in the West, 10 May to 28 July 1940. After its foray into Holland *Leibstandarte* pushed south through Belgium and into France. After the evacuation of the BEF from Dunkirk, *Leibstandarte* advanced deep into central France until the Armistice on 25 June. After the victory parade in Paris did not take place, the unit transferred to Metz awaiting its next mission. It would train there from July 1940 to February 1942.

In the map:

ENGLAND

NETHERLANDS

Haarlem
Amsterdam
Zwolle
Appeldoorn
Amelo
Rotterdam
Deventer
Hengelo
Gertruidenb
Nijmegen
Hertogenbosch
Gemert
Venlo
Roermond
Calais
Dunkirk
Gris Nez
Düsseldorf
BELGIUM
Wormhoudt
Köln
Abbeville
Hesdin
Arras
Valenciennes
Huy
Cambrai
Le Quesnoy
Amiens
Fins
Avesnes
Dinant
St. Quentin
Sedan
Soissons
LUX.
La ferté Milon
PARIS
Metz
FRANCE
Fontainbleu
Maas (Meuse)
Sens
Rhein
Toucy
Auxerre
St. Amand
Nevers
Luzy
Seine
St. Remy
Roanne
Clermont-Ferrand
St. Etienne

The Campaign in the West
10th May – 28th July, 1940

0   50   100   150   200
KILOMETRES

WHAT'S IN A NAME?

As with many SS units, *Leibstandarte* went through many changes between 1933 and 1945, usually getting larger and more strongly armed. The name changes over this period were as follows:

SS-*Stabswache* Berlin	from 17/3/33
SS-*Sonderkommando* Berlin,	from end 4/33
SS-*Sonderkommando* Zossen	from 10/5/33
SS-*Sonderkommando* Jüterbog	from 8/7/33
Adolf Hitler-*Standarte*	from 3/9/33
Leibstandarte Adolf Hitler	from 9/11/33
Leibstandarte-SS Adolf Hitler	from 13/4/34
Infantry Regiment (mot) LSSAH	from 24/8/39
SS-Division LSSAH	from 9/5/41
SS-Panzergrenadier Division LSSAH	from 24/11/42
1. SS-Panzer-Division LSSAH	from 22/10/43

vicinity of Arras (the canal line), in an attempt to stop a rush northward by the German forces. The only hope appeared to be an attempt to cut the German line of communications, thereby establishing a firm position from the Somme to the Scheldt. Gort attempted to drive southwards from Arras to cut the head of the advance, but promised French support failed to materialise and the attack failed in the face of determined resistance by German units. The next day the French Army finally counter-attacked with two divisions from the salient it held southeast of Lille, but this too failed. Now trapped in a pocket surrounding Dunkirk, its only remaining port, pressed by Army Group A from the south along the fragile canal line and the east by Army Group B through Belgium, where the Belgians appeared on the brink of collapse, the BEF position had become untenable.

After the battles in Holland, *Leibstandarte* was afforded a brief interlude, during which it remained under the command of Eighteenth Army. Subsequently, it was transported south, and on 20 May, crossed into France, where it transferred to XXXXIV Corps of Sixth Army, Army Group B. On 22 May, the French forces trapped in the east attempted to break out of the German trap and *Leibstandarte* was rushed into the line to stem these attacks. It was then moved into position on the Aa canal, part of the defensive perimeter around the trapped Allied forces, waiting for rescue from Britain.

That afternoon, Hitler ordered a halt in the advance, persuaded by Göring's assurances that his Luftwaffe would destroy the enemy on the beaches. However, by the time the order reached the front, the *Verfügungs* Division was already attacking the British perimeter. In response to instructions from Guderian, to whose Panzer Corps *Leibstandarte* was subordinated, the regiment was preparing to assault at Wattan. On 25 May, disregarding Hitler's orders, Dietrich ordered Jochen Peiper to lead the assault across the Aa Canal, and eliminate the British artillery positions on the Wattenberg heights, which commanded the surrounding flatlands. Guderian appeared at Dietrich's command HQ during the middle of the attack demanding to know why orders were being disobeyed, but suitably appraised of the situation and encouraged by the early successes, gave his approval and brought up the armour of the 2nd Panzer Division in support, and the bridgehead was secured.

The next day, 26 May, the British government authorised Lord Gort to begin evacuating the BEF from Dunkirk, and the following night the BEF began withdrawing to a shallow perimeter around the port. During the retreat, they were doggedly pursued by German troops. *Leibstandarte*'s 2nd Battalion,

Below: The Blitzkrieg in the West was a resounding success for the German forces. Soldiers of the Waffen-SS receive the Iron Cross, 2nd Class.

tasked with capturing the key town of Wormhoudt, encountered stubborn resistance from men of the British 48th Division, and on 28 May the town was still in British hands. As fighting continued, a number of the 4th Cheshire Regiment were captured and herded into a barn, which was then raked with fire. Grenades were tossed in, and by the time an officer had halted the slaughter, 65 of the 80 POWs were dead. Those who did survive implicated Wilhelm Mohnke as the officer who gave the execution order — not the last such crime in which this fervent Nazi would be implicated. Dietrich, however, was cleared of any involvement in the war crime, as he claimed to have spent the entire day pinned down in a ditch after troops of the British Gloucestershire Regiment shot up his staff car around Esquelbecq. The incident has been the subject of controversy and numerous attempts to bring the perpetrators to justice, and remains a dark stain on *Leibstandarte* history.

With the BEF evacuation underway, and its destruction entrusted to the Luftwaffe, attention turned to the south, where the French held a line stretching along the Somme and Aisne rivers. This hastily constructed 'Weygand Line' was badly compromised by the fact that during its advance to the Channel the German forces had captured vital bridgeheads on the Somme. *Leibstandarte* and SS-*Verfügungs* Division, hastily reinforced and briefly rested after the action around Dunkirk, were attached to von Kleist's armoured group for an advance from the northwest on Paris by Bock's Army Group B.

Attacks on the Weygand Line began on 5 June, with *Leibstandarte* advancing across the Somme south of Amiens. Along the Aisne, von Rundstedt's Army Group A launched the main attack on the 9th, and with the destruction of the Oise Bridge much of von Kleist's group, including *Leibstandarte*, was rushed to the north-east into the area around Guiscard to reinforce Army Group A, capturing Laon and then Chateau-Thierry. On 11 June, despite spirited resistance, the French were forced to

Above: Junior NCOs of the Waffen-SS, all of whom have just received the Iron Cross, 2nd Class for their part in the campaign in the West.

Above: Young and confident. Troops of the Waffen-SS wearing their distinctive camouflage smocks and helmet covers photographed riding in an armoured troop carrier.

fall back on the Marne in deference to their open left flank, but this last line of defence was breached and on the next day four armoured divisions under Guderian broke through the line at Châlons-sur-Marne. Subsequently, Paris was declared an open city and abandoned. On 14 June Paris surrendered, but for the *Leibstandarte* the advance continued. At the spearhead of Panzer Group Kleist, it battled for crossings over the Seine, and, continuing south in pursuit of the remnants of the retreating Second and Fourth French armies, the regiment seized nearly 250 abandoned French aircraft, 4,000 men and untold other materiel at the Clermont-Ferrand aerodrome. By 17 June von Kleist was at Nevers on the Loire; to the east Guderian had reached Dijon and the Swiss border, cutting off 500,000 French troops in the Maginot Line, who were pressed from the east by Army Group C under von Leeb.

For the advance south Dietrich was placed in command of XVI Corps and tasked with attacking the rear of the French Alpine Corps, which was defending against the penetration made by the Italian Army into the French Riviera. *Leibstandarte*, whose line of advance took it west of Lyon, faced brave but ultimately futile resistance. On 22 June, the ageing Marshal Pétain called for a ceasefire, and three days later, France capitulated with armistice.

In total the campaign in France cost the *Leibstandarte* some 500 casualties. Along with the other Waffen-SS units that had fought in Poland, it had performed well in battle, and for this it was amply rewarded. During July, with the regiment quartered at the German city of Metz on the reserve of Army Group C, George Keppler, Paul Hausser and Sepp Dietrich received the Knight's Cross at the Führer's victory celebration in the Reichstag, Berlin, and on 7 September, at a ceremony at Fort Alvensleben in Metz, Himmler presented a revised colour standard to the regiment.

Although the army remained sceptical of SS discipline, in light of fresh instances of SS brutality against French colonial troops and other 'racial inferiors', Hitler now had no misgivings about expanding the SS further. In August *Leibstandarte* was upgraded to brigade status and began amphibious training for Operation *Sealöwe* — the proposed invasion of Britain. For this it was attached to XXXXV Corps, First Army, Army Group C, and in September to XXV Corps. But on 13 October, having failed to defeat the RAF over Britain, Hitler was forced to postpone *Sealöwe*. In December *Leibstandarte* transferred to LX Corps, Army Group D.

YUGOSLAVIA AND GREECE

In the spring of 1941, events in the Balkans conspired to bring about the invasion of Yugoslavia and Greece by German forces. Mussolini, hungry to emulate German successes in northern Europe, launched a disastrous and humiliating invasion of Greece on 28 October 1940, but solid defence by the Greek armies and counter-attacks launched in the new year soon had the Italian armies on the back foot. The events underlined the instability of the region, and convinced Hitler of the need to stabilise his southern flank prior to the invasion of Russia, and equally importantly, protect the vital Romanian oilfields.

In February 1941, in response to the crisis in the Balkans, *Leibstandarte* transferred from Metz to Campalung in Romania, under XIV Corps, Twelfth Army (List), in preparation for the upcoming campaign — codenamed Operation 'Marita'. Then, in March, a coup d'état in Yugoslavia against the pro-Axis regent installed a new government with an anti-German stance, blocking German access to the Greek border. Hitler now prepared another operation against Yugoslavia, codenamed 'Strafe', to run concurrent with the attack on Greece. *Leibstandarte* moved again to Temesvar, Bulgaria, where it joined *Grossdeutschland* Division and *Hermann Göring* Brigade, XXXX Corps, Twelfth Army, which was to conduct the campaign in Greece while the Second Army (Weichs), von Kleist's First Panzer Group and the Hungarian Third Army moved on Yugoslavia.

Generalfeldmarschall Wilhelm List's Twelfth Army numbered eight infantry divisions and two tank divisions, the 2nd and 9th Panzer Divisions. They were faced by troops of the British Expeditionary Force under British General Henry Maitland Wilson, that held a short line facing north-eastward along the Vermion Mountains and lower Aliakmon River, between the Greek forces holding the front in Albania and those in the Metaxas Line covering the Bulgarian border. The BEF comprised some 75,000 men, including the 6th Australian Infantry Division, the 2nd New Zealand Division and the 1st Armoured Brigade, and could field some 100 tanks. The Australian 7th Division and a Polish brigade were intended for Greece as well, but were held back for North Africa, as Rommel was at that time advancing into Cyrenaica.

The German Second Army under Maximilian von Weichs thrust south into Yugoslavia from Austria at 05:15hrs on 6 April, while von Kleist's First Panzer Group pushed towards Belgrade from Bulgaria and the Twelfth Army attacked Thrace, sending XXXX Corps westwards through the Vardar region toward Macedonia and

Above: Motorised Waffen-SS infantry supported by an anti-tank gun.

Left: SS-Obergruppenführer Sepp Dietrich discussing strategy with German Army Gebirgsjäger officers during the Greek campaign, 1 May 1941. He is accompanied by his Adjutant, Max Wunsche.

the Monastir Gap. *Leibstandarte* advanced into Yugoslavia with the 9th Panzer Division from the border town of Kustendil, heading toward Skopje in the southern Yugoslavia on the northern arm of the two-pronged advance. On 7 April the Kriva Pass and Skopje were taken after heavy fighting with the Yugoslav Third Army and *Leibstandarte* turned south, heading for the strategically important Monastir Gap, the gateway into Greece. On the open flank of the British line along the Vermion mountains and the Greek front in Albania, Monastir was taken only three days after crossing the Bulgarian border, and List's Twelfth Army, having pierced the Metaxas Line, took Salonika on the 9th, cutting off eastern Thrace and the Greek Second Army.

As it advanced to the border, the Brigade's Reconnaissance Battalion, under SS-Sturmbannführer Kurt 'Panzer' Meyer, was divided, one element forging ahead to reconnoitre the Monastir Gap and the other to skirting round the northern shore of Lake Preapa to link up with Italian forces to the west. On 10 April the *Leibstandarte* attacked through the Klidi Pass on the border with Greece and the next day won it from ANZAC troops. The British immediately began to withdraw to a temporary defensive line west of Mount Olympus, and the Greek First Army began to pull back from Albania.

Meyer's battalion was then ordered to advance through the Klissura Pass and on to Lake Kastoria. In his postwar memoirs Meyer recalled an incident during the assault when, pinned down by enemy gunfire, his soldiers could only be motivated to attack the heavily defended Allied positions when Meyer tossed a grenade at their feet! The pass was duly taken from its ANZAC defenders, and with it secured, Meyer's battalion moved on, taking Kastoria on 15 April.

On the 20th, at the Katara Pass, entrance to Epirus through the Pindus Mountains, Dietrich accepted the surrender of 16 Greek divisions from General Tsolakoglous, signalling that Greece was lost, and forcing the British and Imperial forces to begin withdrawing to the Thermopylae Line. The Metsovan Pass fell on 21 April, cutting the Greek First Army's route of escape from the area around and north of Ionnina. Three days later what remained of the Greek Army surrendered. Hounded through the Pindus and down the Aegean coast to Athens by the Luftwaffe and the pursuing *Leibstandarte*, by 25 April the British had retreated into small beachhead at Kalamata, and were evacuating towards Crete and Egypt. Having taken Patros, *Leibstandarte* crossed the Gulf of

Below: *Leibstandarte*'s campaign in the Balkans, 4 March to 30 April 1941. In a brilliant campaign the British were pushed out of Greece with great loss of life as the German forces secured their southern flank before the attack on Russia. *Leibstandarte* played a major part in the campaign.

SENIOR PERSONNEL OF MOTORISIERTE BRIGADE DER SS-LEIBSTANDARTE ADOLF HITLER SPRING 1941

CO Sepp Dietrich
Staff
Ia SS-Stubaf Keilnaus
Ib SS-Stubaf Ewert
IIa SS-Hstuf Max Wunsche
III SS-Stubaf Knote
IVa SS-Stubaf Bludeau
Band

1st Infantry Battalion (mot)
CO SS-Stubaf Fritz Witt
1st Company SS-Ostuf Gerd Pleib
2nd Company SS-Hstuf Schulze
3rd Company SS-Hstuf Shiller
4th Company (MG) SS-Hstuf Krocza
5th Company (Hy) SS-Hstuf Grob

2nd Infantry Battalion (mot)
CO SS-Stubaf Theodor Wisch
6th Company
7th Company SS-Hstuf Rudolf Sandig
8th Company SS-Ostuf Beutin
9th Company (MG) SS-Hstuf Wielk
10th Company (Hy) SS-Hstuf Scappini

3rd Infantry Battalion (mot)
CO SS-Stubaf Weidenhaupt
11th Company SS-Hstuf Frey
12th Company SS-Hstuf Hubert Meyer
13th Company SS-Hstuf Hempel
14th Company (MG) SS-Hstuf Max
    Hansen
15th Company (Hy) SS-Ostuf Olboeter

IV Infantry Battalion (mot)
    (from 10 June 1941)
CO SS-Sturmbannführer Jahnke
16th Company SS-Hstuf Klingemeyer
17th Company SS-Ostuf Wandt
18th Company SS-Hstuf Kling
19th Company SS-Hstuf Meiforth
20th Company SS-Hstuf Kolitz

Guard Battalion
at Berlin-Lichterfelde

Artillery Regiment (mot)
CO SS-Staf.

1st Group CO—SS-Stubaf Sukkau
    1st Battery SS-Hstuf Teufel
    2nd Battery SS-Hstuf Cischek
    3rd Battery SS-Ostuf Horns

2nd Group CO—SS-Stubaf Mertsch
    4th Battery (hy) SS-Hstuf Schroder
    5th Battery (hy) SS-Ostuf Heberer
    6th Battery SS-Hstuf Fend
    7th Battery SS-Ostuf Dr Naumann
    8th Battery SS-Hstuf Urbanitz

SS-Pionier Battalion (mot)
CO SS-Stubaf Christian Hansen
1st Company SS-Hstuf Anhalt
2nd Company SS-Hstuf Wendler
3rd Company SS-Ostuf Tscholtsch

Signals Battalion (mot)
CO SS-Ostubaf Keilhaus

Support Column (mot)
CO SS-Stubaf Bernhard Siebken

Flak Battalion
CO SS-Hstuf Bernhard Krause
1st Battery SS-Hstuf Ullerich
2nd Battery SS-Hstuf Mobius
3rd Battery SS-Hstuf Kappus

Heavy Infantry Battalion (mot)
CO SS-Stubaf Steineck
1st Company (Lt IG) SS-Ostuf Jurgensen
2nd Company (Hy IG) SS-Ostuf Wiest
3nd Company (PzJg) SS-Ostuf Woest

Reconnaissance Battalion
CO SS-Stubaf Kurt Meyer
1st Company (MC) SS-Ostuf G. Bremer
2nd Company (MC) SS-Hstuf Hugo Kraas
3rd Company (Lt AC) SS-Ostuf Bottcher
4th Company (Hy) Nachrichtenzug

Sturmgeschütz Battalion
CO SS-Stubaf Schönberger
1st Battery SS-Hstuf Wiesemann
2nd Battery SS-Hstuf Prinz

Abbreviations
Ostuf   Obersturmführer
Hstuf   Hauptsturmführer
Stubaf   Sturmbannführer
Ostubaf Obersturmbannführer

Above: German troops being greeted with obvious enthusiasm by Greek women, some of whom are giving the 'German Greeting' — the 'Heil Hitler' salute — May 1941.

Corinth into southern Greece in pursuit of the BEF, but through a skillfully executed withdrawal the bulk of the British forces were evacuated by sea.

On 27 April *Leibstandarte* was at Pirgus, and the following day the remaining British troops in Greece surrendered. In all the Greek campaign cost the British some 12,000 men killed, wounded or captured, most of them in the final desperate defensive battles around the evacuation ports. The cost to *Leibstandarte* was 93 killed, 225 wounded and three missing, and it was afforded a few days' rest. On 8 May the victorious German Army paraded through Athens, where the passing motorcyclists were handed flowers from cheering Greeks.

In Yugoslavia, Wehrmacht forces took a mere 12 days to bring Yugoslavia under heel. By 13 April German motorised and armoured elements had linked up in Belgrade, and on the 15th, Sarajevo was occupied. Finally, on the 17th, the Yugoslavs formally surrendered. Some 6,000 officers and 338,000 NCOs and men became prisoners of war, although the larger part managed to escape and form an army of partisans around Tito.

OCCUPATION DUTY — CZECHOSLOVAKIA

After the Balkan diversion, *Leibstandarte* was transferred back to Prague, Czechoslovakia, for rest and refitting in preparation for the delayed invasion of the Soviet Union. At this time it was upgraded to divisional status, becoming *1. SS-Motorisierte Division Leibstandarte Adolf Hitler* (1st SS-Motorised Division *LAH*), but even with the addition of a motorised infantry battalion and other reinforcements, strength stood at only 10,796, half that of the *Das Reich, Totenkopf* and *Wiking* divisions. The shortfall was due to a manpower shortage that was already beginning to manifest itself at home. The Wehrmacht had placed restrictions

Above: Troops of the advance guard from *Leibstandarte* after crossing the Gulf of Corinth, 27 April 1941.

Left: Waffen-SS troops were also employed on duties other than fighting. Here a guard examines the pass books of new recruits about the join the Waffen-SS. Recruitment into the SS was not as straightforward as Himmler or Hitler would have liked, because the regular army was reluctant to let go men from its manpower pool. The SS was forced to look elsewhere — initially at the police force and then outside Germany, mainly at 'ethnic Germans' or those with 'Nordic blood'. Himmler certainly wanted to expand the organisation internationally and of the 39 SS divisions set up between 1933 and 1945, eight were fully or partially composed of 'ethnic Germans', and 19 of other nationalities, including Yugoslavs, Dutch, Italians, Belgians, French, Scandinavians, Ukrainians, Russians, men from the Baltic states and Hungarians.

WAFFEN-SS UNIT STRENGTHS ON 22 JUNE 1941 FOR OPERATION 'BARBAROSSA'

1st SS Division	10,796
2nd SS Division	19,021
3rd SS Division	18,754
4th SS Division	17,347
5th SS Division	19,377
6th SS Division	10,573
Himmler's Command Staff	18,438
Administrative	4,007
Reserve	29,809
Concentration Camp Inspectorate	7,200
SS Guard Battalions	2,159
Garrison posts	992
Officer/NCO schools	1,028
SS Volunteer Battalion Nordost	904
TOTAL	160,405

on the number of men it would permit to join the Waffen-SS, and so Reichsführer Himmler began to fill the ranks of the SS with increasing numbers of *Volksdeutsche* from the occupied territories. However, *Leibstandarte* remained a unique exception to this new policy, as Himmler was determined that it should remain 'racially pure'. For the time being its exclusive entry standards were maintained.

RUSSIA — OPERATION 'BARBAROSSA'

As the French campaign drew to its conclusion, Hitler began to feel that an attack on the Soviet Union was the best means of achieving two important strategic aims. Firstly, by denying Britain a potential ally, he could force its people to accept negotiated peace. Secondly, it presented an opportunity to satisfy a fundamental ambition of Nazism — the acquisition of territory to extend its living space (*Lebensraum*). Equally importantly, he had an inherent hatred for Bolshevism, was contemptuous of Slavic peoples and mistrusted the Soviet Union's ambitions in Europe. Thus even before the fall of France, the OKH was planning for an invasion of Soviet soil, and this gathered increasing impetus as hopes for a swift victory over Britain diminished.

For 'Barbarossa', some 3,350 tanks in four Panzer armies were available, in addition to 3,050,000 men, another 750,000 from Finland and Romania, 7,184 artillery pieces, and 600,000 motor vehicles, with support from over 3,000 aircraft. The ground forces were organised into three army groups under three newly promoted field marshals — Wilhelm Ritter von Leeb had the north, Fedor von Bock the centre and Gerd von Rundstedt the south. All of them agreed that the war hinged on the use of the Panzer armies, acting independently ahead of the infantry, but for the start of the Russian campaign, they were to be in close cooperation with the infantry in battles of encirclement that aimed at netting the Soviet forces before they could retreat behind the safety of the River Dnieper

German Army estimates, which were approximately correct, placed the total initial strength of the Soviet forces at 203 divisions and 46 motorised or armoured brigades. Of these 33 divisions and five brigades were in the east, leaving about 2,300,000 men to meet the European invasion. The Soviet air forces were numerically twice as strong as the Germans, but mostly equipped with obsolete types. Russia had 10,000 tanks, including a few of the excellent T-34 that was not yet in full production. The T-34s that did see action had a sobering effect on the Germans, leading to an immediate re-evaluation of the PzKpfw III and IV, the mainstays of the *Panzerwaffe*. The reaction to the T-34 would be the PzKpfw V Panther, the best medium tank of the war. The other surprise to soldiers who had been taught that the Slavs were subhuman was the determination and tenacity of the ordinary troops. An example of this was seen at the citadel of Brest-Litovsk where individual soldiers resisted for weeks after the main strongpoint had fallen. In fact, the real weakness of the Soviet forces was its officer corps, within which almost none of those who had survived the brutal purges of the 1930s had military competence or experience. This weakness was first exposed during the 1940-41 Winter War with Finland, and was again during 'Barbarossa'.

Badly delayed by excursions in the Balkans and complicated reorganisation and refitting, on 22 June 'Barbarossa' was finally unleashed on a 1,800-mile front against the Soviet Union. The Red Army was totally unprepared to meet the onslaught, and the seven divisions opposing von Leeb in the Baltic states were rapidly swept aside. By the end of the month, having destroyed an estimated 15 Soviet divisions, the

Right: Troops from LSSAH drive through a village somewhere in the east. The reaction towards the advancing Germans was mixed. In most areas they were treated as invaders but in areas that had felt the worst effects of the Soviet purges, the Germans were welcomed.

ORGANISATION OF 1. SS-MOTORISIERTE DIVISION LEIBSTANDARTE ADOLF HITLER IN MAY 1941

Divisional HQ, HQ Staff and Band

4 x Infantry Battalions
Staff
3 x Inf Companies
1 x MG Company
1 x Hy Company
of 2 x A/tk Platoons, 1 x Mortar
Platoon, 1 x Pionier Platoon

1 x Heavy Weapons Battalion
(created 10 June 1941)
Staff
1 x Lt Inf Gun Company (75mm)
1 x Hy Inf Gun Company (150mm)
1 x A/tk Company (47mm)
1 x Field Gun Company (75mm)
1 x AA Company (37mm)

Guard Battalion (4 x Companies
at Lichterfelde Kaserne)

1 x Artillery Regiment
Staff
1 x Battalion (3 x 150mm btys)
1 x Battalion (2 x 150mm, 1 x 88mm)
1 x Lt Arty Column

1 x Reconnaissance Battalion
2 x MC Companies
1 x AC Company
1 x Hy AC Company
1 x Sig Platoon

1 x AA Battalion
2 x 3.7cm Batteries
1 x 2cm Battery

1 x Pionier Battalion
Staff
3 x Companies
1 x Bridging Column
1 x Lt Pionier Column

Sturmgeschütz Battalion
(Abteilung Schönberger)
1 x StuG Battery
1 x PzJg (4.7 cm) Company

1 x Signals Battalion
1 x Telephone Company
1 x Wireless Company

Supply Services
Staff
1 x Workshop Company
1 x Weapons Workshop Platoon
2 x Fuel Columns
6 x Motorised Columns
1 x Bakery Company
1 x Butchery Company
1 x Rations Office
1 x Field Post Office

Medical Services
2 x Medical Companies
1 x Field Hospital
1 x Ambulance Platoon
1 x Surgery

Left: Waffen-SS troops manning a mortar in the tundra somewhere on the Finnish-Russian border. It's likely to be the 8.1cm GrW34 (GrW= *Granatewerfer* =mortar) that proved better than the smaller 5cm light mortar (GrW36). Experience on the Russian fronts led to the development of a 12cm mortar (the heavy GrW42) often on a two-wheel trolley, and German troops made use of captured Russian heavy mortars whenever they could.

Below: German troops closing the ring around the Soviets holding out in Kiev.

Right: Waffen-SS troops proudly display a captured Communist banner.

Inset: Large numbers of Russians were taken prisoner in the early stages of 'Barbarossa'. Here, prisoners, stripped of their arms, equipment and helmets, are made to stand with their arms raised. The woman prisoner in the front row is presumed to be a female commissar.

Below right: A reconnaissance detachment from a Waffen-SS unit holds a meeting in open ground from the back of a four-wheeled armoured car — probably an SdKfz 261 with frame antenna in raised position.

Army Group North drew up on the western Dvina River. Meanwhile, Bock's Army Group Centre crossed the border on 27/28 June in the wake of 7th Panzer Division, and advanced on the northern fringes of the impassable Pripet Marches, moving toward its main objective — Moscow. At Bialystock it encircled a vast army and again at Minsk another large encirclement yielded more than 150,000 Soviet prisoners.

During the initial attack *Leibstandarte* was undergoing reorganisation into a division as part of the reserve of the First Panzer Army, Army Group South (Rundstedt) in the Lublin area, and as such took no part. It moved on to Ostorwiecz and finally, a week after the invasion, crossed the Vistula and headed into the western Ukraine, entering the battle attached to von Mackensen's III Panzer Corps, itself part of von Kleist's First Panzer Army, and which included the SS *Wiking* Division and the 13th and 14th Panzer Divisions.

Initially Army Group South (Sixth, Eleventh and Seventeenth Armies), which was tasked with cutting off and destroying Soviet forces west of the Dnieper River, 300 miles into southern Russia, made stunning progress. The line of advance took it along the main road to Kiev, a major objective on the route towards the grand prize, Rostov. Such was the pace of the advance that the infantry began to be left behind, inviting attacks on the vulnerable German flanks; furthermore, the Russian forces of the Kiev Military District under General Kiroponos were sited in better-prepared defences than on the north and central fronts. In this situation, *Leibstandarte* was again able to demonstrate the advantages of motorised infantry by filling the widening gap between the armoured spearhead and the slower (largely horse-drawn or pedestrian) infantry. In one instance 73rd Panzer Division met with unexpectedly fierce counter-attacks by Russian armour at Dubno and Olyka; *Leibstandarte* was rushed in to support, and although the ensuing battle cost 683 killed and wounded, it prevented the Soviets from cutting the lengthening line of communications.

Consistent with the conventional military doctrine at that time, which emphasised defence, a fortified line running from the Gulf of Finland to the Black Sea was built in western Russia during the 1930s. Behind this the Russian forces of the Southern Front retreated, while launching fierce counter-attacks against von Kleist's armour, which was advancing on the left flank at an average rate of 20 miles a day. On 3 July Stalin announced that the Soviet government would welcome aid from the west and called for a scorched earth policy, which would leave the invaders with 'not a kilogram of grain or a litre of gasoline', while rallying the populace to the defence of the motherland.

The Stalin Line, despite its innumerable obstacles, proved too weak to hold the German armour. Von Kleist broke through east of Zhitomir at Miropol on 8 July, driving a wedge between the two Soviet armies. Moving quickly on the main road to Kiev, *Leibstandarte* ran into strong enemy forces north of Romanovka. At the same time the renamed Southwest Front under General Budenny launched a concerted Soviet counter-attack along the whole of the south-western front and the brigade was temporarily forced onto the back foot, defending the prizes it had won during the advance. But the huge losses incurred by the Soviet forces soon brought a respite in the attacks and *Leibstandarte* was soon on the attack again. Shepetovka was taken and then, in support of the 13th Panzer, Zhitomir itself.

Although von Rundstedt now stood poised to take Kiev, Hitler paused to contemplate a move on Uman, a major transport hub for the Crimea. Such a move had the added attraction of encircling the Soviet forces holding up the Seventeenth and Eleventh Armies in the centre and on the right flank. In the event his hand was forced. Budenny began advancing a section of his forces on Odessa, leaving the

Below: Mosquitoes and flies could prove to be an unbearable nuisance during the summer season on certain sectors of the Eastern Front. As a form of protection this Untersturmführer has covered his head with a mosquito net.

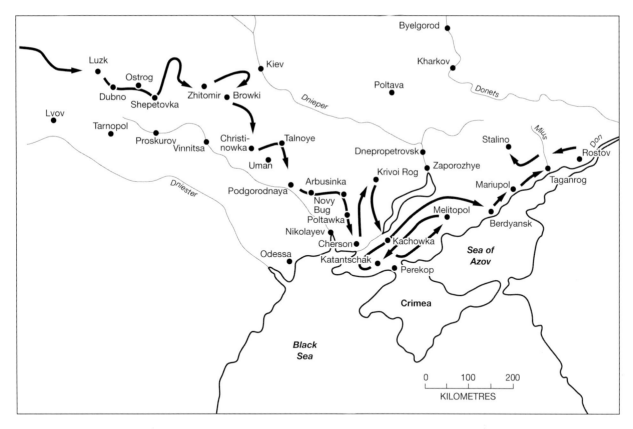

Above: The Russian campaign — *Leibstandarte* in the Ukraine, 2 July 1941 to 26 July 1942.

remainder in defence of Uman, and the German Sixth Army was ordered to move south-east from in front of Kiev on the left flank of Army Group South. *Leibstandarte* was again instrumental in preventing Soviet counter-thrusts from piercing the flanks of von Kleist's armoured column, spearheading the advance. Taking the cities of Novo Ukraina and Kirovograd on 25 and 30 July, the Sixth Army met the Seventeenth Army (Manteuffel and Schobert) on the Southern Bug River some 50 miles east of Uman on 8 August, trapping two whole Soviet armies and a large part of another. In an attempt to break the encirclement, the Soviets threw armour, cavalry and scores of infantrymen into the battle, and for its part in defeating these relentless attacks *Leibstandarte* earned considerable praise from corps commander, Generalmajor Werner Kempf.

Soviet forces in the Uman pocket were finally eliminated on 22 August, but the focus of the advance had already switched to the industrial centre of Cherson, north-east of Odessa. After bitter fighting *Leibstandarte* took Bubry and subsequently the road junction at Sasselje. Arriving at Cherson on 17 August, *Leibstandarte* fought through the streets for three days before the defenders finally abandoned the city.

During the march south another atrocity had allegedly taken place. According to a postwar account of a Waffen-SS journalist serving with the 4th Battalion, east of Gejgova, men from the battalion found the mutilated bodies of six fellow SS troopers who had been previously captured and executed in the town's NKVD headquarters. In reprisal, Dietrich ordered *Leibstandarte* to shoot all surrendering Soviet troops for three days, and in the ensuing slaughter an estimated 4,000 were killed. For want of reliable evidence, the allegations remained unproven.

Above: A command post somewhere on the Eastern Front.

Left: Destroying enemy armour is thirsty work. Men of the Waffen-SS, one from the *Totenkopf* Division, take a pause to drink from a field flask with a burning tank behind them, 18 August 1944. Note the tank destruction badge on the right sleeve of the soldier drinking.

Opposite, Above: The encirclement battle of Uman. Ready for action in their camouflaged smocks and helmet covers these Waffen-SS gunners start firing their 75mm LG18 light infantry gun at the Soviet stronghold, 3 September 1941.

Opposite, Below: The defence of Breslau near to the Czech border. Roadblocks were set up to deny or slow down the enemy advance. Men of a Waffen-SS unit prepare an anti-tank rifle.

Above: The division's chief medical officer examining the wound of a young SS-Grenadier (note the *Leibstandarte* cuff title). The 1941 battles in Russia decimated the brigade, which lost — as did the whole of the German forces — many of its most experienced NCOs and young officers. By early 1942, while still on the offensive the writing was on the wall: Russian numbers would ensure that the German forces would lose a battle of attrition. Altogether, by early 1942 *Leibstandarte*'s initial complement of 10,796 had suffered 5,281 casualties.

KIEV AND THE UKRAINE

By mid-August the first, highly successful, phase of the campaign against the Soviet Union was nearly ended. Fighting on the Central Front had been characterised by rapid advances across the flat empty steppes of central Russia as far as the area south of Smolensk, against sporadic and limited resistance. The capture of Smolensk on 7 August brought 850,000 Russian captives, and towards the end of the month the ferocious fighting in the vicinity of Vaskovo-Chochlovka-Rudnaya began to slacken off. Army Group Centre was then moved into defensive positions to hold the salient that had been put into the Soviet line west of Yelnya by the 360-mile wide advance.

The OKH now felt that the maximum effort should be directed against Moscow, but Hitler was unconvinced of the strategic value of this target. Encouraged by confident predictions that the war was already won, he decided to redirect some of Army Group Centre to the south to take the Crimea and the Donets Basin industrial region thus cutting the Russians off from the oilfields of the Caucasus. He also looked north with a view to taking Leningrad. He was insistent that only after Leningrad had been secured, and Army Group South had made significant inroads, would the advance on Moscow resume.

Acting on these orders, on 25 August the Second Army and the Second Panzer Army turned southward from the Army Group Centre flank. The advance was slowed by rain and mud but the defences of the Soviet Army were breached on 12 September, and on 16 September the lead elements of the Second Army and the First Army, which had moved northward from the Dnieper bend, met 150 miles east of Kiev. Denied permission to withdraw by Stalin, the seven Soviet armies inside the Kiev pocket surrendered on the 19th after five days of resistance. In addition to those lost at Uman in the south, this amounted to nearly 1.5 million men — or half of the current active strength of the Soviet army.

After the battle of Uman, *Leibstandarte* was placed on the reserve of XXXXVIII Corps, First Panzer Group, Eleventh Army, for a much-needed period of rest. It was soon on the advance south again, now under command of the XXX Corps, Eleventh Army (von Manstein), into the dry, dusty steppes of the Nogai Steppe. On 6 September, Hitler had another change of heart and decided that operations against Moscow would resume, and reinforced Army Group Centre with elements of Army Group South. On 6 October, after a fateful delay, it returned to action in front of Moscow.

In the Ukraine, having advanced as far south as the Black Sea, *Leibstandarte* turned east toward Rostov on the River Don. Capturing Romanovka, at Melitopol the brigade was met by a fierce Soviet counter-attack, which broke the sector of the line held by the Third Romanian Army and threatened an envelopment. *Leibstandarte* was again rushed into the line to beat back the attackers, and subsequently took Berdyansk on the Sea of Azov. Moving along the north shore of the lake, it took Taganrog, where according to some accounts, troops executed Soviet prisoners on Dietrich's orders as a reprisal for the brutal execution of SS men by the district NKVD. On 20 October von Manstein's exhausted forces attacked the five-mile wide Perekop Isthmus, guarding the gateway to the Crimea, and 10 days later broke through and poured onto the peninsula, aiming toward Kerch and Sevastopol.

Even after this most dramatic advance the sheer numerical superiority of the Red Army, the vastness of the terrain and the coming of winter rains that turned the roads into quagmires began to make a quick victory increasingly improbable. Army Group Centre's attacks stopped dead in their tracks on the heavily defences of

Moscow, despite the fact that the troops were fighting in the capital itself, and in the south the advance on Rostov began to bog down.

On 15 November Army Group South reached the Don River, the last natural obstacle before Stalingrad. It had penetrated some 600 miles into Russian territory, in five months of bitter fighting. *Leibstandarte* was transferred to the command of III Corps, First Panzer Army, and on the 17th began the attack on Rostov on the Don from the Black Sea coast. The 3rd Company assaulted across the main railway bridge and captured it intact, earning SS-Hauptsturmführer Heinrich Springer the Knight's Cross. Kleist's armour poured over this vital crossing and on 21 November took the city. For *Leibstandarte* came the prize of 10,000 prisoners, 159 artillery pieces, 56 tanks and two armoured trains.

It was a brief victory. During the following week the army, racked by sickness, badly overstretched and plagued by shortages, was battered by a fierce counter-offensive by Timoshenko's Ninth and Thirty-seventh Armies, and although retreat from Rostov was soon the only viable option, Hitler refused to countenance any such move. Responding to Hitler's 'no retreat' order of 30 November, von Rundstedt stated, '. . . it is madness attempting to hold. In the first place the troops cannot do it, and in the second place if they do not retreat they will be destroyed. I repeat that this order be rescinded or find someone else.' Hitler sent back a message that same night, telling him to give up his command. He was replaced by Walther von Reichenau.

Defeat at Rostov exposed how badly overstretched the German forces were and the inherent flaws in Hitler's decision to halt the advance on Moscow. The battles in Rostov left *Leibstandarte* decimated. At the end of November it was pulled out

Above: Among all the signs of a fierce firefight — empty cartridge boxes and shell cases strewn around them — these men of a Waffen-SS infantry unit pause after repelling an enemy assault. During the first winter in Russia temperatures fell as low as -40°C: even the best winter clothing — and there wasn't much of that available — could not protect men and machines and thousands suffered from the extreme conditions. A new winter uniform was designed and available for the next winter, 1942–43, but it had one drawback: it was used so frequently that it got dirty. Too heavy to wash comfortably, the easiest solution was to wear white overalls or snow suits over the top.

and spent December in defensive positions outside Rostov behind the Mius. Here during the first winter of the Russian campaign, it engaged in defensive battles in temperatures that sank as low as –40°C. A deep carpet of snow made movement almost impossible, and partisan actions ensured that little or nothing in the way of supplies got through. During this time the daily food ration fell to only 150 grams. For the troops, the troubles were heightened by Hitler's ban on the distribution of winter clothing, which he reasoned would be detrimental to morale.

Within the ranks of *Leibstandarte*, Dietrich devolved command to the independent unit commanders, which no doubt saved the *Leibstandarte* further casualties. But even in these straits, the unit earned plaudits. In a Christmas communique with Himmler, III Panzer Corps Commander General Eberhard von Mackensen wrote: '. . . Every unit wants to have the *Leibstandarte* as its adjacent unit. The unit's internal discipline, its refreshing eagerness, its cheerful enthusiasm, its unshakable calmness in a crisis and its toughness are examples to us all . . . This truly is an elite unit.'

For the coming year prospects on the Eastern Front were bleak. The combat experience of the early Blitzkrieg years had been lost on the steppes of Russia through battle and weather casualties. And the new year promised a different Soviet Army, one now supplied with better tanks, guns and aircraft, and supplies from the US and United Kingdom. Furthermore, behind the German lines partisan forces were becoming a serious threat to the overstretched supply lines, which crossed hundreds of miles of overrun but not conquered territory.

At the beginning of 1942 *Leibstandarte* was firmly entrenched in positions outside Rostov, in anticipation of an expected Soviet offensive. At this time a Panzer Battalion was added to the order of battle. It was comprised of three companies equipped with PzKpfw IIIs and IVs.

In February *Leibstandarte* was transferred to the command of XIV Corps in the Mius area, and for the remainder of the winter, sub-zero temperatures rendered movement next to impossible as the brigade fought containing actions against

Below: The victors of Kharkov. Troops from the *Leibstandarte-SS Adolf Hitler, Das Reich and Totenkopf* divisions, all of whom took part in the battle for Kharkov, being congratulated by Reichsminister Dr Goebbels in his Berlin residence, 1 April 1943.

limited Soviet actions in the Mius and Donets area. As the first winter in Russia drew to a close, 5,281 men of the *Leibstandarte* had lost their lives in Russia.

In Berlin, recriminations for the failure of the Moscow campaign saw 35 leading generals, including all of the army group leaders and Guderian and Höpner, dismissed. Hitler appointed himself as direct Commander-in-Chief of the Army, and during the spring assumed the role of commander-in-chief for all operations on the Eastern Front from his headquarters at Rastenburg (the *Wolfschanze* or Wolf's Lair). Here he outlined his plans for the summer operations. He ordained that these would be limited to a full-scale offensive in the south, towards the Don River, Stalingrad and the Caucasus oilfields, the capture of which he saw as the decisive stroke. Not only would this cut the Soviets off from their fuel, but also achieve an even more important objective, namely the 'final destruction of the Soviet Union's remaining human defensive strength.' Hitler's plan was for a series of successive converging attacks; the first phase was to be an enveloping thrust on the Kursk–Voronezh line, which would carry the German front to the Don River. Then the attack would proceed to Stalingrad and across the Kerch Strait to the Taman Peninsula.

The Soviet High Command, which had also planned to take the initiative when the good weather returned, got their attack in first, launching a disastrous strike on the South-west Front toward Kharkov on 12 May. South-east of Kharkov the Soviet South-west Front (Timoshenko) broke through the lines near Dnepropetrovsk, where the German forces had captured a huge power plant. *Leibstandarte*, as part of III Corps, was rushed in to fill the breach in the line, and held fast in these positions until the Soviet attack was beaten off. Although initially successful, the Soviets met with strong German resistance and on 25 May a German armoured force struck into the Izyum bridgehead, sealed off the pocket and netted 240,000 prisoners. The plans for a Soviet summer offensive collapsed at a stroke.

Above left: A Grille — a 15cm sIG33 on a PzKpfw 38 (t) chassis — supporting Waffen-SS infantry somewhere on the Eastern Front, July 1943.

Above: Camouflage comes in many forms. Here a soldier of the Waffen-SS on sentry duty has camouflaged himself with bunches of reeds held to his body by his waist belt. Presumably, he was operating in a reeded, watery area.

**UNITS OF
1st SS-PANZERGRENADIER
DIVISION LEIBSTANDARTE ADOLF
HITLER AS AT NOVEMBER 1942**

1st Panzergrenadier Regiment
2nd Panzergrenadier Regiment

Panzer Regiment 1 (from November
    1942)
    1st Battalion (PzKpfw III, IV)
    2nd Battalion (PzKpfw III, IV)
    Panzer Workshop Company
    Panzer Pionier Company

Artillery Regiment
    1st Battalion (150mm, 88mm)
    2nd Battalion (88mm)
    3rd Battalion (88mm)

Reconnaissance Battalion
Flak Battalion
Panzerjäger Battalion
Sturmgeschütz Battalion
Pionier Battalion
Signals Platoon
Supply Troops
Workshop Company
Weapons Workshop Platoon
Bakery Company
Butchery Company
Rations Office
Field Post Office
Medical Battalion
Field Hospital

REFIT AND REDESIGNATION

A month later, on 28 June, the Second and Fourth Panzer Armies of Army Group South opened the German summer offensive. *Leibstandarte*, having been transferred to the reserve of First Panzer Army, moved in May to Stalino for an intended refit and took no part in this campaign. Subsequently, in June it returned to III Corps in the Rostov area before being pulled back to France, to meet a feared Allied invasion of Northwest Europe. Stationed in the Evreux region, west of Paris, and attached to the SS-Panzer Corps, Fifteenth Army, Army Group D, it participated in a ceremonial parade through Paris in front of Generalfeldmarschall von Rundstedt, and during the summer underwent a much needed rest and refit. The formation, which had already received a tank battalion (see page 40), was upgraded and began training as a panzergrenadier division. Significantly, due to manpower shortages, *Volksdeutsche* ('ethnic Germans' — ie people born outside Germany but, according to Nazi racial rules, of German racial descent) were for the first time allowed into the division.

In October, *Leibstandarte* moved south for a spell of occupation duty in Vichy France and also spent time in Normandy. On 22 October it was formally redesignated a panzergrenadier division, and renamed SS-Panzergrenadier Division *Leibstandarte* SS Adolf Hitler. Panzergrenadier units were required to accompany armour over difficult terrain into action, and were provided with both supportive firepower and safety against enemy fire by purpose-designed *Schützenpanzerwagen* (SPW/armoured personnel carriers). Suffice to say that although they pioneered the concept of mobile infantry warfare, Germany was never able to fully complete the formation of Panzergrenadier units, because until the very end of the war it was unable to produce enough armoured transports to equip even a fair proportion of the Panzergrenadier units. (For a detailed discussion of the development of the Panzergrenadier see the 'Spearhead' series title *2 Grossdeutschland*.)

In November *Leibstandarte* was still on occupation duty in southern (Vichy) France, as part of the reserve of Army Group D, where its armour was reorganised into two battalions in a panzer regiment. The next month two new companies were added, equipped with the new PzKpfw VI Tiger Is. At this time division strength was a nominal 678 officers, 20,166 NCOs and men, but many of these were poorly trained and inexperienced and, furthermore, at the end of December some of the veteran NCOs were transferred to form the cadre for the 9th SS-Panzer Division

A *Leibstandarte* veteran remembered: 'It was those defensive battles in Russia which I shall always remember for the sheer beauty of the fighting, rather than the victorious advances. Many of us died horribly, some even as cowards, but for those who lived . . . it was well worth all the dreadful suffering and danger. After a time we reached a point where we were not concerned for ourselves or even for Germany, but lived entirely for the next clash, the next engagement with the enemy.'

During the winter of 1942–43 the tide of the war turned against Germany, which now found itself matched on all fronts. On the Eastern Front it was contending with a enemy vastly different from the one it had attacked 18 months previously. Elsewhere, better leadership and equipment was also beginning to tell against the German armies. But in the east it was most obviously losing the war of supply and of numbers, where the Soviet Union was beginning to exhibit its vastly greater capacity to replace losses of men and materiel. Furthermore, by now the best Russian aircraft and tanks had achieved a parity with German equipment. In the coming battles the German forces, firmly on the defensive, would be tested to the limit.

On 19 November 1942, the Russians attacked the Romanian Third Army positions north of Stalingrad and destroyed its front within hours. The next day came another attack, on the Romanian corps to the south, and by 22 November the Soviet forces had met at Kalach, trapping the German Fourth Panzer Army around Stalingrad. Then, on 16 December, the Soviets rolled over the Italian Eighth Army positions on the right flank of Army Group B and thus extended their offensive west of the city. Finally, on 14 January of the new year, with nearly 300,000 Germans and Romanian troops still trapped in the pocket, the Russians moved up the Don again, this time to strike the Hungarian Second Army on the flank of Army Group B (now commanded by Maximilian von Weichs) south of Voronezh. The Hungarians collapsed, opening a 200-mile front between Voronezh and Lugansk (Voroshilovgrad). The Soviets then turned southwards to the Donets, threatening to envelop the remnants of Army Group B and Army Group Don, which was still battling to keep open Army Group A's lifeline to the west at Rostov. Ten days later they struck again at the German Second Army north of Voronezh, and in three days had encircled two of its three corps.

With Army Group South now close to collapse in the face of this renewed offensive, *Leibstandarte*, currently on OKH reserve, Army Group B, was recalled from France in mid-January and sent to reinforce the weak points in the Ukraine as part of the newly created SS Panzer Corps, under Hubert Lanz. Hitler had agreed to the formation of an SS Corps in 1942, which would allow Waffen-SS divisions to fight together as a coherent force, rather then being distributed throughout the different army groups. Lanz was ordered to hold Kharkov at all costs, and sent *Leibstandarte* into defensive positions along the River Donets, with *Das Reich* in positions to the east of the river. Although already overstretched on a 70-mile front, the division was further weakened by the deployment of Fritz Witt's Panzergrenadier regiment to defensive positions at Kupyansk, and the detachment of the 7th Battalion to the front as SS-Brigade Schuldt.

The Red Army advance ground on through January and into early February, slowly pushing back Army Group Don, and with it *Das Reich*, on to the Mius/Donets defensive line. On the flanks of the SS positions, the 320th Infantry Division crumbled in the face of a concerted Soviet assault, and in headlong retreat to the Donets with 1,500 wounded was surrounded. Led by the SS-Sturmbannführer Jochen Peiper, who was to distinguish himself on numerous future occasions, the 3rd Battalion of *Leibstandarte* made a daring penetration behind the enemy lines and extricated the division from disaster.

KHARKOV

The encirclement and destruction of Axis forces at Stalingrad in February 1943 was a catastrophe of the worst kind for Germany. With the annihilation of the Sixth Army, and the destruction of the greater part of Fourth Panzer Army, five of the seven divisions of the Romanian Third Army, and nearly the whole Sixth Romanian and Seventh Italian Armies, almost immediately a vast gap was formed in the front line, through which Russian troops stormed toward toward Rostov, Kursk and Kharkov. On 8 February Kursk fell. Not wishing to risk another encirclement, Hitler gave his permission on 6 February to withdraw Army Group Don to the line of the Mius and Donets Rivers, and in nine days this was achieved. But with the Soviet advance still

Below: *Leibstandarte* at Kharkov, 22 January–23 March 1943. One of the greatest of Erich von Manstein's victories, the recapture of Kharkov finished the Soviet 1942–43 winter offensive and, albeit at great cost, straightened the lines on the Eastern Front except for the salient at Kursk. Had the German counter-attack continued, the salient may have fallen to the victorious German armies. Instead indecision let the advantage swing over to the Russians against whose defensive bulwarks the might of the German Panzers would be blunted.

Right: Men and armour — in the shape of a snow-camouflaged PzKpfw IV — from the LSSAH Division moving up to the front, March 1943.

Below right: A three-man MG34 machine gun crew operating in deep snow. The MG34 was a brilliant weapon — almost too well made, because German companies found it hard to keep manufacturing quantities high. It was, therefore, superseded by the MG42 (see caption below) although MG34s would remain in service throughout the war.

Below: Motorcycle troops preparing to move off check their ammunition and weapons. The machine gun in the foreground is an MG42, probably the best machine gun of the war. Easier to manufacture than the MG34, it was made from simple metal pressings. With a 1,200 rpm rate of fire, and a quick-release barrel change that allowed a skilled operative to do so in only a few seconds, over 750,000 MG42s were made by the end of the war.

moving at full speed, the right flank of Army Group B was forced back on to Kharkov, and on the southern front, where von Manstein had taken over command, the forces had been severely weakened by the savage fighting.

Although von Manstein did not share Hitler's views on the need for strong fixed defences and was convinced that the numerically inferior German forces could only match the Red Army by taking full advantage of their superiority mobility in a fluid defensive pattern, the Führer concluded that no more territory was to be lost, and ordered both armies to hold. Hitler, remembering the way the Waffen-SS units had defended themselves during the winter of 1941, ordered SS-Panzer Corps (under former SS-VT commander Paul Hausser) to hold Kharkov. For *Leibstandarte* Kharkov was a familiar battleground, but to contemplate defending the city in winter against Soviet forces seven times greater in numerical strength was nothing less than suicidal. On 15 February Hausser, who had no desire to preside over a second Stalingrad, ignored Hitler's orders and allowed SS-Panzer Corps to pull out of the city towards Krasnograd. There they held firm and destroyed the Soviet vanguard, bringing the Kharkov offensive to a standstill.

However, with the withdrawal, a 100-mile wide gap appeared between the right flank of Army Group B and Army Group Don, through which the six Soviet tank corps of the Popov Group struck southward and westward across the Donets, moving to cut Army Group Don's remaining communications lines. To the south the Donetsk railroad was cut and on the 19th the Soviets reached the Sinelnikovo railroad junction 20 miles east-south-east of Dnepropetrovsk. By this time Army Group A had begun evacuating from the Taman Peninsula to reinforce Army Group South (as Hitler had renamed Army Group Don on 12 February), and von Manstein had initiated a series of manoeuvres that were to produce the last great German victory of the war.

He ordered the headquarters of the Fourth Panzer Army to move to Dnepropetrovsk to close the gap in the centre of the German line between the First Panzer Army and the southern flank of the former Army Group B (which had been divided between Army Group Centre and South). He then set about preparations for a counter-attack against the Russian salient that had formed at Kharkov. Despite the inherent risks of advancing in the spring thaw, both Hausser and von Manstein knew that the Soviet offensive was losing momentum, and that their lines of supply were now dangerously outstretched and the troops were tired from months of relentless fighting. Von Manstein asked for and received 12 tank divisions — the largest concentration of armour the Germans had thus far fielded — for an armoured counter-attack. He envisaged an assault from three sides, with the SS-Panzer Corps at the head of a pincer movement that would destroy the Russian divisions around Kharkov. While still ostensibly a Panzergrenadier division, *Leibstandarte* had already been strengthened by SS-Panzer Regiment 1, and with it a Tiger company — designated 13th (Heavy) Company of SS-Panzer Regiment 1.

The assault began on 23 February in a south-easterly direction, and on 28 February, after five days of bitter fighting, the spearhead units made contact with Fourth Panzer Army. *Leibstandarte*, and the entire body of the SS-Panzer Corps, then swung into action towards Kharkov itself. The Fourth Panzer Army reached Kharkov itself on 11 March, trapping several Soviet divisions, and after days of bitter fighting through the city, Kharkov was retaken on 14 March. The battle cost the Soviets 20,000 dead or wounded, together with 600 tanks. Casualties were also high on German side. The SS-Panzer Corps lost 12,000 killed or wounded and *Leibstandarte* alone suffered the loss of 167 officers and 4,373 NCOs and soldiers — 44 percent of its fighting strength. The army took its advance 30 miles farther north and on

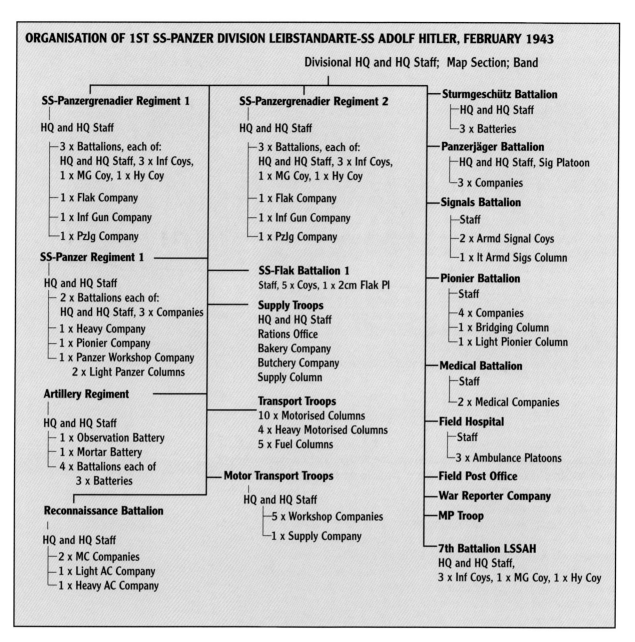

ORGANISATION OF 1ST SS-PANZER DIVISION LEIBSTANDARTE-SS ADOLF HITLER, FEBRUARY 1943

Divisional HQ and HQ Staff; Map Section; Band

SS-Panzergrenadier Regiment 1

HQ and HQ Staff

- 3 x Battalions, each of:
  HQ and HQ Staff, 3 x Inf Coys,
  1 x MG Coy, 1 x Hy Coy
- 1 x Flak Company
- 1 x Inf Gun Company
- 1 x PzJg Company

SS-Panzer Regiment 1

HQ and HQ Staff

- 2 x Battalions each of:
  HQ and HQ Staff, 3 x Companies
- 1 x Heavy Company
- 1 x Pionier Company
- 1 x Panzer Workshop Company
  2 x Light Panzer Columns

Artillery Regiment

HQ and HQ Staff

- 1 x Observation Battery
- 1 x Mortar Battery
- 4 x Battalions each of
  3 x Batteries

Reconnaissance Battalion

HQ and HQ Staff

- 2 x MC Companies
- 1 x Light AC Company
- 1 x Heavy AC Company

SS-Panzergrenadier Regiment 2

HQ and HQ Staff

- 3 x Battalions, each of:
  HQ and HQ Staff, 3 x Inf Coys,
  1 x MG Coy, 1 x Hy Coy
- 1 x Flak Company
- 1 x Inf Gun Company
- 1 x PzJg Company

SS-Flak Battalion 1
Staff, 5 x Coys, 1 x 2cm Flak Pl

Supply Troops
HQ and HQ Staff
Rations Office
Bakery Company
Butchery Company
Supply Column

Transport Troops
10 x Motorised Columns
4 x Heavy Motorised Columns
5 x Fuel Columns

Motor Transport Troops

HQ and HQ Staff
- 5 x Workshop Companies
- 1 x Supply Company

Sturmgeschütz Battalion
- HQ and HQ Staff
- 3 x Batteries

Panzerjäger Battalion
- HQ and HQ Staff, Sig Platoon
- 3 x Companies

Signals Battalion
- Staff
- 2 x Armd Signal Coys
- 1 x lt Armd Sigs Column

Pionier Battalion
- Staff
- 4 x Companies
- 1 x Bridging Column
- 1 x Light Pionier Column

Medical Battalion
- Staff
- 2 x Medical Companies

Field Hospital
- Staff
- 3 x Ambulance Platoons

Field Post Office

War Reporter Company

MP Troop

7th Battalion LSSAH
HQ and HQ Staff,
3 x Inf Coys, 1 x MG Coy, 1 x Hy Coy

18 March, the SS-Panzer Corps retook Byelgorod, thus regaining the defensive line of the Donets to Byelgorod, and correcting the tactical situation brought about by the Stalingrad disaster.

Previously, on 9 March, SS-Werfer Abteilung 102/502 (a Nebelwerfer unit) was assigned to the division, and shortly after taking Kharkov SS-Brigade Schuldt was disbanded. Despite the enormous losses, Kharkov was a timely victory, gained in no small part through the efforts of *Leibstandarte*. In every other theatre on every front the German armies were in retreat, and its propaganda value was immense. The red square in Kharkov was even renamed '*Leibstandarteplatz*' in the division's honour and on 21 March, Hitler awarded Dietrich Swords to his Knight's Cross.

It should be noted that, postwar, Soviet authorities alleged that *Leibstandarte* troops massacred 700 wounded Soviet troops in their hospital beds.

The late spring on the Eastern Front was quiet, a respite that afforded the division desperately needed time for rest and refitting. While attached to the reserve of Army Detachment Kempf in the Kharkov area, 2,500 Luftwaffe troops were transferred-in allowing time in May for some of the Leibstandarte veterans to visit their homes in Germany.

KURSK—OPERATION 'ZITADELLE'

Since June 1941, German attention had centred on the Russian front, but in the early months of 1943 the strategic situation began to change. The defeat of Rommel's Africa Korps in North Africa brought with it the prospect of an

Above: An SS motorcycle crew relaxes. The extreme cold, tiredness and the effort needed to ride the machine with its sidecar under these conditions is evident in the exhausted appearance of the rider and his passenger, April 1943.

invasion of Italy, and with the launching of daylight raids on the Ruhr by the USAAF 8th Air Force, German industrial production was threatened. There was also the looming threat of a Second Front in north-west Europe. So, although the Kharkov victory did much to restore German morale, with attention and resources now focused elsewhere no German commander believed that the next summer would see significant gains in Russia. However, on a limited level, the failure of Hitler's defensive doctrine during the winter had produced a substantial bonus, in that the long winter retreats had dramatically shortened the front and created a surplus strength on the Eastern Front equivalent to two armies. These two factors offered von Manstein and the OKH the temptation of an attack on the Soviet salient centred on Kursk. Although there was enthusiasm for the prospects of an incisive victory, most favoured defence. There were sharp divisions at the top, and even Hitler prevaricated. Some argued for the construction of an East Wall, a permanent line of fortifications across the USSR, and small local attacks that would wear down the Red Army. Guderian, recalled to active duty, told Hitler at a meeting on 9 March: 'The task for 1943 is to provide a certain number of tank divisions with complete battle efficiency capable of making limited objective attacks.'

Guderian's opinion, that only in 1944 would the Germans be able to go on the offensive again as the present situation showed that the divisions were much too weak, was shared by almost the entire senior army command. Von Manstein thought differently, believing it essential to deal the Soviet Army a series of powerful blows, and remove the Soviet threat to the Ukraine and Crimea. For three months Hitler deliberated, before finally deciding that he needed one more big victory in Russia, 'that will shine like a beacon around the world.' On 12 June he finally announced that he intended to execute Operation 'Zitadelle' (Citadel).

The plan for 'Zitadelle', developed by Hitler with Kurt Zeitzler, the OKH Chief of Staff, in March, projected converging strikes by Ninth Army (Walther Model, Army Group Centre) and Fourth Panzer Army (Hoth, Army Group South) on the northern and southern flanks of the Kursk salient to achieve a double envelopment. Hitler favoured a large build up of men and material for a great attack in the future, which Guderian bitterly contested. He insisted upon the need for immediate action, arguing that further delay would allow the Russians time to build further strength. Zeitzler shared von Manstein's beliefs, and these were presented to Hitler on a number of times after 19 March. When the attack was postponed by Hitler. Zeitzler and von

Above: The PzKpfw IIs and IIIs (seen here) were obsolescent by the time of Kursk but *Leibstandarte* still had some on strength in spring 1943.

Below: A StuG 40 heavy assault gun moves forward, August 1943. The long-barrelled 75mm StuK 40 was an improvement on the StuG III's StuK 37 and started reaching units in 1942. Note the condition of the *Schürzen*.

Manstein became increasingly sceptical, and privately the Führer himself expressed his reservations.

They were well-founded. Prewarned of the German intentions by intelligence sources (the 'Lucy' spy ring), the Soviet forces under Georgi Zhukov were able to fortify the salient heavily, preparing defences in depth as well as building up massive troop concentrations in the area. Those defences consisted of six defensive belts, complete with some 22,000 guns, 3,306 tanks, vast minefields and trenches, manned on the northern half of the salient by Konstantin Rokossovsky's seven armies and in the southern half by Nikolai Vatutin's six armies, which included a tank army and two Guards tank armies. The Germans planned to assault the salient with 43 divisions, of which 17 were armoured, and two tank brigades, grouped in the Ninth and Fourth Panzer Armies.

The defenders were of a much stronger calibre than in 1941, and well equipped. The Germans however, were not only losing manpower, but also firepower. While a 1941 Panzer regiment had three battalions of about 70 tanks, a 1943 Panzer regiment had only two battalions of about 50 tanks, with a third battalion equipped with some 30 Sturmgeschütz IIIG vehicles. The tanks themselves were admittedly of much better quality. The mainstays, the PzKpfw II and III, were now being slowly replaced by numbers of the PzKpfw IV series and, more importantly, by PzKpfw V Panther and PzKpfw VI Tiger tanks, but these were untried in battle and the latter had had a disastrous debut. The heavy company of the *Leibstandarte* had 12 Tigers ready for the assault, with 72 PzKpfw IVs, 16 PzKpfw IIIs and IIs and 31 assault guns. The SS-Panzer Corps had a total of 425 tanks with 110 assault guns.

In June Dietrich finally handed over command of *Leibstandarte* to Teddy Wisch. Promoted to the unique rank of SS-Obergruppenführer und Panzergeneral der Waffen-SS, upon returning to Berlin he set about creating I SS-Panzer Corps from elements of *Leibstandarte* and 12th SS-Panzergrenadier Division *Hitler Jugend*. It was perhaps inevitable that so able a commander, and an unshakeable supporter of the Führer, would rise through the hierarchy, even if by this time he had begun publicly to express his doubts about the likelihood of a decisive victory in the east.

For the attack on the Kursk salient, already badly compromised, *Leibstandarte* was again part of Hausser's II SS-Panzer Corps, Fourth Panzer Army, which was to drive through the Soviet defences on the Voronezh front before turning north-east to take Prokharovka, where a decisive action was expected. II SS-Panzer Corps was assigned the left flank of the Fourth Panzer Army attack, and *Leibstandarte* was to assault in its centre. On its left was the elite Wehrmacht Panzer division *Grossdeutschland*, part of XXXXVIII Panzer Corps. Having been brought up to full strength, at the end of June the division began the march to the SS-Corps troop staging area north of Tomarovka.

The attack was launched at 03:30hrs on 5 July. On the southern spearhead the three SS divisions moved on three parallel lines of advance. Fighting through the heavy minefields north of Byelgorod, *Leibstandarte* was by 19:30hrs on the southern outskirts of Jakovleva, a village within the second defensive line some 14 miles into Soviet territory, and had already suffered 97 killed and 522 wounded. In the north, Model's Ninth Army ran into difficulties in the thickly sown minefields that were heightened by the loss of over three-quarters of his new Panthers through mechanical problems.

After a night marked by continuous infantry battles in pouring rain, at dawn the next day the SS divisions assaulted bunkers and fortified positions in the second line of defensive works. In a day of heavy fighting, *Leibstandarte* armour engaged the 1st Guards Armoured Brigade, destroying a large part of it, and carrying the front line to Pokrovka, south-west of Prokharovka.

The following afternoon, having torn a large hole in the Soviet line, the push began to Oboyan, 37 miles south of Kursk on the River Psel. Second SS-Panzer Army moved north-east on the Teterevino–Prokharovka road, aiming at Prokharovka on the Kursk–Byelgorod railway, where the Soviets had already begun to concentrate their armour reserves. However, during the characteristically rapid advance, which had carried II SS-Panzer Corps some 25 miles deep into Soviet lines, the three Waffen-SS divisions became separated, and both corps flanks were left wide open as Kempf's armoured detachment, advancing on the right flank, and XXXXVIII Panzer Corps, on the left, fell behind. *Totenkopf* (Hermann Priess) was moved to the flanks, and the advance proceeded.

On 8 July the Soviet Fifth Guards Tank Army mounted an armoured counter-attack that aimed at cutting II SS-Panzer Corps' supply route on the Byelgorod–Oboyan road, but was savaged by the Luftwaffe. By the end of the day the Corps HQ was able to report that 290 Russian tanks had been destroyed in the three days of fighting, but the next day, the advance of the Ninth Army ground to a halt. II SS-Panzer Corps regrouped; *Das Reich* was placed on the defensive, and *Leibstandarte* was ordered to push onwards.

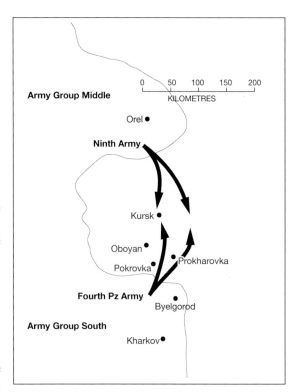

Above: The Battle of Kursk, 29 June–29 July 1943. The biggest tank battle of the war to date, by the end of it the SS-Panzer Corps would have its disposal only 30 PzKpfw VI Tigers, 69 PzKpfw IVs, 80 PzKpfw IIIs, four PzKpfw IIs and 64 assault guns along with a number of command vehicles and captured T-34s.

Below: Supported by a Tiger, infantry of the Waffen-SS move across uneven ground advancing against the enemy.

Above: The epitome of an *Ostkampfer*—an East Front fighter—August 1943.

Below: Wearing loose white covers to help him blend into the snow-covered terrain, this Waffen-SS Unterscharführer poses for the camera somewhere on the Eastern Front.

On the 10th, *Totenkopf* moved from the left to rejoin the *Leibstandarte* and *Das Reich* in the van for the assault on Prokharovka. Fighting through a sea of mud to the banks of the Psel River, to the west of the town and the last natural obstacle before Kursk, SS formations had by late afternoon assaulted across the river and were in position to attack the rear of the Soviet concentration. To the south III Panzer Corps began battling toward Prokharovka, attempting to link up with II SS-Panzer Corps before more Soviet reserves could be brought up.

On the plain outside the small town scene the forces massed for the largest tank battle yet seen, and the final decisive encounter on the Eastern Front. For the battle the Germans fielded some 600 tanks, and the Russians about 850, and with III Panzer Corps threatening from the south a pre-emptive strike was clearly advantageous to the Soviet commander, Vatutin. On 12 July Rotmistrov's Fifth Guards Tank Army launched a series of unco-ordinated strikes with the intention of separating the SS divisions. In an area of only a few square miles, firing at almost point-blank range across the dust-choked plain, the superior range of the German tank guns counted for nothing against suicidal attacks by Soviet tank crews. In the heavy fighting that ensued, the heavy company (the 13th) of *Leibstandarte*'s Panzer Regiment 1 engaged the Russian 181st Tank Regiment, and destroyed the whole unit without loss — but on both sides the losses were enormous. At the end of the day a thick pall of smoke hung over the wrecks nearly 700 tanks, nearly half of those engaged.

The Soviet attack was driven off, albeit with tremendous losses of men and materiel, and the Germans now held the area around Prokharovka and the railroad. III Panzer Korps managed to break through the Soviet line to the south that same day, but too late to effect the Kursk battle. Nevertheless, with the advance of the Fourth Panzer Army gathering pace, Von Manstein felt that he was close to success, so 13 July saw no let-up in the fighting at Kursk. While *Leibstandarte* rested, the *Totenkopf* and *Das Reich* divisions, attacked between Pravorot and Prokharovka, exploiting a gap in the enemy lines.

In the north, however, the Soviets had launched a strong counter-attack behind the Ninth Army north of Orel, which threatened to cut off the salient, forcing Model to redeploy forces and halting his advance. With the situation in the north around Orel becoming increasingly precarious, Hitler cancelled 'Zitadelle' on 13 July. There were still 80 miles, filled with defensive structures and Russian armour, between the two arms of the pincer, and the strength of the Soviet reserves could only be guessed at. Furthermore, on 10 July Allied troops had landed on Sicily, and the Soviets were threatening the Donets basin. To counter both of these threats Hitler needed troops. Although operations continued in von Manstein's sector, and II SS-Panzer Corps managed to link up with III Panzer Corps and destroy several Soviet units, heavy rainfall brought the advance, and German hopes of victory, to a halt on the night of 15 July.

At Kursk *Leibstandarte* paid heavily — 2,753 casualties, including 474 dead, and 19 tanks knocked out, or over 30 percent of its armoured strength. In total Hausser lost 420 of his tanks, while for the campaign Army Group South alone had expended 20,700 men killed and wounded. Soviet losses included 2,100 tanks, and the number of killed and wounded can only be guessed at. But having taken the initiative, the Soviets ensured there was no let up. In the immediate wake of the battles around Kursk, the Soviet commanders launched fierce counter-attacks against the Bryansk–Orel railway line that forced Model to withdraw from the Orel salient by 26 July.

In Italy a fresh emergency soon arose. In the wake of the Allied landings, the Fascist Grand Council led by Marshal Badoglio had begun secret negotiations with the Allies, and on 25 July it deposed Mussolini. Hitler was determined not to allow the Allies bases from which to attack the Romanian oilfields and expose his southern flank, and had already issued a contingency plan on 22 May, code-named Operation 'Alarich', that provided for the occupation of northern Italy and evacuation of the southern peninsula in the event of Italian capitulation to the Allies. In fact the negotiations between Italy and the Allies were protracted, allowing Hitler time to complete his occupation of Italy in September. On 3 August, as part of Alarich and against the bitter opposition of the front commanders, *Leibstandarte* was sent to Italy. Before entraining, it was stripped of all its remaining tanks, which passed over to *Das Reich* and *Totenkopf*, which now comprised the III SS-Panzer Corps. *Leibstandarte* then moved into Italy from Austria via the Brenner Pass, and occupied Bolzano. August passed on occupation duty in Milan, where the division was assigned new armoured vehicles, and helped to disarm surrendering Italian troops in the Po Valley.

In early August a strong Russian attack was launched by General Rodion Malinovsky's forces at the sector from which the Fourth Panzer Army had launched the attack against the Kursk salient. Malinovsky's attack tore a 35-mile wide gap in the German line. Through this breach the Russians poured, taking Byelgorod on 5 August and heading south-west toward the Dnieper River. As the fighting retreat continued along the Central Front towards Bryansk, Smolensk and Roslavl, Hitler finally accepted that retreat on the Eastern Front was inevitable and ordered work to begin on the defensive line (the 'Eastern Wall') previously suggested to him. This which was to run from Melitopol in the south to the shores of the Gulf of Finland at Narva — and it was to prove as unsuccessful as the Western Wall.

In the last two weeks of August the Soviet offensive was expanded to the north and south, where Fedor Tolbukhin's Southern Front drove in across the Donets south of Izyum and on the Mius River east of Snigrevka to threaten an envelopment of Army Group South. To the north, Kharkov was abandoned on 22 August and in the following week Army Group Centre's front was penetrated in three places. At the end of the month, the German Sixth Army withdrew from the Mius to the Kalmius, and three days later Army Group A began evacuating from the Taman peninsula.

Through the autumn the Soviet drive continued west, and on 15 September, with the northern flank of Army Group South threatening to disintegrate and the Soviets pressing at Smolensk, Hitler gave permission for the two army groups to retreat to the line of the Dnieper, Sozh and Pronya rivers. In most places the retreat was already underway, and in the last week of the month, as Bryansk, Smolensk and Roslavl were retaken, it developed into a race for the river lines.

Below: The north of Italy — *Leibstandarte* was transferred here on 1 August 1943 following the invasion of Sicily. The operation to take and hold north Italy proved remarkably successful. *Leibstandarte* left for Russia again in November, but the forces that remained showed that the thought that Italy would prove the 'soft underbelly of Europe' for Mark Clark's Fifth Army was entirely incorrect. In spite of Allied air superiority the German defence of North Italy proved dogged and efficient and the Germans would still hold some Italian territory in 1945.

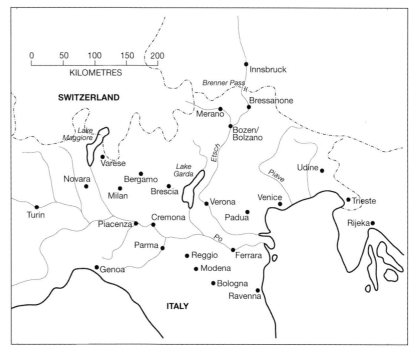

Above: Waffen-SS Grenadiers riding on the back of a Panzer IV. Apart from the dangers of the enemy and weather, troops travelling on the engine deck of tanks had another enemy — carbon monoxide poisoning, not unknown in Russia.

Above right: A welcome stop. A column of Waffen-SS motorcyclists pause during an exhausting move.

Below right: A stretcher bearer photographed during the Battle for Byelgorod.

Leibstandarte, stationed in northern Italy as part of II SS-Panzer Corps, was enjoying a welcome respite in the Italian sun. The sojourn was not without incident. Shortly after the surrender of the Italian government on 8 September, a detachment of the regiment was involved in Operation '*Eiche*' (Oak), the daring mountaintop rescue of Mussolini from captivity at the Campo Imperatore hotel on the Gran Sasso d'Italia high in the Abruzzi Apennine mountains.

On 19 September, reacting to a report that renegade Italian troops had captured two SS officers and were planning to attack the division, SS-Standartenführer Jochen Peiper shelled the town of Boves, killing 34 Italian civilians. Postwar, Italian authorities accused Peiper of war crimes for the attack, but the charges were dropped for lack of evidence. Further allegations were made that divisional troops helped round up Jews around Lake Maggiore for transfer to concentration camps: again these are as yet unconfirmed.

DEFENCE ON THE DNIEPER

The Dnieper River offers the strongest natural defensive line in western European Russia, but the losses incurred in battles to the east of the river denied Hitler the resources adequately to man and fortify the line and, coupled with the fact that the Red Army had established five bridgeheads over the river, the position the German armies held was at best tenuous. The stark reality of the situation was that in just two and a half months Army Group Centre and South had been forced back for an average of 150 miles on a front 650 miles long, and in so doing, had lost the most valuable territory taken during the advances of 1941–42. As for the East Wall, nothing had been done. Much of the proposed line had yet to be even surveyed.

After a brief interlude in the first week of October, as the Russians paused to regroup and bring up new forces, 45 divisions of the 4th Ukrainian Front attacked the Sixth Army positions between Melitopol and the Dnieper, and in three weeks it was driven back onto the lower Dnieper, trapping the Seventeenth Army in the Crimea. On 15 October a fresh onslaught began, this time at the First and Eighth Panzer Armies south of Kremenchung. Here the Soviets threw the full weight of the 2nd and 3rd Ukrainian Fronts, opening a 200-mile wide bridgehead between Cherkassy and Zaporozhe, while to the south the 3rd Ukrainian Front threatened important iron and manganese mining areas near Krivoi Rog and Nikopol. Then, south of the bridgehead at the confluence of the Pripyat and Dnieper, the Soviets broke out of two smaller bridgeheads and on 6 November, Kiev was retaken by the 1st Ukrainian Front, creating a large salient in the front.

In November *Leibstandarte* was ordered back to the Eastern Front. It travelled via Lvov to Ternopol as part of XXXXVIII Corps of the Fourth Panzer Army, and was rushed east into positions on the southern flank of the Kiev salient for a counter-attack that aimed at Zhitomir, and the Soviet bridgehead on the Dnieper. The attack was launched on 19 November and initially it achieved some success. Zhitomir was taken, and although it would soon have to be relinquished, Soviet supply routes between the city and Kiev were cut. Next *Leibstandarte* moved on Brusilov, where it met a strong concentration of V and VIII Guards Armoured Corps, and I Guard Cavalry Corps. With the 1st Panzer and 9th Panzer Divisions attacking the northern and southern flanks, and *Leibstandarte* from the west, on 24 November the concentration was encircled and destroyed. But despite inflicting substantial losses on the enemy, the Germans were unable, for lack of manpower, to hold the positions they captured and carry the advance further. On 16 December, amid biting cold and blinding snowstorms the division advanced east with the 1st and 7th Panzer Divisions from Korosten, aiming at encircling the Soviet armies around Meleni. This was achieved, but with so few troops that the positions could not be held and soon attack turned to retreat.

As the year drew to a close, the Fourth Panzer Army was pushed back west and south of the city by a fresh offensive launched on Christmas Eve by the combined forces of four Russian armies plus two independent corps of the 1st Ukrainian Front against the southern rim of Kiev. The next day it developed a second thrust west, which threatened to destroy the entire left flank of Army Group South, and succeeded in recapturing Zhitomir and the road linking it to Kiev. While recognising that this thrust could be employed to drive the two army groups back against the Black Sea and the Carpathian Mountains, Hitler saw that the southern attack posed the danger of an envelopment of Army Groups South and A between the Dnieper and Dniester Rivers, and considered it the greater danger. Fourth Panzer Army was ordered to bring it to a halt.

Although December had brought some respite, enabling the German forces to regain some of their balance, the best solution to the German predicament at this stage would have been to order Army Group South to withdraw to the next major line of defence, the Bug River. This Hitler would not consider, and instead the armies were told to hold their positions for the winter, and informed that they would have to do so without extra resources that were needed for defence against the expected invasion of north-west Europe. And so, now in the third winter of the Russian campaign, the men of *Leibstandarte* could again reflect on a year in which they had time and again been used to reinforce weak points in the German lines and incurred huge losses, many of them from the experienced core of veterans.

As the war in the east entered its fourth year, Zhukov's 1st Ukrainian Front moved across the Dnieper against Kirovgrad, taking advantage of the now severely weakened Army Group South right flank. Two days later Kirovgrad was in Russian hands, despite spirited defence by 11 German divisions. Fighting a continuing series of defensive engagements in the area around Zhitomir, Korosten and Beredichev, *Leibstandarte* at Beredichev temporarily checked the Soviet advance. By mid-January the Soviet First Tank Army, spearheading the 1st Ukrainian Front's southern advance, had gained 65 miles and was approaching Uman. In knee-deep mud, sleet and blizzards, Army Group South fought desperately to prevent its front from collapsing.

A new attack, begun on 25 January by Koniev's 2nd Ukrainian Front, in four days linked up with Vatunin's 1st Ukrainian Front and encircled six German divisions totalling 100,000 men at Korsun-Shevchenkovsky, north-west of Cherkassy. Hitler

Above: On the Eastern Front, March 1944. A messenger checks his horse's hooves prior to mounting. For all the attempts to motorise the army, Germany forces used more horses in World War II than World War I.

Below: Dutch SS Volunteers manning a 20mm flak gun in the ground role, July 1944. By the pile of expended ammunition at right they have seen heavy action. Dutchmen would make up two SS-Freiwilligen Divisions formed in 1945 — the Panzer Division Nederland and the Grenadier Division Landstorm Nederland

refused to countenance any breakout attempt, insisting that von Manstein instead link up with the trapped forces and thus re-establish the Dnieper line.

For the rescue attempt von Manstein concentrated most of his tank strength in XXXXVI and III Panzer Corps, and attached *Leibstandarte* to the latter. On 11 February the breakout began, with *Leibstandarte* attacking on the northern flank with the 1st, 17th and 16th Panzer Divisions assaulting to the south. Conditions could not have been worse with thick fog and heavily bogged roads rendering rapid movement virtually impossible. Zhukov threw in the Fifth Guards Tank Army to counter the German thrust and halted the northern flank when it was barely eight miles from the trapped pocket. Realising that the link-up he envisaged had failed, Hitler consented to a break-out attempt on 16 February, and that night a slow-moving column formed. Leaving the wounded and most of their equipment behind, 35,000 men began moving toward III Panzer Corps positions south-west of Dzhurzhentsky. Men of the *Leibstandarte*, covering the retreat, exhibited considerable bravery. In one documented incident two NCOs of the 6th Company, 2nd Panzergrenadier Regiment, held off two companies of Soviet troops before they could be relieved. In all 32,000 troops escaped from the pocket, about half of the number that had been trapped. Had it been totally surrounded Army Group South would almost certainly have been destroyed.

At the end of the month Army Groups South and A held a weak but almost continuous line about halfway between the Dnieper and the Bug. Its actions at Cherkassy and in holding this line left *Leibstandarte* badly mauled. Pulled back into the line north-east of Uman to face the advance of the 1st Ukrainian Front, by 28 February, it had only three tanks and four assault guns operational.

These straits afflicted all of von Manstein's divisions. In a pitifully weakened state they faced a mighty assault by the 1st, 2nd, and 3rd Ukrainian Fronts between the Pripet Marshes and the Carpathian mountains early in March, and in the north were driven behind the 1939 Polish border nearly to Kovel. In the centre the attack fell on Eighth Army east of Uman and in the south drove through the centre of the Sixth Army below Krivoi Rog. Manstein was obliged to make a gradual withdrawal to the Dniester River on the border with Romania, but Hitler's insistence on holding the mines near Nikopol and Krivoi Rog meant that by the end of the month the Sixth Army had nearly been encircled. On the left flank, the Soviet advance in the vicinity of Shepetovka opened a gaping hole in the German line. *Leibstandarte*, fighting as part of XXIV Corps, was unable to stem the onslaught, and by 15 March, the division had been all but annihilated — less than 1,250 men remained. In the last week of the month, together with the whole of the First Panzer Army, it was encircled at Kamenets-Podolski. Precious fuel and supplies were airlifted in to the pocket, and on 27 March, as the 4th Panzer Division (with 9th SS-Panzer Division *Hohenstaufen* and 10th SS-Panzer Division *Frundsberg*) launched a diversionary attack, the remnants of *Leibstandarte* fought out of the pocket to the west. By mid-April it was safely back in German lines.

THE WESTERN FRONT

On 18 April the division, although what remained scarcely warranted the name, entrained for north-western France for rest and refitting, to counter the expected summer invasion of north-west Europe. From 25 April it was headquartered at Turnhout, Belgium, as one of the elements of Dietrich's newly created I SS-Panzer Corps which was given the title *Leibstandarte* Adolf Hitler, with units at Hasselt and Herentals. Here over 2,000 troops were transferred into the division from the 12th SS Division, and on 3 May Hitler decreed new equipment for the division, much of it to come straight from the factory. With these and other replacements, by June 1944 *Leibstandarte* had been rebuilt to a strength of 20,000. However, it is worth noting that it was still some 208 officers and 2,234 NCOs and men below its notional establishment, and that the reinforcements were mostly raw recruits. In material strength, the division had 42–45 self-propelled guns, 48–50 PzKpfw IVs, 38 PzKpfw V Panthers, and 29 PzKpfw VI Tigers.

In early June, with German forces all along the Western Wall poised for the Allied invasion, which was expected to fall on the Pas de Calais, *Leibstandarte* was at Enghen, Belgium, on the reserve strength of OKH. For the invasion the Allies, under the command of General Eisenhower, had two army groups under Montgomery, plus an invasion fleet of 5,000 ships and most importantly a huge air armada that included 13,000 American aircraft alone. For the most part, with the exception of those who had fought in the desert and in Italy, the Allied soldiers were without experience, poorly trained and less politically motivated than their adversaries, particularly the SS infantrymen. The Allied soldier was also dependent on equipment untested in battle, tactics that were hopelessly outdated and had achieved nothing like the German level of co-ordination with armoured forces that were equipped with tanks greatly inferior to the Germans. It is hard to remember that the success of 'Overlord' was by no means a foregone conclusion. Crucial to the success were the elaborate deception operations (such as Operation 'Bodyguard') that preceded it, under which a fictitious army, the American First Army, was assembled in south-east England to reinforce the view held by von Rundstedt, C-in-C West, that the invasion would come in the Pas de Calais region. Thus on 6 June, when the Allies launched the second front in Normandy, Hitler still firmly believed that Normandy was merely a decoy operation to hide a larger invasion to come, and denied Rundstedt reinforcements for a counter-attack, instead relying on the two Panzer divisions in the area to face the weight of the combined air, sea and land offensive.

Severe moving sanctions were imposed on *Leibstandarte* and the 19 other divisions of the Fifteenth Army held in the Pas de Calais. *Leibstandarte*, as part of the strategic reserve, could not be called into action without the express permission of the Führer himself. The situation was further complicated by a muddled chain of command and communications, which meant that *Leibstandarte* was separated from the other elements of Dietrich's I SS-Panzer Corps — namely 12th SS-Panzer Division *Hitler Jugend*, 21st Panzer Division and Panzer Lehr. These had been transferred to the Normandy area prior to the invasion and, as the only three German divisions in the area, bore the full brunt of the initial assault. While *Leibstandarte* hurried to make ready its combat and supply vehicles for the move south, the *Hitler Jugend* became heavily involved in the fighting for Caen, 10 miles south-west of the mouth of the River Orne. The town and its surrounding heights were the primary target of the Anglo-Canadian forces at the eastern end of the invasion front over the first two weeks, but all attempts to capture the town were repulsed by stern defence, and the Allies suffered costly losses before they were be able to break out towards open terrain.

Above: A short pause in the fighting somewhere on the Eastern Front. Farm buildings burn in the background, behind this MG34 gunner. The experience gained by such troops on the Eastern Front meant that the fresh US and British troops coming ashore in Normandy faced forces with a proportion of veterans in their ranks. However, such was the attrition in Russia that the core of veterans was often quite small and the divisions were bulked out by well-motivated — and at this stage in the war still well-trained — but inexperienced troops.

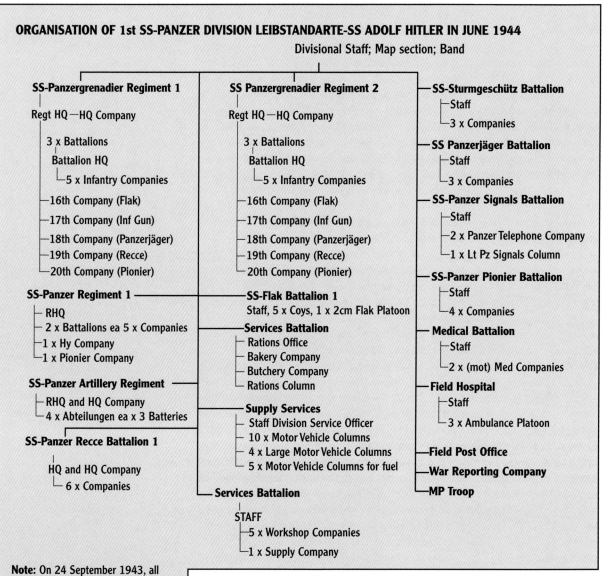

ORGANISATION OF 1st SS-PANZER DIVISION LEIBSTANDARTE-SS ADOLF HITLER IN JUNE 1944

Divisional Staff; Map section; Band

SS-Panzergrenadier Regiment 1

Regt HQ—HQ Company

3 x Battalions
Battalion HQ
└ 5 x Infantry Companies
—16th Company (Flak)
—17th Company (Inf Gun)
—18th Company (Panzerjäger)
—19th Company (Recce)
—20th Company (Pionier)

SS-Panzer Regiment 1 ——————
├ RHQ
├ 2 x Battalions ea 5 x Companies
├ 1 x Hy Company
└ 1 x Pionier Company

SS-Panzer Artillery Regiment ———
├ RHQ and HQ Company
└ 4 x Abteilungen ea x 3 Batteries

SS-Panzer Recce Battalion 1
HQ and HQ Company
└ 6 x Companies

SS Panzergrenadier Regiment 2

Regt HQ—HQ Company

3 x Battalions
Battalion HQ
└ 5 x Infantry Companies
—16th Company (Flak)
—17th Company (Inf Gun)
—18th Company (Panzerjäger)
—19th Company (Recce)
—20th Company (Pionier)

SS-Flak Battalion 1
Staff, 5 x Coys, 1 x 2cm Flak Platoon

Services Battalion
├ Rations Office
├ Bakery Company
├ Butchery Company
└ Rations Column

Supply Services
├ Staff Division Service Officer
├ 10 x Motor Vehicle Columns
├ 4 x Large Motor Vehicle Columns
└ 5 x Motor Vehicle Columns for fuel

Services Battalion
STAFF
├ 5 x Workshop Companies
└ 1 x Supply Company

SS-Sturmgeschütz Battalion
├ Staff
└ 3 x Companies

SS Panzerjäger Battalion
├ Staff
└ 3 x Companies

SS-Panzer Signals Battalion
├ Staff
├ 2 x Panzer Telephone Company
└ 1 x Lt Pz Signals Column

SS-Panzer Pionier Battalion
├ Staff
└ 4 x Companies

Medical Battalion
├ Staff
└ 2 x (mot) Med Companies

Field Hospital
├ Staff
└ 3 x Ambulance Platoon

Field Post Office

War Reporting Company

MP Troop

Note: On 24 September 1943, all Panzer divisions of the Heer (with the exception of 21st Panzer Division and Panzer Division Norwagen) were reorganised as Type 43 Panzer Divisions. Subsequently, the Waffen-SS expanded to 17 divisions, seven corps, plus miscellaneous guard, support and special forces troops, and on 22 October, the division was renamed 1st SS-Panzer Division *Leibstandarte*-SS Adolf Hitler. A Sturmgeschütz battalion and a medical company were transferred to 12th SS Panzer Division *Hitler Jugend*

On 9 June, acting on intelligence based on a intercept of Allied radio traffic suggesting an imminent attack in the Pas de Calais, *Leibstandarte* was ordered to an assembly area of east of Bruges to meet the assault. But this too was, in fact, part of the deception plans. Finally, six days after the invasion Hitler ordered *Leibstandarte* to make all haste in its preparations and join *Hitler Jugend* near Caen, under the command of I SS-Panzer Corps.

Despite some significant successes, including the heavy defeat of the 7th Armoured Division at Villers-Bocage on the 13th at the hands of former *Leibstandarte* officer Michael Wittmann, now commander of the 2nd Company of the 101st Heavy Panzer Battalion of I SS-Panzer Corps, by the 21st the Allies had a secure bridgehead on the Normandy beaches, and vast quantities of men and materiel were flooding ashore. With the understrength German divisions in Normandy committed at Caen, the Americans were able to break out of their bridgehead on the 18th and take Cherbourg on 27 June. German troop and materiel movement across northern France was seriously hampered by the effective disruption of the transport network by Allied bombing, and *Leibstandarte's* PzKpfw V Panther tanks could not be transported across France, to be unloaded at Rouen, until the last week of the month. Divisional HQ was established 15 miles south of Caen. Finally on 28 June the 1st Panzergrenadier Regiment arrived Caen, and on the next day *Leibstandarte* units reached the invasion front. But it was be another week before the division was up to full strength, robbing Dietrich of the opportunity to use *Leibstandarte* for a combined counter-attack with *Hitler Jugend* to push the Allies back onto the beaches. In the interim, *Hitler Jugend* suffered grievously in the face of a concerted attempt to take high ground to the west of Caen by the infantry and armour of British VIII Corps (Operation 'Epsom'), launched on 25 June and preceded by a massive bombardment from sea and air. Gradually the division was driven back and relinquished part of the city to the British, albeit at a heavy cost to the attackers.

On 6 July the Allies launched Operation 'Charnwood' to secure the rest of the city. *Leibstandarte*, along with other German units, was rushed to the British sector and until 9th was fully engaged in repulsing the attack, which cost the life of former *Leibstandarte* regimental commander and current *Hitler Jugend* commander Fritz Witt, killed in his HQ by naval gunfire.

Although he had been held again at Caen, this concentration of German forces in the Caen sector was much as Montgomery planned (according to his own account), as it allowed American preparations for a major breakout in the western sector to go unmolested. In their sector, the only Waffen-SS divisions available were 2nd SS-Panzer Division *Das Reich* and 17th SS-Panzergrenadier Division *Gotz von Berlichingen*, which were without any of their heavy armour.

On 11 July, *Leibstandarte* took over the Caen sector from the seriously depleted *Hitler Jugend*. Here, over the coming week, it played its most crucial role in the Normandy battles. Beginning on 18 July, three British armoured divisions attempted to break through the gap between Caen and the eastern heights, across a small bridgehead over the Orne River and through the four lines of man-made and natural defences, then across the hills at Bourguebus and to the open ground beyond. The operation was preceded by a three-hour bombardment by some 2,500 Allied aircraft, followed immediately by the armoured assault. 'Goodwood' began well for the British, who seized all their primary objectives, but then *Leibstandarte* was rushed in from Falaise, south of Caen. Arriving late in the afternoon, *Leibstandarte* launched a counter-attack along with the 21st Panzer Division and the British attack was halted on the left flank. The next morning fighting was sporadic, and it appeared that 'Goodwood' had petered out, but in the early afternoon, having brought up reinforcements, the British attacked again. The armoured spearhead quickly overran the forward German units and pressed on, but as the leading tanks approached the hill at Bourguebus at 16:00hrs, they came under accurate and concerted fire by the Panthers and PzKpfw IVHs of *Leibstandarte*, which had taken up positions on the hill itself. Heavy casualties were inflicted on the British 7th and 11th Armoured Divisions.

Inevitably, the weakened German defences began to lose the battle of attrition. Few reinforcements arrived, and free-roaming Allied aircraft destroyed supplies from the air before they could reach the lines and made movement by day in the maze of narrow lanes impossible. By the 21st, despite failing to break out of the Orne bridgehead, the Allies had expanded the bridgehead by some five miles and finally taken Caen from its defenders. *Leibstandarte* held firm defensive positions on the Caen–Falaise highway until the end of the month, against repeated Allied attacks. On the 28th, the number of killed, wounded, missing or captive

Above: On 31 July 1944 the Allies broke through the German lines around Avranches. Although badly mauled the battered SS divisions still proved to be dangerous opponents. This Wespe 105mm mounted on a PzKpfw II chassis was produced from 1943 and first saw action at Kursk.

Below: An SdKfz 231 eight-wheeled armoured car from the *Hitler Jugend* Division amidst the ruins of a French town. The 12th SS-Panzer Division *Hitler Jugend* was an attached unit to I SS-Panzer Corps during the Battle of Normandy.

SUBSIDIARY UNITS OF 1st SS-PANZER CORPS LEIBSTANDARTE ADOLF HITLER IN NORMANDY, 1944

Corps HQ I SS-Panzer Corps/101
Aircraft Staffel (Flight)
SS-Corps Map Unit
SS-Rocket Launcher Battery (mot)
    101/501
SS-Corps Signals Battalion 101/501
SS-Hy Observation Battery 101/501
SS-Military Geology Battalion 101
SS-Corps Supply Troops 101
SS-Lorry Company 101
SS-Corps Hospital Abteilung101
SS-Artillery Command I
SS-Artillery Battalion 101/501
SS-Flak Battalion 101
SS-Flak Company
SS-Ambulance Platoon 501
SS-Field Post Office (mot) 101
SS-War Reporting Company (mot)
SS-MP Company 101 (mot)
SS-Korps-Sicherungs-Kompanie 101
SS-Field Replacement Brigade
SS-Field Hospital 501

Attached units
1st SS-Panzer Division
    Leibstandarte-SS Adolf Hitler
12th SS-Panzer Division Hitler
    Jugend
Panzer Lehr Division (for the
    Normandy Campaign, 1944)
Heavy SS-Panzer Abteilung 101
    (501) (for the Normandy
    Campaign, 1944)

was 1,500 and Panzer strength stood at 33 PzKpfw V Panthers, 30 PzKpfw IVs and 22 Sturmgeschütz IIIs.

In the last week of July, the US forces launched Operation 'Cobra' from the vicinity of St Lô, a concerted attempt to break-out of the 'bocage' terrain that had stymied their advance, carrying Omar Bradley's First Army to Avranches at the base of the Cotentin Peninsula. At the beginning of August, Hitler ordered a German counter-attack, aimed at splitting the First Army, now commanded by Courtney Hodges, and Patton's Third. New reinforcements brought *Leibstandarte* strength up to 20,395. The plan called for two co-ordinated thrusts, one of which headed west towards Avranches, and the other in an encircling movement towards St Lô. Launched on the 6th, initially gains of a few miles were made, but it was soon halted by a murderous barrage of rocket fire by Allied fighter-bombers. On 7 August, under a blanket of protective cloud, *Leibstandarte*, together with four other SS-Panzer divisions and three Wehrmacht Panzer divisions, renewed the attack. *Das Reich* managed to recapture Mortain, and a *Leibstandarte* armoured battle group under Jochen Peiper advanced as far as Bourlopin, but was again stopped by massive concentrations of Allied aircraft. Another attempt was mounted the next day, but it too failed. The Canadian First Army then launched a powerful thrust south-west to Falaise, and an encirclement of the German forces threatened. Three days after it began the Avranches attack petered out, and *Leibstandarte* was pulled back into defensive positions at St Barthelemy.

On 13 August, *Leibstandarte* arrived at Argentan on the Orne, south-east of Falaise. The following day, with the noose tightening around Seventh Army in the 'Falaise Pocket', Dietrich again requested permission to pull back, but was refused. Encircled by the Allied forces, and under a hail of aircraft and artillery fire, Hausser, commander of Fifth Army, was told by von Kluge (who had succeeded von Rundstedt as Commander-in-Chief West) to withdraw II SS-Panzer Corps (*Hohenstaufen* and *Frundsberg*), his motors and his administrative personnel, and between 21 and 24 August *Leibstandarte* crossed the Seine near Elbeuf and was withdrawn to positions behind the river. Although 35,000 escaped from Falaise, some 50,000 other German troops and much of the equipment were captured.

Having jumped the Seine and captured Paris on 25 August, the Allies began the pursuit of the disorganised German forces across northern France and into Belgium. Already, on the 15th, supplementary landings had been made in the south of France between Cannes and Toulon (Operation 'Dragoon') in support of the Normandy invasion rendering the German position in France increasingly precarious. Pulled back through Marle and Montcornet, by the end of the month *Leibstandarte* reputedly had no tanks or artillery pieces and had suffered an estimated 6,000 casualties. There was no let up in the fighting. On 3 September there were minor defensive skirmishes with British troops in Philippeville, Fleurus and in Mons, Belgium, where the division was again threatened with encirclement, this time by the US First Army. Another 25,000 German troops fell captive, but *Leibstandarte* slipped through the net at Jodoigne, Tirlemont, Hasselt and Diest, and into the Bree–Neerpelt–Lommel Mol area. On 4 September, with the US Army preparing to cross the Meuse, *Leibstandarte* received orders to withdraw to the area around Bitburg, Germany, and into the defences of the Western Wall.

Despite three months of successful advances the Allies had yet to capture any of the Channel ports, and their overstretched supply lines ran all the way back to the Normandy coast. Thus at the beginning of September there was a notable loss of momentum, which allowed the Germans time to reorganise. Through the month, poorly conceived operations against Antwerp and three important Dutch river positions at Arnhem (Operation 'Market Garden') were successfully beaten off, as Montgomery and Patton engaged in a race to the Rhine that further stretched the supply lines. Von Rundstedt, who had been reappointed as C-in-C West by Hitler in an attempt to bolster morale, now marshalled the 63 depleted divisions along the Western Wall running along the line of the German/Dutch frontier for the defence of the homeland. Although this not was considered practicable by the field commanders, the alternative, a retreat to the Rhine, was not even considered by Hitler.

THE ARDENNES — OPERATION 'HERBSTNEBEL'

In fact, with the Allies halted in the north by II SS-Panzer Corps and in the south by a determined defence from 11th Panzer Division and several Volksgrenadier divisions, and the knowledge that the Allied supply lines had been overstretched, Hitler was already confidently preparing a counter-offensive at the southern flank of the US Third Army — the offensive was called Operation '*Herbstnebel*' or 'Autumn Mist'.

His ambitious plan, essentially a repeat of the 1940 offensive, centred on a rapid drive to Antwerp to split the British and American forces and stabilise his western front. Both von Rundstedt and Model voiced their reservations, but they were ignored. Thus through the late autumn and into December 25 German divisions, 11 of them armoured, secretly made ready for the offensive. For the attack they were arranged into three armies, under Dietrich, Manteuffel and Brandenberger. Dietrich's Sixth Panzer Army, commanding I (Herman Priess) and II (Willi Bittrich) SS-Panzer Corps, was by far the most powerful, and as the first wave tasked with the main effort of breaking through the US XVIII Corps' (Matthew Ridgway) lines in the Ardennes, seizing the high ground of Elsenborn Ridge and control of the roads in the north, and then moving to capture the vital bridges across the Meuse between

Below: Reinforcements being rushed forward to the Normandy front. The heavy camouflage on this PzKpfw IV reflects the problems caused by Allied air supremacy.

ORGANISATION OF 1st SS-PANZER DIVISION LEIBSTANDARTE-SS ADOLF HITLER IN AUTUMN 1944

SS-Kampfgruppe Hansen
1 x SS-Panzergrenadier Regiment
1 x SS-Panzerjäger Abteilung
    (21 x Jagdpanzer IV, 11 x 75mm
    PaK)
1 x Artillery Abteilung (towed
    105mm guns, 24 x Nebelwerfers)

SS-Kampfgruppe Sandig
1 x SS-Panzergrenadier Regiment
1 x Flak Abteilung
1 x Nebelwerfer Abteilung
1 x Pionier Abteilung

SS-Kampfgruppe Knittel
1 x SS-Recce Battalion
1 x Battery towed 105mm guns
1 x SS- Panzer Pionier Company

SS-Kampfgruppe Peiper
1 x SS-Panzer Regiment (72 x
    PzKpfw V Panthers and PzKpfw
    IVHs)
1 x Heavy SS-Panzer Abteilung
(No 501 with 45 x Königstiger)
1 x Flak Abteilung (No 84)
1 x SS-Panzergrenadier Battalion
1 x SS-Panzer Artillery Battalion
1 x Sturmgeschütz Company
2 x SS-Panzer Pionier Companies
1 x SS-Panzer Signals Company

Liège and Huy. A second wave with Kurt Student's Fifteenth Army was then to advance on Antwerp, trapping four Allied armies in the north. Manteuffel's Fifth Panzer Army on the south-western flank aimed at Brussels, and Brandenberger's Seventh Army was to hold the southern flank. The start date was set at 16 December.

During late October and early November *Leibstandarte*, as part of LXVI Corps, Seventh Army, refitted at Osnabrück. New equipment was found, although munitions and fuel were becoming increasingly scarce, and 3,500 replacements, many of them with only a minimum of training, were drafted in. Between 9 and 18 November, assigned to Sixth SS-Panzer Army, the division assisted in rescue efforts to save German civilians at Köln (Cologne), after the devastating Allied bombing on the city. By December 1944, division strength was at 22,000 (estimated), 84 tanks, and 20 self-propelled guns Finally on 14 December the heavy veil of secrecy that had masked preparations for the winter offensive in the Ardennes lifted. I SS-Panzer Corps was placed at the spearhead between Hollerath and Krewinkel, with *Hitler Jugend* on the right and *Leibstandarte* on the left. *Leibstandarte*, now in the command of Wilhelm Mohnke, was instructed to divide into four Kampfgruppen, under Hansen, Sandig, Knittel and Peiper.

The attack began at first light on 16 December with a concerted artillery barrage on the American lines, thinly held by six divisions of resting and newly arrived troops. At spearhead of the I SS–Panzer Corps, Kampfgruppe Peiper — the most powerful Kampfgruppe — began moving through the heavy snow with Kampfgruppe Sandig following closely behind. Passing through the heavily wooded and congested Losheim Gap into Belgium, where 12th Volksgrenadier Division had swept aside weak defence, progress was at first slow, but by early evening the vanguard of *Leibstandarte* was past Losheim and moving west through more open terrain toward Lanzerath. Here it met with 9th Fallschirmjäger Regiment and struck out towards Buchholz railway station on the Buchholz–Honsfeld road. By first light on the 17th *Leibstandarte* was in Honsfeld, which it took with comparative ease.

But hour by hour, Pieper's limited fuel reserves were rapidly diminishing. Disregarding specific orders to avoid the area, he turned north toward the American fuel depot at Büllingen, bypassed Heppenbach and captured the depot, and 50,000 gallons of precious fuel with comparative ease. Pressured by accurate artillery fire, his Kampfgruppe moved out in two columns on the Büllingen–St Vith road shortly before midday, then toward Ligneuville on the route to Stavelot, taking Schoppen, Ondenval and Thirimont. South east of Malmédy *Leibstandarte* ran into Battery B of the US 285th Artillery Observation Battalion, who were quickly captured and herded into a field adjacent to a crossroads near Baugnez. According to the reports of survivors, at least 86 of them were subsequently executed when a passing SS soldier began firing into the group. When details of the massacre became public a few days later, Dietrich's headquarters ordered an investigation, but that met with denial. The incident is, perhaps, the most notorious of the atrocities for which *Leibstandarte* soldiers stood trial.

At Ligneuville, Peiper was delayed by a few American tanks but soon took the town. Continuing on towards Trois Ponts and Beaumont, at Stavelot the lead units met with fierce defence and were forced to wait for daybreak to carry on the advance. By 10:00hrs, after a heavy German artillery barrage, the Stavelot bridge was firmly in German hands. Peiper immediately headed for the three crossings — two over the Salm and one over the Amblève — in the Trois Ponts area, from where he intended to move on Werbomont. On 18 December Peiper's lead elements reached Stavelot and Trois Ponts on the north side of the Amblève. Moments before his arrival, the 291st Engineers had blown three bridges — one over the Amblève at Trois Ponts and two on the Salm River, south of Trois Ponts.

Peiper was now forced to turn north to La Gleize, rather than follow his planned crossing of the Amblève for the most direct route to the objective. To complicate matters further, the river on his left and the high wooded hills on the right limited his route of advance to the vulnerable valley road. In the late afternoon the fog that had hampered air operations cleared, and the battle group came under attack by fighter-bombers. These succeeded only in delaying the column, but on the night of 18/19 December Kampfgruppe Peiper was in woodland surrounding Stoumont, and appeared poised to break out of the valley and into the open country to the north.

Opposite: Troops of the Waffen-SS resting in the bocage of Normandy.

Below: Kampfgruppe Peiper's progress during the Ardennes campaign 16 December 1944–20 January 1945. Initially good progress was halted by tenacious American defence, although Peiper did secure much-needed fuel at Büllingen. He also had the opportunity to attack northwards from there to encircle the American divisions on the Elsenborn ridge. While this would probably have had no impact on the course of the campaign, it would certainly have had an immediate tactical effect.

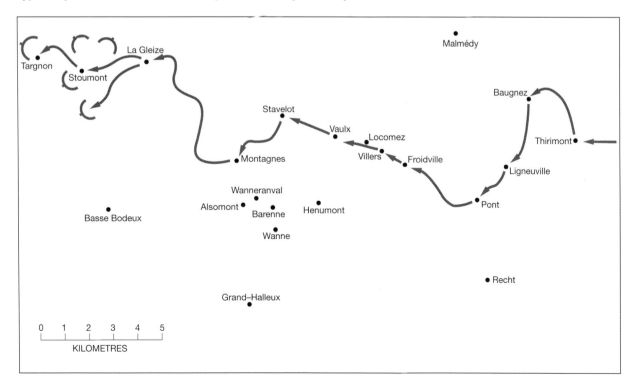

Above: Captured as he crouched in a foxhole this boy soldier was taken prisoner by a unit of the US Seventh Army. He claimed to be 14 years and seven months old and was one of the youngest soldiers captured by the American unit. He is wearing Waffen-SS garments with all the insignia removed.

It was, however, isolated at the head of a long salient and suffering another fuel crisis. Furthermore, Dietrich had still failed to capture the Elsenborn Ridge on the right flank and Allied HQ had woken up to full extent of the attack, which initially had been interpreted as a local attack on Monschau. As reinforcements were rushed into the line, opposition began to stiffen considerably.

Peiper moved on Stoumont on the morning of the 19th, where a desperate battle ensued with units of the 30th Infantry Division before the town was finally taken. Dangerously low fuel supplies now forced him to halt, unaware of the vast fuel depot located in the area. But as he waited at Stoumont for fuel and reinforcements to cross the Stoumont bridge and continue the drive, Stavelot was attacked by US troops, and by the evening the northern approach to the bridge had been destroyed. The noose was tightening on Peiper. Although he had found an intact bridge over the Amblève at Cheneux, his advance in that sector was halted by the 82nd Airborne Division, which had built a front on the south side of the Amblève extending east to the Salm.

Now trapped, Peiper sought and was refused permission to withdraw back to the *Leibstandarte* lines. A battalion of the 2nd SS-Panzergrenadier Regiment managed to reach him with vital fuel on foot via a footbridge across the Amblève east of Trois Ponts at Petit Spa, and on the afternoon of 22 December they attacked the US aid station at Petit Coo. Fierce fighting raged on into the night, but efforts to reinforce Peiper from the east and to retake Stavelot by other elements of the *Leibstandarte* on the 19th were beaten off and an attempt in mid-afternoon by the combined forces of Kampfgruppe Sandig's two battalions and Peiper's two Königstiger battalions, with a co-ordinated attack westward by Gustav Knittel's command, also failed under accurate and heavy artillery fire.

Abandoning its plans for attack, on 21 December Kampfgruppe Peiper withdrew to La Gleize, a small hamlet containing nothing more then a circle of white houses with a church and a schoolhouse, near to the vital Cheneux bridge. In the schoolhouse basement Peiper established his HQ, and was soon under fire from US heavy artillery located at Stoumont. In the streets savage battles finally forced the Germans back, and on 23 December Peiper was given permission to try to break out to the east, with the other elements of the *Leibstandarte* tasked with providing cover. Kampfgruppe Hansen reached Petit Spa and there tried to cross the Amblève river, but the bridge was blocked by a stricken tank and a push north was met by firmly entrenched American armour and infantry armed with anti-tank weapons.

Leaving behind 150 American prisoners and his wounded to destroy the remaining tanks, at 04:00hrs on Christmas Day Peiper and the 1,800-strong column was retreating along a small track that led into the Amblève valley to Le Venne (Wanne), south of Trois Ponts, and the *Leibstandarte* lines. Moving only in darkness, they paused for rest at daybreak, but were soon on the march again. There was more fighting with airborne troops from the 82nd Airborne Division, and a crossing of the cold, fast-flowing Salm River, before finally the 800 survivors of the Kampfgruppe, including an exhausted Peiper, stumbled into the German positions. Thus the exploits of the once mighty Kampfgruppe Peiper were ended, and with it the Sixth Army role in the Ardennes offensive. Starting with about 5,800 men, 60 tanks (some Tigers), three Flak tanks, 75 halftracks, 14 20mm Flak wagons, 27 75mm assault guns, plus 105 and 150mm SP howitzers, the group was now reduced to 800 survivors.

HUNGARY — OPERATION 'FRÜHLINGSERWACHEN'

Following the Soviet re-conquest of Romania in 1944, forces under Marshal Malinovsky advanced toward Hungary on two fronts, breaking through via Arad on 22 September and joining Petrov's 4th Ukrainian Front to launch a strong drive on the capital, Budapest. Outside Budapest Malinovsky stalled in bad weather, but on 3 December on the southern flank Tolbukhin's 3rd Ukrainian Front reached Lake Balaton, encircling the city. Still believing he could manipulate the situation in the east, in early January 1945 Hitler began to assemble a large concentration of SS divisions for an attack in the east, with the goal of stabilising the situation in Hungary and saving the link to the oil from wells near Lake Balaton. But on 12 January Soviet forces along the Vistula launched one of the greatest offensives of the war, aimed at driving the German army out of Poland. Heavily outnumbered, the Germans were forced to relinquish much of the country by the end of the month.

In Hungary the attack moved up the Danube Valley toward Budapest and Vienna, and drove most of the German forces out of eastern Hungary. In Budapest the SS garrison hung on tenaciously, and launched a series of failed counter-offensives. Three attempts to relieve it, including one by VI SS-Panzer Corps also failed. On 27 January the 3rd Ukrainian Front attacked and in mid-February the final German positions in the city were overrun.

With the 3rd Ukrainian Front now threatening the Balaton oilfields, in mid-February Sixth Panzer Army began transferring in from the Ardennes, and with it I SS-Panzer Corps. Rushed from the western front, *Leibstandarte* and *Hitler Jugend* were thrown into battle, with the objective of destroying the Seventh Guards Army bridgehead at Gran. Although between them they could muster only some 150 tanks

Below: Panzer IIIs and IVs and of the Waffen-SS passing a war photographer. Dietrich would say, towards the end, that his Sixth Panzer Army was so called because it had only six tanks left!

and assault guns, the bridgehead was smashed, and with it 8,500 Soviet troops. With Gran relieved and a threat on Vienna averted, the larger operation — aimed at destroying the Red Army between the Danube, the Plattensee and the Drava, and establishing a line east of the Balaton fields — could begin.

Immense secrecy surrounded the operation, codenamed 'Frühlingserwachen' (Spring Awakening). SS-Sturmbannführer Otto Günsche, Hitler's adjutant, briefed Dietrich verbally, and no reconnaissance was permitted. But the ambitious plan was already compromised by British intelligence. Tolbukhin, commander of 3rd Ukrainian Front, was briefed by Stavka that that the main thrust would come between the Plattensee and the Velenczsee, and in response ordered extensive defences to be laid. Here Dietrich's Sixth Panzer Army, renamed Sixth SS-Panzer Army after the Ardennes offensive and including I (Leibstandarte and Hitler Jugend) and II (Das Reich and Hohenstaufen) SS-Panzer Corps, two cavalry divisions and IV SS-Panzer Korps (Wiking and Totenkopf), was ordered to attack south, on either bank of the Sarviz Canal.

For the thrust Dietrich placed the Leibstandarte, now commanded by SS-Brigadeführer Otto Kumm, at the spearhead, with II SS-Panzer Corps to the left and I Cavalry Corps to the right. Kumm's goal was to cut the Russian communications across the Danube and, if successful, drive north for Budapest. For the attack he had 12,461 troops and 14 operational PzKpfw IVHs, 26 Pzkpfw V Panthers, and 15 Jagdpanzer IVs and StuG IIIGs. The heavy tank unit, SS-Panzerabteilung 501, had a mere four Königstigers battle ready.

Having moved into its positions, Leibstandarte began preliminary attacks on 3 March. The main assault was launched at dawn four days later. It was supposed to fall a day earlier, but to retain the element of surprise, troops were held 12 miles from their assembly areas and the long, tiring march through the mud created by an early thaw left them exhausted and in need of rest. Hitler's plan had not taken into account the appalling conditions created by an early thaw, in which normally frozen ground became heavily water-logged. Not even tracked vehicles could operate off the paved roads, and these inevitably became badly clogged with traffic. Dietrich reported after the war that 132 vehicles were trapped in the mud, and 15 Königstigers sank up to their turrets in the mire. Furthermore, there were shortages of ammunition.

Below: A member of the Waffen-SS lies dead in a field in France. Someone has searched through his pockets discarding what they considered of no interest or use.

Leibstandarte's I SS-Panzer Regiment made the deepest penetration and was only 20 miles from the Danube, its first objective, when the Russians counter-attacked on 16 March, trapping the overextended Sixth SS-Panzer Army. Das Reich fought and held open a narrowing pocket through which the trapped divisions escaped, but with Hungarians formations deserting en masse, the full weight of the Russian 2nd and 3rd Ukrainian Fronts was brought to bear on the SS formations. With the spectre of defeat hanging, a fighting retreat back to Germany and Austria began. But Hitler had decided to inflict another humiliation on the SS. Reacting to reports by Balck on 23 March that the men had lost confidence in their leaders who added that the Waffen-SS formations were on the brink of collapse, the

Führer in a fit of pique ordered the Waffen-SS divisions to remove their regimental honour titles.

Goebbels wrote in his diary: 'The Führer has decided to make an example of the SS formations. He has commissioned Himmler to fly to Hungary to remove their armbands . . . The indignation of the SS commanders in the field can well be imagined and Krämer, Dietrich's chief-of-staff, suggested asking Führer headquarters whether the armbands of the men killed between the Plattensee and the Danube should also be removed . . .' In the end, the order was never carried out. It did not go unnoticed, however, and Dietrich reportedly stated that he would sooner shoot himself than carry out such an order.

Little more than a week after they had launched the attack, the 2nd and 3rd Ukrainian Fronts broke through on either side of Lake Balaton and by the end of the month had crossed the border into Austria. General Lothar Rendulic, recently appointed the command of Army Group South, was told to hold Vienna and the Alpine passes. Dietrich's Sixth SS-Panzer Army, as part of the group, did what it could to defend the city with what little it had, but as the strength of the *Leibstandarte* and *Hitler Jugend* combined was down to only 1,600 men and 16 tanks Hitler's demands that the city be held to the last man were wishful thinking in the extreme. On 6 April the Red Army was on the outskirts of the city and by the middle of the month was approaching the centre, while to the north and south of the city the Soviets were threatening an envelopment.

Already, on 1 April, the Red Army had launched its last great offensive of the war, and sealed the fate of the Third Reich. With the Ruhr encircled and Silesia gone, tank, artillery and ammunition production at a mere ebb, and gasoline in hopelessly short supply, the only thing prolonging the war was the Führer, who grimly held on to hope for another miracle similar to the one that had saved Frederick the Great during the Seven Years' War. None was forthcoming, and on 16 April on the Oder–Niesse Line the 1st Belorussian and 1st Ukrainian Fronts broke through toward Berlin. On 21 April Sokolovski's 1st Belorussian Front reached Berlin and with the 1st Ukrainian moving from the south-east, by 24 April the city was encircled.

In mid-April *Leibstandarte* was forced back from Vienna by the advance of Malinovsky's 2nd Ukrainian Front, and retreated with the remnants of the Sixth Panzer Army to positions to the west of the city. In Berlin, loyal to the last, the honour guard battalion of the *Leibstandarte*, SS Guard Battalion I, commanded by Wilhelm Mohnke, battled hand-to-hand with the Soviet forces closing on Hitler's underground bunker. On 30 April Soviet troops entered the Reichstag and the Führer shot himself and his wife. Berlin surrendered two days later on the night of 6/7 May. Desperate to escape capture by vengeful Soviet troops, from whom they expected no quarter, what troops remained of Hitler's guard fled south toward US lines. Of the other elements of *Leibstandarte* Dietrich himself surrendered at Kufstein, south-east of Munich.

Above: Guarded by Canadians, these youthful members of the Waffen-SS captured during the fighting in Normandy gave their ages as being between 16 and 20.

INSIGNIA, CLOTHING
& EQUIPMENT

INSIGNIA

RZM — *Reichzeugmeisterei* — the Nazi HQ organisation based in Munich, oversaw the design and manufacture of all Nazi uniforms and insignia. Generally, SS insignia can be classified as follows (military speciality insignia, qualification badges, decorations and campaign medals are, for reason of brevity, excluded): national emblem, honour title cuffbands, shoulder straps, *Totenkopf* badge, SS runes, collar *Tresse*, rank insignia, camouflage insignia, vehicle insignia.

National emblem (das Hoheitsabzeichen)

The national emblem of the Third Reich was an eagle clutching a swastika in its talons, a version of which was worn by every uniformed organisation — military, political or civilian — in Germany. The SS in general wore the eagle mounted either on the top front of the officer's cap, above the capband, on the front or left side of soft crush caps, or more unusually on the upper left arm of the combat, service and walking-out dress.

Honour title cuff bands

Cuff bands bearing unit 'honour titles' were worn by at least 50 elite German army and Luftwaffe formations during the war. Names were chosen after geographical regions or racial designations, contemporary Nazi heroes or historical figures. The cuffband was a strip of black cloth about 3cm wide, and was worn on the left-hand sleeve of an SS greatcoat or tunic. The font used for the *Leibstandarte* cuffband was unique to the unit. Officers sometimes had their bands tailor-made — Dietrich had his 'Adolf Hitler' cuff embroidered in gold.

Shoulder boards

Shoulder straps were constructed of black wool material and secured to the shoulder by a loop at the shoulder seam and a button near the uniform collar. Officers wore the shoulder straps corresponding to their rank with appropriate pips and metal monograms. NCOs' shoulder straps were trimmed with *Tresse* and also displayed the appropriate pips. Depending on the unit, shoulder boards were trimmed with various colours — white for infantry, yellow for reconnaissance, pink for Panzer troops and so on. In addition, the *Leibstandarte* had a

Below: Shoulder boards showing the monogram 'AH' identifying the wearer as a member of the Leibstandarte.

Bottom: Different forms of Leibstandarte *cuff title.*

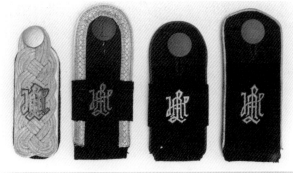

Above: Displayed is the enlisted and NCO grade peaked cap with leather chinstrap. The piping is white denoting infantry. The pavilion shows a very common 'front line crush' favoured by many NCOs. *Wade Krawczyk*

Right: Re-enactor showing off the uniform of a *Leibstandarte* (note cuff band) Panzergrenadier in front of a Russian T-34 tank. The man wears his *Zeltbahn* (the shelter quarter that doubled both as a poncho and as part of a pup tent) in a variation of 'Plane Tree' camouflage patterns. His weapon is an StG44 (StG=*Sturmgewehr*=assault rifle, the magazines for which are carried in canvas pouches (three each side) slung around his chest. Into his webbing are stuck two M24 stick grenades and an entrenching tool. In his left hand he holds a Tellermine 35 — usually detonated by a friction plate. His bayonet hangs from his belt and his gas mask container is slung over his shoulder with a grey cloth gas cape bag. *Peter Amodio*

special 'AH' (Adolf Hitler) shoulder board monogram, either of early (large) or late (small) style. NCO monograms were of silver metal, and officers' were gold metal.

SS Totenkopf (death's head)

The *Totenkopf* (death's head) symbol is, along with the SS double lightning bolts, the most distinctive of SS insignia. Its origins lay in the Prussian and Imperial German army, and during World War I it was used by the elite Brandenburger units. It was then appropriated by the Freikorps, and thereafter by the SS. Every SS unit wore the *Totenkopf* on the front of an officer's cap, in the centre of the headband or on the top front of soft crush caps. The *Totenkopf* was also the adopted symbol of the original concentration camp *Standarten* — which eventually became the 3rd SS-Panzer Division *Totenkopf*.

SS Runes

The 'Sig' rune is an ancient Germanic symbol of Thor, the Norse god of thunder, and is representative of a lightning bolt. It was designed in 1933 by Walter Heck, who used a double sig rune as a visual alliteration to the double 'ss' in Schutzstaffel. Waffen-SS troops of purely German heritage (*Reichsdeutsche*) were permitted to wear the SS runes on the right collar patch. Waffen-SS units of troops who could claim some German ancestry (*Volksdeutsche*) and other foreign volunteers without ethnic Germanic origins (*Freiwilligen*) had a special unit collar patch created in lieu of the runes.

Collar Tresse

The SS collar *Tresse* were of the diamond Wehrmacht pattern and were required to be worn on all tunics (with the exception of camouflage tunics) and optional on overcoats. The *Tresse* were affixed to the forward and bottom edge of the collar on all tunics, and a subdued colour was optional on field uniforms. *Sigrunen* were always worn on the right, with the rank tab on the left collar. Officer's collar *Tresse* were outlined with a thin white or aluminum border. SS non-commissioned officers (SS-Unterscharführer to SS-Hauptscharführer) wore silver *Tresse* to denote their status as NCOs. For example, an SS-Sturmmann wore a black wool or felt inverted chevron on the left sleeve with silver NCO *Tresse* in the shape of a 'V', and two strips of sutash on their left collar tab, and SS-Rottenführer wore the same chevron on the left sleeve with the addition of a second NCO *Tresse* strip, with four strips of sutash on their left collar tab.

Sleeve Rank Insignia for unrated ranks

SS-Panzerobergrenadiers wore a black wool or felt circle containing a white or silver embroidered diamond on the left sleeve.

Vehicle Insignia

Adopted in 1940, the basic *Leibstandarte* vehicle insignia was a skeleton key (which translates into German as 'Dietrich'). In 1941 the key was enclosed in a shield, changed to a bevelled shield in 1943, and with the award of Oakleaves to Dietrich's Knight's Cross in 1944 these were added. There were also symbols and numbers to distinguish particular units.

PERSONAL IDENTIFICATION

Soldbuch

Each soldier carried at all times his *Soldbuch* (soldier's pay book) containing information such as place of birth, name, equipment numbers, pay records, leave

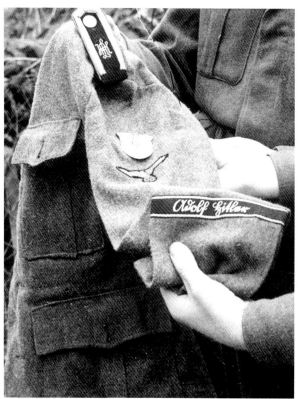

Above: An unnamed SS-Sturmmann of the LSSAH wearing shoulder straps with the prewar fourth, and final, pattern LAH cipher. This cipher dates this photo as been taken late in 1938 or early in 1939.

Above right: A tunic being examined by British field intelligence somewhere in Normandy, 1944. The cuff-band 'Adolf Hitler' together with the prewar, third-pattern shoulder strap with its distinctive pointed end clearly indicate an SS-Unterscharführer.

Right: A heavy artillery SS unit on coastal defence duty somewhere in France, October 1940. This photo clearly illustrates the distinctive helmet insignia carried, at least during the early part of the war, on the steel helmets of the Waffen-SS. Black runes on a white shield worn on the right side and a black swastika standing on its point set against a white disc within a red shield on the left. The red, white and black represented the then national colours of Germany and the Swastika the official emblem of both the Party and the German State. The chalk drawing of an umbrella is a reference to the former British Prime Minister, Neville Chamberlain who was frequently caricatured carrying an umbrella.

Left: SS-Hauptscharführer Hubert Walter wearing service dress with breeches.

papers, photo ID, money, mementos of home — pictures, letters of family, wives, girlfriends and memories of battles in which he had fought.

Identification disc

Every SS soldier was also issued identification discs, which he was required to wear suspended around his neck by a cord at all times. The oval zinc disc was divided by perforations. Information on the disc detailed the soldier's roster number, his unit, and his blood type. This information was duplicated on the other half of the disc, and in the event of death, the disc could be snapped in two. The portion with the cord stayed on the body and the other half went to his family.

Most, although not all, Waffen-SS troops also had their blood type tattooed under their left arm. The purpose of the tattoo was for medics to quickly determine a wounded man's blood type. After the war, Allied investigators used the tattoo to identify war crimes' suspects, prompting many SS members to burn or disfigure their skin to avoid capture. This only applied to ORs as officers were not obligated to get the tattoo.

Below and Bottom: Waffen-SS collar tabs for the rank of Sturmmann. The collar tabs usually featured the Nordic double-runes' symbol associated with the SS that were worn on the right-hand side. The SS drew heavily on Nordic symbology when creating their own system of ranks and associated insignias. The silver stripe denotes this particular rank; this was worn on the right side. Peter V Lukacs WW2 Militaria AB

UNIFORMS

Particularly in the latter stages of the war, the Waffen-SS had a great variety of different uniforms and equipment. Here I have focused on those particular to *Leibstandarte*. The black uniform was the most striking and part of its enduring image. Identical to that worn by the *Allgemeine-SS*, it consisted of black wool blouse, brown shirts, matching black tie, tapered trousers and high polished boots, worn with swastika armband, rank insignia, the honour cuffband, and a brown belt upon which ordinary troops attached three leather K98 ammunition pouches. NCOs and officers had a leather cross belt to support the sword scabbard carried on the left. In the mid-1930s a white belt and cross belt was substituted.

Although impressive as a parade uniform, it was not practical for use in the field, and in the summer of 1933 a grey-white cotton drill uniform was procured for the fledgling armed SS units. Commissioned officers' and NCOs' drill jackets were of similar cut to the original black tunic and were designed to incorporate both collar patches and shoulder straps. Non-rated soldiers were issued a tunic with standing collar, although it was not as finely tailored as those of officers and NCOs. In early 1935, an earth-grey uniform was adopted by the soldiers of the *Leibstandarte* and the SS-VT. The SS political armband was thought too striking for field use, and so it was replaced with the national emblem, which was worn on the left arm.

Field service blouse

In 1937, both the earth-grey and earth-brown uniforms were phased out as *Leibstandarte* switched to the field grey of the army. They were kitted out from army

Left: The M44 combat uniform in camouflage was used extensively in the Ardennes and Normandy. This squad leader carries the MP40 machine-pistol and a P38 pistol. He also has a hand grenade tucked into his belt behind the ammunition pouch for the MP40. *Wade Krawczyk*

Far left: Displayed on the cover of an original SS photo album impressed with the famous 'Double Runes' (*Doppelrunen*) is an SS officer's belt buckle; a Waffen-SS enlisted grade sleeve eagle; LAH officer's gilt shoulder strap cipher; enlisted rank's machine-woven cuff title bearing the signature 'Adolf Hitler'; uncut *Totenkopf* insignia for the field cap; and an enlisted grade belt buckle bearing the legend '*Meine Ehre heißt Treue*' (Loyalty is my honour!). *Peter V Lukacs WW2 Militaria AB*

Below: This Waffen-SS general's peaked cap (*Schirmmütze*) is piped in silver designating general officer rank. The silver chinstrap cords denote an officer. *Peter V Lukacs WW2 Militaria AB*

Right: The Führer salutes the troops of the *Leibstandarte* drawn up with their colour on the Berlin Lichterfelde parade ground. Hitler is accompanied (on his left) by SS-Obergruppenführer Sepp Dietrich.

Below right: Winter clothing — SS-Obergruppen-führer und General der Waffen-SS Sepp Dietrich (wearing sheepskin coat) accompanied by senior divisional officers including SS-Obersturmbann-führer Kurt Meyer (on his left).

Below: An LSSAH guard of honour presents arms to Hitler during the 1938 Munich conference when the British Prime Minister, Neville Chamberlain, and the French Premier, Daladier, confronted Hitler and Mussolini. To appease Germany the fate of Czechoslovakia was sealed when, to all intents and purposes, large sections of the country were handed over to the Germans without consultation with the Czech government. Six months later the rest of Czechoslovakia was absorbed into the Greater German Reich.

stocks of M1936 pattern field grey jackets, to which were added SS insignia. In 1940, the distinctive dark green collar and shoulder straps of the SS were changed to field grey. A variation in 1942 was the discontinuation of pocket pleats as a labour and material saving measure, although material quality was already in decline. Further labour and material saving measures came in 1943, including the elimination of the pocket flap points and the internal suspenders, the use of rayon for the jacket lining and a 70/30 percent wool/cellulose blend for the new outer material, which also had less of a 'green' tint. The 1944 pattern tunic introduced changes to colour, now olive brown or '1944 field grey' and a reduction in the number of belt hooks to two. The design was tested and adopted for all German ground forces, including the Waffen-SS, in July 1944, although uniform material manufactured at this time of the war was very poor, in some cases containing 90 percent artificial fibres.

Officer's field service blouse

Officers of the Waffen-SS adopted field grey as their uniform colour at the same time as the other ranks — much the same as the army. However, the basic design was retained throughout the war. Key features were turnback cuffs, dark green pointed collar and scalloped pockets. Material quality fell dramatically during the war, and it was not unusual for officers' uniform to adopt modified enlisted mens' issue field blouses when their own kit wore out.

Field service trousers

The 1942 mountain-style trousers or *Keilhosen* were the most widely used trousers in the German Army after 1941, although less often used by the Waffen-SS, which continued to produce the M37 straight-leg service trousers. They have the same button-down loops to take a cartridge belt and trouser suspender hooks as the army version. The ankles taper and feature an adjustable stirrup to hold the trouser legs inside the gaiters.

Sturmartillerie/Panzer uniform

Tank and assault gun crewmen were issued with a uniform designed to be practical within the tight confines of an armoured vehicle. They were essentially of the same cut and made of black cloth. The blouson-style jacket was cut at the waist and fastened with a row of buttons arranged vertically on the right-hand side. The collar was large and worn open but could be fastened at the neck with a hook and eye. The trousers were tapered toward the ankles giving a bloused effect over boot top. The trousers had an integral belt and front pockets with pocket flaps. Standard insignia were worn on these uniforms.

Summer combat uniform

The need for a lighter, cooler uniform blouse for the summer prompted the SS to introduce its

own version of the Army's HBT field blouse, although it kept the traditional five-button front. The design remained the same throughout the war

Cold weather suits

These mouse-grey suits were actually the same as the German Army's cold weather suits introduced for the winter of 1942–43. The Waffen-SS had its own camouflage version of this uniform for the winter of 1943–44 which was identical in cut, except for slight stylistic changes to the pocket flaps. Various camouflage patterns were used.

Tropical uniforms

The Waffen-SS had a full line of uniform items for use in hot weather territory. These uniforms were used by Waffen-SS in Sardinia, Italy, Greece and Southern Russia.

Helmet (Stahlhelm)

The steel coal scuttle design dates back to the First World War and was standard issue for the infantry units. Painted in field grey it had a black leather chinstrap and air vent holes on the sides.

Footwear

Leibstandarte members were shod in the familiar German high marching boot, but by 1944–45 leather shortages meant that the boot been much reduced in height, and some new recruits were issued with a new style ankle boot, trialled by the German Army in 1935 and reintroduced in 1942. The

Left: This SS-Oberscharführer wears a reversible 'oakleaf' camouflage smock with a 'plane tree' pattern camouflage helmet cover. The Waffen-SS was innovative in the production and issue of camouflage clothing on a unit-sized basis. *Wade Krawczyk*

Right: *Soldbuch* for SS-Sturmmann Fritz Lederer. He wears the SS pattern Panzer wrap with the LAH cipher slides on his shoulder boards as a member of the 7th Company of Panzer Regiment 1. *Wade Krawczyk*

Below: Waffen-SS officer's sidecap. This sidecap belonged to Sturmbannführer Alfred Arnold, who wore it through the campaign in France and in Russia as a member of SS Infantry Regiment 9 and the *Totenkopf* Division. The front displays the SS pattern national eagle and the death's head (*Totenkopf*) badge. Arnold was killed in combat in October 1944. *Peter V Lukacs WW2 Militaria AB*

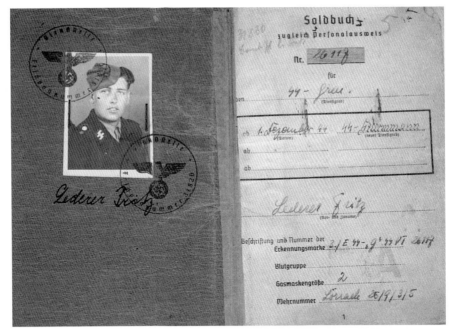

Below: This typical officer grade peaked cap (*Schirmmütze*) is piped in red designating artillery and displays the SS pattern national eagle and *Totenkopf*. The silver chinstrap cords denote an officer. *Wade Krawczyk*

Bottom : LAH cuff title. *Peter V Lukacs WW2 Militaria AB*

style varied; some were all eyeholes, others eyeholes and hooks. Heavy canvas gaiters were issued that provided the wearer with some ankle support, and also prevented stones and twigs getting into the boots. In the bitterly cold Russian winters, other types of lined boots such as those worn by Russian troops were a popular non-regulation alternative.

CAMOUFLAGE

Although it had been pioneered on ships and aircraft during World War I, the Waffen-SS was the first to use camouflage as an integral part of the soldier's standard combat uniform and equipment. A huge catalogue of camouflage patterns and styles for clothing, helmet covers and shelter tarps were developed. These camouflage items utilised by the Waffen-SS help one to distinguish the SS from the Wehrmacht, but it has to be noted that, due to late-war production shortages, many SS units also wore Italian or Wehrmacht camouflage items.

Camouflage smocks (Tarnjacken)
Two types of smock were issued, both of lightweight canvas or cotton duck material, and sometimes also waterproofed. All were reversible with a spring foliage pattern on one side and autumn foliage on the other. Multiple camouflage patterns were created during the war, of which the most recognisable are the 'oak leaf' (early war) and 'plane tree' (mid-war) patterns. There are countless others, details of which may be found in any comprehensive history of German uniforms. Other features of the smock were an elastic waistband, elastic cuffs, a drawstring front closure and shoulder loops to attach foliage. The first pattern had a shorter skirt than the second and also had two vertical slash-type openings on the left and right sides of the chest covered with a straight cut pocket flap. In 1943, while stationed in Italy, *Leibstandarte* seized vast amounts of Italian camouflage clothing, and this was later used to equip the 12th SS-Panzer Division *Hitler Jugend* and *Leibstandarte*'s own recruits. Italian-style camouflage fur anoraks are of much the same cut as the standard SS green fabric fur anorak, first used during the Ardennes offensive.

Camouflage helmet cover (Stahlhelm Tarnüberzug)
Made from the same material as the smock and reversible, the helmet cover was fastened to the sides and rear of the helmet by clips, and at the front by a reinforced lip of material overhanging the bill of the helmet. Sometimes loops were included for attaching foliage.

BASIC WAFFEN-SS FIELD EQUIPMENT

Black leather belt (Koppel) and belt buckle (Koppelschloss)
A black leather belt, 1.5 inches wide, was used for walking-out dress and for field use by all ranks. Brown belts were optional for officers. In addition to enhancing appearance, the belt was used to support the field equipment. Additional 'D' rings and leather equipment straps were also used to attach equipment to the belt.

Ammunition pouches (Patronentaschen)
The original Mauser Kar98K pouches were constructed of black leather, either sewn or riveted together, and worn in pairs. Attachments for the belt and 'Y' straps were provided. G43 pouches were constructed of a canvas material, with the same leather attachments for the belt as the K98 pouches, and could hold two 10-round magazines for the G43. Usually one of these pouches and one K98 pouch was worn on the belt.

Right: A member of the *Leibstandarte* captured near Trun seems almost relieved to have been taken prisoner by the Canadians. Although his pockets appear to have been searched, he still retains all his insignia.

Below right: SS volunteer from Bosnia and Herzegovina engaged in anti-partisan warfare, May 1944.

Below: Festooned with equipment, this Waffen-SS soldier is firing an aimed shot from his rifle. Although he is wearing all his issue equipment he is not wearing it in the prescribed manner — his mess tin is slung over his shoulder rather than attached to his belt; the water bottle is slung at left rather than at right; and his gas mask container is slung over the incorrect shoulder. It is unlikely that anyone other than a pedant would worry about this in the field!

MP40 pouches were similarly constructed of canvas with leather attachments for the belt and 'Y' straps, with capacity for three magazines per pouch. One of the pouches had an extra flap to hold the reloading tool. MP44 pouches were constructed of canvas, held three magazines per pouch and attached to the belt and 'Y' straps in the same fashion as the MP40 pouches.

In addition, machine gun crews carried an ammunition can and an MG belt loader, machine gunners' tool pouch (MG34 or MG42) and machine gun spare barrel carrier.

Bread bag (Brotbeutel)

The bag was constructed of heavy canvas, with attachments for securing it to the rear of the belt, in colours varying from olive drab to reed green. The flap had two leather straps for attaching the water bottle and/or mess tin. Eating utensils were usually carried in it, and a lard/butter container was also issued.

Water bottle (Feldflasche)

Constructed of aluminium, with a capacity of one litre, the covering of the *Feldflasche* was made of felt and the cup was large made of aluminium or smaller and made of bakelite. It was generally carried on the right side of the bread bag.

Yoke straps

Leather straps helped support the waist belt and field equipment, and were connected at the front to the back of ammunition pouches, and to the waist belt itself at the back.

Mess tin (Kochgeschirr)

For cooking and eating in the field, the mess tin could be carried on the 'Y' straps, small 'A' frame or the left side of the bread bag. Food was cooked on an Esbit stove.

Gas Mask Canister (Tragebuhse)

The distinctive fluted canister was usually strapped over the right shoulder, and the closed end had a retaining strap and hook to secure it to the waist belt.

Entrenching Tool

Both World War I and World War II pattern entrenching tools were carried by the Waffen-SS. Late war versions included a pick. It was carried in a leather pouch on the waist belt at the left hip.

Poncho/shelter quarter (Zeltbahn)

This was produced in waterproof materials of various camouflage patterns, with Spring/Summer on one side and Fall/Winter. on the other. It was variously used as a poncho, or shelter half, and rolled and either strapped to the "A" frame, or hooked to the yoke straps.

Bayonet, scabbard and frog (Seitengewehr und Scheide)

The standard issue bayonet was produced with both wooden and bakelite handles, and was carried in a scabbard suspended from the belt on the left hip. As an added measure of camouflage the scabbard was usually blued or painted flat black.

Optional equipment included an A frame for mounting equipment, a bag for personal items, flashlight, blanket, trench knife, goggles and gas cape bag. Depending on their needs officers, NCOs, artillerymen, field police and machine gun crews were issued map cases, binoculars, compasses and whistles (for signalling).

Right: This is an M40 combat tunic for an SS-Sturmmann. It displays the machine-woven cuff title of the LSSAH as well as the slip-on shoulder strap ciphers bearing the letters 'LAH'. Piping is in white for infantry. Until 1940 the Waffen-SS used the M1936 army uniform with a distinctive dark green collar and shoulder straps. After that date they dispensed with the coloured collar and straps, reverting to the Wehrmacht field grey. The M40 combat tunic was only superseded in 1942 — and then only in limited numbers — by a new combat tunic produced by the SS clothing works (*SS-Bekleidungswerkel*). Note the pleated pockets and *Hoheitsabzeichen* (national emblem) on the left sleeve.
Wade Krawczyk

Right: Waffen-SS camouflaged Panzer wrap tunic.
Intended as an overgarment or summer tunic, this
example displays the 'dot' pattern camouflage used
towards the end of the war. The only insignia is a
subdued cloth sleeve eagle. *Wade Krawczyk*

Above left: The warning *'Abstand 30m'* (Stand back 30m) was a slogan peculiar to the motorised vehicles of the LSSAH. It was painted on the rear of all their vehicles on the express instructions of Sepp Dietrich as an aid to keeping safe distances between vehicles in convoy. Note also the skeleton key, the division's vehicle insignia.

Left: The Day of Fallen Heroes (*Heldengedanktag*), 21 March 1943. Adolf Hitler, accompanied by senior officers representing the Luftwaffe (Göring), the Kriegsmarine (Dönitz), the OKW (Keitel), the police (Himmler), together with Milch (Luftwaffe) and von Bock (Army). Drawn up in review order in front of the *Ehrenmal* — the World War I war memorial — the contingent nearest the camera is from the *Leibstandarte*-SS Adolf Hitler with their 1st Battalion colour.

Above and **Above right:** In order to operate in the open during the severe weather conditions warm clothing was essential. The Waffen-SS were frequently issued with better quality clothing and equipment — as seen here. The man on the left is wearing white single-piece snow overalls and pouches for his MP40 spare magazines.

Right: Massed 'Germany Awake' SS standards paraded at Nuremberg during the 1937 *Reichsparteitag*.

Above: Amongst the many flags and standards captured by the victorious Soviet forces was the standard of the 'Adolf Hitler' Regiment shown here, minus its cloth banner, being carried by Russian soldiers during the Victory Parade held in Moscow on 24 June 1945.

Above left: Paris, France, July 1942. Sepp Dietrich and Generaloberst Haase (right), Commanding General of the Fifteenth Army, inspect and admire the newly produced, and unique, artillery guidon about to be presented to a detachment of the LSSAH.

Left: The colour for the infantry battalion from LSSAH being used for swearing-in new recruits at the division's barracks, Berlin-Lichterfelde.

Right: Massed SS standards paraded during the seventh Party Congress, the Party Day of Freedom, held at Nuremberg from 10 to 16 September 1935. It was at this congress, on 10 September, that the German Citizenship Law and the Law for the Protection of German Blood and German Honour — thereafter known as the Nuremberg Laws — were proclaimed. Flags and standards were of particular importance to the Nazis, and used to great effect at the Nuremberg rallies.

PEOPLE

JOSEF 'SEPP' DIETRICH

Undoubtedly the most celebrated of *Leibstandarte* soldiers was its founder, first and long-time commander Oberstgruppenführer Sepp Dietrich. Dietrich was born and raised in Bavaria, served as a sergeant-major in World War I, and after the war was attracted into the Freikorps volunteers. Subsequently he became a member of the SA and participated in the Munich Beer Hall Putsch. In 1928 he switched to the SS, and was one of the small group of bodyguards from which the *Leibstandarte* grew. Hitler expected and had their absolute loyalty, and after he had risen to power he called on Dietrich to formalise the unit. For more than 10 years Dietrich led the *Leibstandarte*, overseeing its growth from a tiny elite hand-picked ceremonial troop into the most feared of all the SS divisions. From his men he demanded excellence and gave in return genuine care and respect, which earned him their adulation and loyalty.

Below: Dietrich as an SS-Gruppenführer photographed just prior to his being promoted by Adolf Hitler to the rank of SS-Obergruppenführer.

The relationship between commander and men in *Leibstandarte* was far closer than in most of the Wehrmacht, but relations with his own superiors were often far less cordial. He had frequent and often bitter rows with Himmler, Reichsführer-SS, and it is unlikely that he would have achieved so much without the protection and patronage of the Führer himself. This friendship brought rapid promotion through the ranks of the SS; in the summer of 1943 he was appointed to create I SS-Panzer Corps. The army generals, von Rundstedt among them, tended to regard him as a good leader of men but a poor strategist, and his brusque manner, common roots and frequent use of gutteral German further alienated them. Perhaps, too, they were envious of the relationship between the Führer and the commander of his bodyguard, which was unique among German commanders, forged out of mutual respect between ex-comrades-in-arms and in the political struggle of the 1920s.

In 1944, Dietrich led I SS-Panzer Corps at Caen and was promoted to command the Sixth SS-Panzer Army for the Ardennes Offensive. His leadership earned him Swords & Diamonds to the Oak Leaves to the Knight's Cross he already had. But Dietrich's career was so peppered with accusations of atrocities — both real and imagined — that postwar saw him tried and convicted for war crimes. Many consider him lucky not to have been executed. When he was released from prison in 1956, he was still an unrepentant and committed Nazi, a firm adherent to the beliefs that he took with him to his grave in 1966.

OTTO KUMM

Kumm, the last commander of the *Leibstandarte*, was born in Hamburg on 1 October 1909, the son of a salesman. At the age of 21 he joined the Nazi Party and SS, and was a soldier in the SS-VT unit *Der Führer*. He rose through the ranks and at the close of the Western campaign as a SS-Hauptsturmführer was awarded the Iron Cross I and II Class. During service in Russia he won promotion to the command of the 4th SS-Panzergrenadier Regiment *Der Führer*, and in February 1942, as the regiment fought in the area of Rzeh Kumm, saw it reduced from 2,000 to 35 men. Subsequently he was awarded the Knight's Cross, and in April 1943 became Chief of Staff of the 5th Panzergrenadier Division *Wiking*. As SS-Oberführer Kumm, in August he took over command of 7th SS Freiwilligen Mountain Division *Prinz Eugen* from Carl von Oberkamp, and during his time with the unit was awarded Swords to the Knight's Cross he had already earned. In November came promotion to to SS-Brigadeführer und Generalmajor der SS and finally, in February 1945, command of 1st SS Panzer Division *Leibstandarte–SS Adolf Hitler*. In April came the Swords to his Knight's Cross, and a month later he surrendered with the remnants of the division. After the war he wrote the history of the 7th SS Division.

Above: Sepp Dietrich was the 41st recipient of the Oakleaves, awarded to him on 31 December 1941 for the part he played in the Balkans campaign as commander of the LSSAH. He was the first Waffen-SS officer to receive the Oakleaves. He is seen here in a SdKfz 251 command vehicle.

KURT 'PANZER' MEYER

After working as a miner and then serving with the Mecklenburg police, Meyer was attracted into the Nazi Party and joined the SS. In 1932 he was promoted to Untersturmführer and two years later as Obersturmführer was selected for the *Leibstandarte*. He served in Poland and France, gaining promotion to SS-Sturmbannführer, and was the commander of the reconnaissance detachment in Greece, where he led the spectacular assault on the Klissura Pass on 15 May 1941 (see page 26). In Russia he won the Oakleaves to his Knight's Cross at Kharkov and promotion to SS-Obersturmbannführer, and from there came command of the 25th SS-Panzergrenadier Regiment (12th SS-Panzergrenadier Division *Hitler Jugend*) as SS-Standartenführer. He led this unit through the early Normandy campaign, where

COMMANDING OFFICERS OF THE LEIBSTANDARTE

SS-Oberstgruppenführer Joseff Dietrich	1 September 1939	7 April 1943
SS-Brigadeführer Theodor Wisch	7 April 1943	20 August 1944
SS-Brigadeführer Wilhelm Mohnke	20 August 1944	6 February 1945
SS-Brigadeführer Otto Kumm	6 February 1945	8 May 1945

Above: SS-Obersturmbannführer Kurt Meyer, commanding officer of the 1st SS-Panzer Reconnaissance Battalion, LSSAH, photographed on the day he was awarded the Oakleaves to his Knight's Cross — 23 February 1943 — for actions on the Eastern Front. He became the 195th recipient of this award.

it bore most of the brunt of the early fighting and sustained enormous casualties. In August, following the death of *Hitler Jugend* commander Fritz Witt, he became at 33 the youngest divisional commander in the German Army. The following month he was captured near Amiens, and postwar was tried and sentenced to life imprisonment for the murder of Canadian prisoners in Normandy. In prison he wrote his memoir *Grenadiere* and was released after 10 years in jail. He died in 1961 a committed Nazi.

WILHELM MOHNKE

Mohnke, who has gained notoriety as the alleged perpetrator of the Wormhoudt and Malmédy massacres, was born in Lübeck in 1911. In 1931 he joined the NSDAP and the SS, served with the Lübeck troop, and then the 22nd SS Detachment, and in 1933 volunteered and was selected to form the core of the *Leibstandarte*. For the campaign in France, he was senior company commander of 2nd Battalion and reportedly ordered British POWs to be executed at Wormhoudt. In 1941, during the Balkans campaign, he lost a foot during an air attack and from 1943–44 was commander 26th Panzergrenadier Regiment, 12th SS-Division *Hitler Jugend*. He became commander of *Leibstandarte* in August 1944, a position he held until the following February. After leading the defence on the Seine, during the Ardennes Offensive Mohnke was accused of instigating the Malmédy massacre.

His final appointment was as commander of the Kampfgruppe Mohnke, tasked with the defence of the Reich Chancellery, and he was present in the Führerbunker when Hitler committed suicide. Captured by Soviets, he was finally released 1955, but despite efforts by the survivors of the massacres he has never been brought to trial.

JOACHIM ('JOCHEN') PEIPER

Joachim (he preferred Jochen, saying it sounded less Jewish) Peiper was, perhaps, the consummate SS hero. His wartime exploits made him at once a hero among ordinary Germans and a murderer to others. Born in 1915, at the age of just 19 he joined the SS-VT. His brothers were in the SS-TK and another in the SD. He went through two years of officer training and in 1936 was posted to the *Leibstandarte*. In 1938 he worked for a three-month long period as adjutant to Heinrich Hammer, during which time he worked with concentration camp commanders and, it is suggested, therefore had knowledge of plans for the Final Solution.

Peiper spent the first wartime campaign, in Poland, as part of Hitler's staff. He saw his first action with *Leibstandarte* in 1940, during the campaign for France. Here he led the assault on the Wattenberg heights and was awarded the Iron Cross 1st and 2nd class for his actions. For a long period he commanded the 3rd Battalion of SS-Panzergrenadier Regiment 2, and established an outstanding reputation as a combat leader. In 1943, he won the Knight's Cross at Kharkov for orchestrating the rescue of the 320th Infantry Division, which was then retreating to the Donets and in danger of being annihilated. Peiper took a small battle group deep into the Russian lines and extricated the survivors. In 1944, for the Ardennes Offensive, he was given his most famous command — SS-Kampfgruppe Peiper — and tasked with leading the spearhead of the German offensive. Subsequently promoted to

SS-Standartenführer, commanding SS-Panzer Regiment 1, he was the youngest regimental colonel in the Waffen-SS.

His name was implicated in massacres in Italy and at Malmédy, and postwar he was sentenced to hang. The sentence was commuted, and he was released from prison in 1956. Finding life in postwar Germany incompatible with his fervent Nazi beliefs, and its people intolerant of his past, in 1970 he moved to France. He was murdered at his home on Bastille Day in July 1976.

THEODOR WISCH

Born in 1907 in Wesselburener Hoog, 'Teddy' Wisch joined the *Leibstandarte* in March 1933 at the age of 25. A thoroughly professional soldier, if reportedly rather uncharismatic, he won rapid promotion through the ranks and by the start of the Polish campaign was a company commander. In Poland he won both the 1st and 2nd classes of the Iron Cross, and after serving in the Western, Balkans and Russian campaigns he was awarded the Knight's Cross in September 1941. The following summer he became commander of the 22nd SS-Panzergrenadier Regiment (part of the 10th SS-Panzer Division *Frundsberg*) and at Kharkov won the German Cross in Gold. In July 1943, at the age of 36, he took command of *Leibstandarte*, a position he held until the Normandy campaign when he was seriously wounded and invalided out. Awarded the Knight's Cross with Swords and Oakleaves, Wisch ended the war at a desk job in the SS-Fuhrüngshauptamt

MICHAEL WITTMANN

The most successful and decorated tank commander of the war, Wittmann was born in the rural Oberfalz region of Bavaria and first joined the regular army. In 1936, as a Gefreiter, he joined the SS-VT and was accepted into the 17th Company of the *Leibstandarte*, retaining the equivalent rank of SS-Mann. His initial training and service was on light reconnaissance vehicles, and at the outbreak of the war he was an SS-Unterscharführer in command of an armoured car. After the French campaign the regiment re-equipped with StuG III self-propelled guns, and Wittmann requested — and was granted — a transfer into the new detachment. Training on the new vehicles was completed in time for the Balkan campaign, in which he was awarded the 2nd class of the Iron Cross for his part in the assault on the Klissura Pass. During the summer, in Russia, he was awarded the 1st Class. Distinguishing himself further in the actions in the Crimea, at the end of 1942 Wittmann was sent to the SS officer training school at Bad Toldt and after passing out with the rank of Untersturmführer, he led the 13th (Heavy) Company of the 1st SS Panzer Regiment. At Kursk, on the first day alone, Wittmann destroyed eight enemy tanks and seven anti-tank guns, but his most famous action was at Villers-Bocage during the battle of Normandy in the West, when as SS-Obersturmführer he led the Tigers of his 2nd Company, SS-Panzer Abteilung 101, against a concentration of British armour threatening the *Panzer Lehr*, and destroyed 23 British tanks and a similar number of half-tracks and light armoured vehicles. Awarded the Swords to his Knight's Cross with Oakleaves for this action, Wittmann refused to accept a training post and was killed on 8 August 1944 in the fighting around Caen.

Below: Michael Wittmann sitting on the mantlet of his Tiger. Note the application of *Zimmerit* paste that produces the characteristic ridges appearance to later war images of German armoured vehicles. Zimmerit was designed to create a surface against which magnetic anti-tank weapons would not stick.
via George Forty

ASSESSMENT

In 1939, the SS-VT was not a favoured body. The army discouraged recruitment to it and, with the exception of *Leibstandarte*, numbers had to be made up from *Volksdeutsche*. In battle, however, the performance of the *Leibstandarte*, and the other elite SS divisions, gave rise to a very different notion: that they could save any situation and turn defeat into victory. Thus they were thrown into the most intense fighting time after time, and received preferential treatment with regard to supplies and equipment. Their feats encouraged Hitler to expand the Waffen-SS, and by 1944 it had swelled to an estimated 900,000 men. Something like 253,000 of these men were killed in action during the war, and an additional 250,000 wounded. But there existed very considerable variation in the quality of the SS divisions, many of which performed poorly in battle and in their treatment of 'enemies'. Appallingly, it is true to say that while the Waffen-SS and the seven elite divisions were among the best of German soldiers, they contained some of the worst characters.

Leibstandarte is considered the finest of the Waffen-SS divisions, and a myth has arisen around the unit that portrays it as a heavily armed army of six-foot blond, blue-eyed warriors charging into battle astride Tiger tanks like latter-day Teutonic Knights. This has more to do with the Nazi propaganda machine than the true facts, which are rather more complex. From its inception the *Leibstandarte* was supposed to represent the ideological elite of the 1,000-year Reich, the very epitome of the SS ideal, a Teutonic elite of physically perfect, impeccably bred specimens. Certainly, in the 1930s, when *Leibstandarte* could afford the luxury of stringent recruitment standards, the propaganda image was rather more accurate. But as war began to eat into Germany's manpower reserves, the SS began to recruit from rather more varied quarters. Although its recruitment standards remained high, the truth is that the men who fought and died under the banner of the Führer were a much more varied bunch. They may not have matched the exacting criteria Himmler set out for the SS at its

Below: Waffen-SS troops resting. While there is no doubt that atrocities committed by soldiers such as these were not uncommon, especially on the Eastern Front, there is also no doubting their qualities as fighting men.

inception but the demands made of them were never anything but superhuman.

Most accounts of the military history of the *Leibstandarte* inevitably focus on the most stunning battles or exciting campaigns. However, it is important to take a closer look at the combat records of the individual *Leibstandarte* to get a clearer picture of its military contribution of the SS during the war.

At the outbreak of the war, tactical command of the Waffen-SS was devolved to the OKH, while Himmler oversaw administration. During the Polish campaign *Leibstandarte* faced combat for the first time, eager to prove itself and disprove its critics in the army, which maintained a lofty contempt for SS troops. Unleashed on the battlefield, this eagerness resulted in high casualties, and while admiring their courage and recklessness, the army felt that overall the SS troops suffered from a combination of recklessness and lack of training. This may have been true, but SS officers countered that the army gave them the most difficult assignments with minimal support. Perhaps both allegations contained a grain of truth and during the invasion of the Low Countries and France *Leibstandarte* showed its true worth as a fighting unit.

Speed was one of the factors underpinning the tactics of Blitzkrieg, and as one of the limited number of motorised units available, *Leibstandarte* had a key role. First it advanced with lightning speed to Rotterdam, next into France where it prevented a French breakout and then audaciously broke through the British defensive perimeter at Wattan. During the advance to Paris, moving again at a breakneck pace at the spearhead of von Kleist's Panzer Group, the division was rushed to reinforce Army Group A, held up in front of the city, and helped force a breach through the defensive line. The successes continued as the *Leibstandarte* pushed into the south and bottled up the the French Army in the Alps. During the April 1941 invasion of Greece, there were several notable incidents; the storming of the Klissura Pass by Meyer's reconnaissance battalion, demonstrates graphically the motivation these men had for battle.

It was in Russia and the Ukraine that the *Leibstandarte* earned its enduring reputation for bravery and steadfastness. Here, during Operation 'Barbarossa' and the subsequent autumn and winter campaign, it made its most valuable commitment and finally won the respect of its peers. For the initial phase it again demonstrated the effectiveness of mobile forces on the battlefield, redeploying to counter attacks on the vulnerable flanks of the armoured thrust toward Rostov, and sealing off the Uman pocket despite concerted attempts to relieve it. For the action at Uman it won praise from Generalmajor Werner Kempf, and later in the year, after the advance through the southern Ukraine to Rostov, German Army General von Mackensen was moved to say of December, 'This truly is an elite unit.'

Already Hitler had begun to expect the impossible from the Waffen-SS. He refused to countenance withdrawal at Rostov, which resulted in heavy casualties for

Above: A PzKpfw III moves past dug-in Waffen-SS infantry on the Eastern Front. Bravery, endurance, skill — *Leibstandarte* and the elite SS units had all of this and Hitler came to expect the impossible from them.

LEIBSTANDARTE STRENGTHS

Date	Men
January 1935	2,531
January 1936	2,650
January 1937	3,177
January 1938	3,607
December 1938	3,626
June 1941	10,796
December 1942	20,844
December 1943	19,867
June 1944	19,691
December 1944	22,000

Above: This photograph, taken somewhere on the Eastern Front, shows an SS despatch rider. He has picked up a Russian weapon .

Leibstandarte, and irrationally denied them adequate clothing for the first brutal winter on the steppes. The result was that in the spring, after further defensive battles around Dnepropetrovsk, the division had to be pulled back to France to be rebuilt. By now the battle-hardened core of the unit was beginning to wither, and it was forced by manpower shortages to accept recruits of a lower calibre. Later in the year it yielded more of its experienced NCOs and officers to the 9th SS-Division *Hohenstaufen*. From here on this cycle of events was repeated with increasing regularity, until by the end of the war the fallen were being replaced by young, barely trained conscripts and draftees.

Always instilled in the troops was the belief that they were the vanguard of the legions forging the new Nazi empire, and thus carrying the expectations of a nation. Above all was the SS creed of self-sacrifice for the glory of the Reich, loyalty to the Führer and the honour of death in battle. It should be remembered that most of the troops had grown up schooled in Nazism, believed in its tenets and held death in contempt. Even after the war, Joachim Peiper, who had joined the SS at 19, expressed his dismay at what he believed to be the selfishness and materialism of postwar Germany. Although it is often pointed out that Germany during the war was by no means united under the swastika, it is safe to say that *Leibstandarte* was Nazi to the core.

1943 was perhaps the high water mark for *Leibstandarte*. The number of SS divisions and corps multiplied, and it won a stunning victory at Kharkov that gave succour after the reversals of the winter months. Summer brought the turning point in fortunes, when at Kursk the combined weight of the *Leibstandarte*, *Das Reich* and *Totenkopf* panzer divisions, despite inflicting enormous losses on the Red Army, failed to make a decisive penetration of the Soviet defences. Defeat came not at the hands of superior generalship but by sheer weight of numbers and the enemy's seemingly endless capacity to absorb losses.

During the long, costly and doomed defence in the east, *Leibstandarte* rushed about the front, plugging gaps in the line, rescuing encircled troops and mounting stubborn counter-attacks. Time and again, *Leibstandarte* displayed a willingness to keep on fighting even when the tactical situation was hopeless, but local successes were undermined by the constant shortages of men and materiel, and despite their bravery, *Leibstandarte* could not stem the red tide.

Hitler was given to remark that 'troops like the SS have to pay the butcher's bill more heavily than anyone else' — and pay they did. With the Reich collapsing, the Führer gave the *Leibstandarte* increasingly unrealistic and impossible orders to attack or to defend to the last man — orders that, at least in the attack, it did not have the capacity to execute. In Normandy, again there were tactical victories, which succeeded in delaying the Allied advance to the homeland. As the spearhead for the Ardennes offensive, *Leibstandarte* showed that it had retained its legendary tenacity in the attack; a breakthrough came tantalisingly close for Peiper's column, only to be thwarted by fuel shortages. In spring 1945 came the final stand in Hungary, where *Leibstandarte* headed the death ride of the Sixth SS-Panzer Army attempting to save Hitler's last remaining fuel supply. Forced back under overwhelming odds, they were berated by the Führer, and ordered to remove the honour cuffbands that were such a source of pride.

Disillusioned and facing inevitable defeat, in these final days of the war *Leibstandarte* men were no longer fighting for National Socialism, for Germany, or for the Führer who, for all their sacrifices, had so callously abandoned them. Instead they transferred the loyalty that they had sworn to the Führer to their unit, their comrades and their commanding officers.

'. . . Our lack of understanding and inner rejection of everything we heard from "up there" or "back home" led us to accept only one last **Heimat**, one final homeland. That was our unit, our "little heap" of men.'

Leibstandarte troops as a whole earned a distinguished combat reputation during World War II, renowned for both stunning offensive victories, tenacious defensive operations and feats of bravery, courage and tactical brilliance for which some 58 of those who served won the Knight's Cross. This reputation is tempered to a large degree by the numerous atrocities carried out by members of the division, and by association with the SS. Without seeking to offer justification for the actions of the division, with the benefit of historical hindsight, it is important to place events in their proper context, and consider the Germany in which these troops were raised.

The average age of the troops was but 19 years old, and many of them had grown up knowing only Nazism. Of course, one should not imagine that *Leibstandarte* troops were simple fools who believed everything Hitler impressed upon them about the superiority of the Germanic races, the invincibility of the Reich and the destiny of the SS as the future master race, but belief in the honour of self-sacrifice bred a disdain for death that accounts for the enormous losses that the *Leibstandarte*, and the Waffen-SS, was able to sustain. It also offers a clue to the disdain SS men showed on occasion for the life of others.

All of the Waffen-SS divisions were to a greater or lesser degree complicit in acts of savagery against enemy troops and civilians. *Leibstandarte*, by no means the worst perpetrator, is by association with the SS and its own actions tainted. After the war Dietrich, Peiper and many others stood trial for these crimes and served sentence for them.

Below: Riflemen and machine gun crews await the order to move forward.

REFERENCE

INTERNET SITES

The main problem with websites on *Leibstandarte*, the Waffen-SS or the SS in general is that they attract apologists of the Nazi cause, those who seek to shift the blame for atrocities away from military units onto unnamed individuals and political racists from the far right. We have not included here any websites that seem to us as being anything other than sites providing information of historical interest.

http://www.tankclub.agava.ru/sign/sign.shtml
Russian-language site with excellent illustrations of the tactical signs of the German armed forces.

http://www.geocities.com/Pentagon/3620/AchtungPanzer!
Site with very detailed information on German armour. Great colour pictures of preserved machines, particularly SPWs.

http://www.feldgrau.com/
This is probably the most comprehensive site dealing with the German Army before and during World War II currently on the Web. Well-written and researched.

http://www.lssah.com/
Website of 1st SS-Panzer Division re-enactors from US and Europe. The site emphasises its historical interests and that it is not political.

http://www.skalman.nu/third-reich/
The Third Reich Factbook — histories, orders of battle and other information on Third Reich military, political and volunteer organisations.

http://www.wssob.com/
Website that concentrates on the Waffen-SS. Plenty of information on history, orders of battle, etc.

BIBLIOGRAPHY

Bender, R. & Odegard, W.: *Panzertruppe – Uniforms, Organisation and History*; Bender, 1980. Panzer formations, crew uniforms and insignia, markings and camouflage.

Butler, Rupert: *SS-Leibstandarte The History of the First SS Division 1933-45*; MBI, 2001. Useful detailed history of the unit, particularly its more famous actions.

Culver, Bruce & Murphy, Bill: *Panzer Colours – Vol. 1*; 170 illustrations with 69 full-colour plates provide the most detailed account of German armour during WWII.

Delaney, John: *The Blitzkrieg Campaigns. Germany's 'Lighting War' Strategy In Action*; Arms & Armour Press, 1996. Describes the origins of the strategy developed during the interwar years; studies how this technique was used during the advances into Poland, Belgium and France then Russia.

Ellis, C. & Chamberlain, P.: *German Tanks and Fighting Vehicles of WWII*; Pheobus, 1976. This tells the story of German armour from the secret training machines of the Weimar period through to the end of WWII.

Erickson, John: *The Road To Stalingrad* and *The Road to Berlin*; Weidenfeld and Nicholson, 1983. Two volumes on Stalin's war with Germany, focusing on Soviet Command decisions.

Fomichenko, Maj-Gen: *The Red Army*; Hutchinson. Studies the development of the Soviet Army and its exploits from June 1941 when Germany launched Operation 'Barbarossa'.

Fugate, B.: *Operation Barbarossa: Strategy & Tactics 1941*; Spa Books, 1989. Studies Hitler's surprise offensive against Russia and analyses his strategy and tactics on the Eastern Front during 1941.

Glantz, David: *From The Don To The Dnieper*. Illustrations with detailed maps are included in this analysis of Red Army operations during eight vital months of struggle that finally ended Hitler's Blitzkrieg against the USSR.

Glantz, David: *Kharkov, 1942*; Ian Allan Publishing, 2000. A detailed appreciation of the battle with extensive quotations from the Soviet postwar study.

Gordon-Douglas, S. R.: *German Combat Uniforms 1939-45*; Altmark, 1970. Concentrates on combat equipment and field uniform.

Guderian, Heinz: *Achtung Panzer!* Classic book by one of the chief protagonists of armour in the 1940s details the development, tactics and operational potential of the German armoured forces and studies the evolution of land warfare and the years of German supremacy.

Haupt, Werner: *A History Of Panzer Troops 1916-1945*; Schiffer, 1990. An illustrated study of German armour from the Battle of Cambrai in 1916 to the 1944 Ardennes Offensive and the struggle to defend Berlin.

Jentz, Thomas L.: *Panzertruppen Vol 1 1933-1942*; *Vol. II – 1943-1945*; Schiffer, 1996. A complete guide to the creation, organisation and combat employment of Germany's Tank force 1933–45.

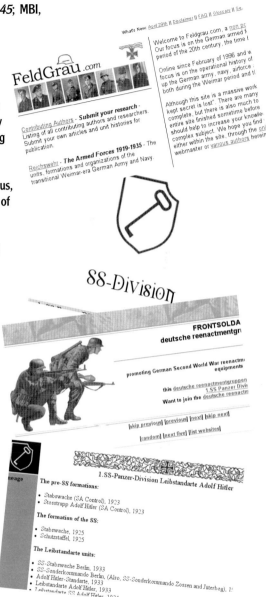

Above: A Waffen-SS machine gunner manages a smile despite the rain. He is wearing his shelter quarter (*Zeltbahn*) as a rain cape and, interestingly, over his helmet cover he is wearing a sniper's face mask, back to front, tied around the helmet.

Keegan, J.: *The Second World War*; Hutchinson, 1989. Excellent general history.

Keegan, J. (editor): *Encyclopedia of World War II*; Bison, 1980. A short, many-sided, history of the war as a whole. It includes biographies, details of major weapons, weapon systems, and details of all major battles. 1977.

Kershaw, Robert: *War Without Garlands*; Ian Allan, 2001. Excellent examination of Operation 'Barbarossa' and the battles of 1941.

Kessler, Leo: *The Life and Death of SS Colonel Jochen Peiper*; Leo Cooper/Secker & Warburg, 1986. Biography of this controversial figure.

Lederrey, Col E.: *Germany's Defeat in the East*; HMSO, 1955. A full account of the Soviet War against Germany during 1941–45.

Lucas, James: *War On The Eastern Front. The German Soldier in Russia 1941-1945*; Jane's, 1979. An account, from the German angle, of the war in the east.

Lucas, James: *Battle Group – German Kampfgruppen Actions of WWII*; BCA, 1994. The story of how Hitler's shock troops, the Kampfgruppen, contributed to German military operations.

Lucas, James: *The Third Reich*; Arms & Armour Press, 1990. A history of Germany's war through the words of German men and women who served with the armed forces or suffered from the devastation of Allied air raids.

Lucas, James: *The Last Year of the German Army* May 1944-May 1945; BCA, 1994. A complete study of structural changes to overcome its depletion and an insight into some of its last battles.

Lucas, James & Cooper, Matthew: *Hitler's Elite: Leibstandarte SS*; Macdonald and Jane's, 1975. Written over 25 years ago with the assistance of many veterans, this is a good account of the *Leibstandarte*, particularly on the unit character and motivation.

Lucas, James & Cooper, Matthew: *Panzer Grenadiers*; BCA, 1977. Excellent background on the panzergrenadier units, which were the first to combine motorised infantry with armoured fighting vehicles.

Mason, David. *Who's Who In World War II*; Weidenfeld and Nicholson, 1978. Presents a survey of the conflict told through the exploits of the main players who participated – military, political and scientific.

Mayer, S. L. (Editor): *Signal-Years Of Retreat 1943-44*; Bison, 1979. Hitler's wartime picture magazine. A facsimile edition of a propaganda journal supervised by Goebbels' propaganda company. A record of the decline and fall of the Third Reich.

Mclean, Donald B. (Editor): *German Infantry Weapons Vol I*; Normount Armament Co, 1967. Originally published in 1943 to assist Allied commanders, details the design and construction of weapons and their ammunition.

Messenger, Charles: *The Art of Blitzkrieg*, Ian Allan, 1995. Excellent discussion of blitzkrieg taking the story into the 1990s.

Messenger, Charles: *Hitler's Gladiator: The Life and Times of Oberstgruppenführer Und Panzergeneral-Oberst der Waffen-SS Sepp Dietrich*, Brassey's, 1988. Definitive biography of the legendary *Leibstandarte* commander.

Mollo, Andrew: *Army Uniforms of World War II*, Blandford, 1977. An easy reference and basic handbook on the uniforms, personal equipment and weapons of 24 nations that took part in WWII.

Pallud, Jean Paul: *Blitzkrieg In The West – Then And Now*, After the Battle, 1991. Fully illustrated Then and Now photographs show how Germany, in just sixty days, caused France to capitulate during 1941.

Piekalkiewicz, Janusz: *Operation Citadel*, Presidio, 1987. A complete illustrated analysis of the Battles of Kursk and Orel — the largest single land-air combat engagement in history which helped shatter Nazi ambitions in Russia.

Quarrie, Bruce: *Hitler – The Victory That Nearly Was*, David and Charles, 1988. An assessment of the situations which could have affected history had Hitler made different decisions, and won the war.

Rosignoli, Guido: *Army Badges and Insignia of World War II*, Blandford Press, 1972. Cap badges, formation signs, regimental badges, tank battle badges, shoulder sleeve insignia are all listed. Countries covered are Great Britain, USA, Italy, Poland, Belgium, and USSR.

Above: An obviously relaxed SS-Grenadier gives directions to a group of Soviet prisoners.

Scheibert, Horst & Elfrath, Ulrich: *Panzers in Russia*, Altmark, 1971. A pictorial record of the German Panzer divisions on the Eastern Front 1941–44. Over 400 pictures, with bi-lingual text, are shown in chronological order.

Seaton, Albert: *The German Army, 1933-1945*, Weidenfeld and Nicholson, 1982. A full length analytical study of the German Army, its rise and fall.

Warner, Philip: *Panzer*, Weidenfeld and Nicholson, 1977. This book gives a fascinating insight into the history of the Panzers. During the Second World War the power and success of these regiments were legendary.

Williamson, Gordon: The SS: Hitler's Instrument of Terror; MBI, 1994. Well illustrated informed general history of the rise and fall of the SS.

SS Ranks
Mannschaften (Enlisted men)
SS-Schütze
SS-Oberschütze
SS-Sturmmann
SS-Rottenführer
SS-Stabsrottenführer

Unteroffiziere ohne Portepee
(Junior NCOs)
SS-Unterscharführer
SS-Standartenjunker

Unteroffiziere mit Portepee
(Senior NCOs)
SS-Oberscharführer
SS-Hauptscharführer
SS-Sturmscharführer

Offiziere (Commissioned Officers)
SS-Untersturmführer
SS-Obersturmführer
SS-Hauptsturmführer
SS-Sturmbannführer
SS-Obersturmbannführer
SS-Standartenführer
SS-Brigadeführer und Generalmajor
der Waffen-SS
SS-Gruppenführer und Generalleutnant
der Waffen-SS
SS-Obergruppenführer und General der
Waffen-SS
SS-Oberstgruppenführer und
Generaloberst der Waffen-SS
Reichsführer-SS

Waffen-SS formations/unit structure
Abteilung Similar to a battalion, a
formation of combined units designed to
be independent on the battlefield.
Armee (army) Comprised of several Korps,
plus any independent formations the
Armee operated on the strategic level.
The only Waffen-SS Armee was Sixth
SS-Panzer Army.
Aufklärung (reconnaissance) Waffen-SS
recce units were well-armed and had two
coys of ACs, plus several MC coys and a
motorised heavy weapons coy.
Bataillon (battalion) Tactical unit of three or
more Kompanien, sometimes with
additional Züge and a strength of
between 500–1,000 soldiers.

Batterie (battery) A group of support
weapons operating as a unit.
Brigade Independent formation, usually of
1-7,000 soldiers. Most Waffen-SS
brigades and/or legions were foreign
volunteer units of varying size and thus
not relevant to the Leibstandarte.
Division Combination of several regiments
and Abteilungen, with manpower of
anything between 10–21,000 soldiers.
Waffen-SS panzer divisions tended to
have a large complement.
Feldersatz (field replacement) When
possible, Waffen-SS divisions would have
an Ersatz, or replacement formation,
often in Germany, which fed new troops
to the front line units.
Feldpostamt (FPA) Military post office.
Flak AA units usually had a mixture of
towed heavy 88mm, motorised med
37mm and lt 20mm quad AA guns.
Kolonne (column) An independent
transportation unit, varying in size,
transporting equipment or supplies such
as a bridge column or a light infantry
column (which consisted of a number of
horse-drawn vehicles capable of
transporting a fixed tonnage).
Kommando (detachment) Tactical military
formation of indeterminate size.
Kompanie (company) Tactical unit of three
or more Züge, with a strength of
100–200 soldiers.
Korps (corps) Ideally the Waffen-SS corps
(formed from 1943) comprised two or
more divisions, plus several attached
Abteilungen, and the HQ staff. Although
the I SS Panzer Korps was the model,
manpower shortages meant that the size
and quality of each varied.
Nachrichten (signals) A signals unit,
comprised Fernsprech (telephone), Funk
(radio) and a Versorgungs units.
Nachschubtruppe Supply troops, which
included non-combatants such as the
veterinary unit, the Backerie-Kompanie
(bakery), Fleischerei (butcher), news and
QM units.
Panzer (armour) Tank battalions were
organised into companies, with one or
more command (Befehl) tanks per
company, and Werkstatt (workshop/

repair) and Versorgungs companies
allocated to each regiment. Each Pz Div
had attached a deep-maintenance
Kraftfahrzeug detachment, including a
workshop, weapons and a spares unit.
Panzerjäger (anti-tank) A PzJg unit usually
contained a mixture of motorised and
stationary anti-tank weapons.
Pionier (assault engineers) In addition to
building bridges and fortifications, Pionier
troops were trained as assault troops,
specialising in urban fighting and
weapons like flamethrowers and satchel
charges. Usually split into an armoured
company, several Pionier and special
companies such as Brücken (bridging)
and assault boat.
Regiment Comprising several Bataillone, with
anywhere between 2–6,000 men.
Sanitätstruppe (medical troops) These
included the Feldlazarett (field hospital
unit), comprising the Sanitäts companies
and the Krankenkraftwagen (motorised
ambulance) section.
Stab (staff) Headquarters unit comprising
officers who would be assigned to a
specific role such as: Ia = operations;
Ib = supply & transport; Ic = intelligence;
Id = training; IIa = personnel matters,
officers; IIb = personnel matters, men;
III = judge advocate; IVa = administration;
IVb = medical; V = motor transport.
Div HQ included the CO, plus staff
officers, cartographers (Kartenstelle), a
signals unit, an MP unit
(Feldgendarmerie), plus an escort force
and transport team.
Trupp (troop) Tactical, sometimes
independent, unit of 10–20 men.
Werfer (mortar) Compared to Allied
formations, German units were much
better armed with mortars. A divisional
Werfer unit typically had three batteries of
six 150mm towed mortars and a battery
of six 210mm towed mortars. After 1943
six battalions of SS Nebeltruppen
(specialised rocket launcher troops) were
raised and equipped with Nebelwerfer (a
multi-barrelled rocket launcher).
Zug (platoon; plural Züge) A tactical unit of
30–40 soldiers.

DAS REICH
Waffen-SS Armoured Elite

Another Soviet attack has been stopped in its tracks. Waffen-SS artillery observers, wearing clean loose fitting snow camouflage coveralls over their parkas, carefully study the enemy lines through their stereo telescope. Any new movement by the Soviets will result in another fire order to bring down artillery fire on the enemy's positions.

ORIGINS & HISTORY

Fame and infamy in equal measure surround the 2nd SS Panzer Division *Das Reich*, the most decorated of all World War II German armed units. With the 1st SS Panzer Division (*Leibstandarte Adolf Hitler*), 12th SS Panzer Division (*Hitler Jugend*) and the 3rd SS Panzer Division (*Totenkopf*), *Das Reich* formed an elite core of highly-skilled, motivated soldiers within the Waffen-SS that won the deserved plaudits of both friend and foe on the battlefields of Europe, and equally deserved condemnation for its actions outside the sphere of military operations. No fewer than 69 Knight's Cross recipients fought in the ranks of *Das Reich* during the five and a half years of war, testimony, if any were needed, to the elite status of this much-vaunted division. The history of the division was both brief and spectacular, but with the other elite Waffen-SS divisions, *Das Reich* has left an indelible mark on the history of arms, both through the ferocity of its actions and for the scale of its achievements. Measure for measure they are unequalled. This title in the *Spearhead* series therefore looks at the career of the 2nd SS Panzer Division, its antecedents and related units, in peacetime and in war.

The story is all the more remarkable when one considers that prior to October 1939 no formal SS Division existed. As with all Waffen-SS units, the elements that coalesced to form 2nd SS Panzer in 1941 were fostered in the violent political scene of 1920s' Germany, by an upstart political party (the Nazi NSDAP) seeking to defend itself from

Right: Pre-war photograph of men from *Germania* during a training march. The SS Standarten (regiments) *Germania* and *Deutschland* were the main constituent elements of the *Das Reich* Division. Both were created in the mid-1930s after the Nazis came to power.

attacks by rival groups and, in turn, harass opponents. The rise of the party through fair means and foul, and the transformation of these political protection groups, is covered in more detail in the companion volume in this series, *Spearhead 5: Leibstandarte Adolf Hitler*. Suffice to say that by 1930, the Schutzstaffel (SS) had been formalised as a personal bodyguard unit for Hitler under the leadership of the ambitious Heinrich Himmler, with detachments in most of the main German cities. There had been a name change, too, to Politische Bereitschaften (Political Stand-by detachments) which had the unofficial status of police squads.

Soon after the *Machtergreifung* (seizure of power) in January 1933 the NSDAP leaders set about consolidating their hold on power, using the Allgemeine (general) branch of the SS, the SA and the Stahlhelm, which were all authorised to act as auxiliary police units, to cast a long shadow over Germany. The Politische Bereitschaften were expanded in the principal municipalities, and rapidly any trace of opposition to the self-proclaimed Nazi 'revolution' was eradicated.

The ruthlessness of such measures was soon graphically demonstrated. Hitler had recognised as early as 1922 the threat that lay within the ranks of the SA membership (this in part prompted him to form the Adolf Hitler Shock Troop that became the 1st SS Panzer Division *Leibstandarte Adolf Hitler*). By the end of 1933 SA membership stood at approximately 3 million, dwarfing the 50,000-strong fledgling Schutzstaffel. The brown-shirted SA regarded itself as the true strong arm of the party, and under Ernst Röhm, a close friend of the Nazi leader, its members had become a significant and increasingly belligerent threat to Hitler's dominance of the party. Furthermore, they had been encouraged to believe that they would replace the German Army as the country's national defence force. The delicate political balance on which the Nazis were still dependent could, of course, countenance no such threat to the status quo and in January 1934, a year after his appointment to power, Hitler used SS murder squads to decapitate the SA during the infamous 'Night of the Long Knives'.

Above: 'Eyes Right!' The 2nd Company of SS Regiment *Deutschland* salutes SS-Obersturmbannführer Keppler and company commander (and later *Das Reich* commander) SS-Hauptsturmführer Willi Bittrich, both of whose heads and upper bodies are cut off in this photograph. The regimental band plays on.

REGIMENT *Deutschland*

Prior to this event, in October 1933, some nine months after Hitler's appointment to the Chancellorship, a group of 35 men selected from each of the Standarten of the Allgemeine-SS was chosen to form the cadre of the 1st Battalion of a new SS regiment. These men were posted to the Munich Regiment of the Bavarian state police and, after selection, began officer training at the SS academy at Bad Tolz. They, together with a group of NCOs, formed the nucleus around which the Waffen-SS and *Das Reich* were built.

Unchallenged by the SA after the savage purge, during the mid-1930s the SS underwent a rapid expansion, under which the SS platoons within the Munich police grew into the Politische Bereitschaft Munich, with a strength in mid-1934 of three infantry companies, one machine-gun company and an infantry-gun company. From this unit we can trace the lineage of the Regiment *Deutschland*, one of the two main formations from which the 2nd SS Panzer was created.

Above: *Deutschland* commander SS-Standartenführer Felix Steiner takes the salute of his regiment in Kufstein, March 1938.

Under orders from Himmler, from late 1934 the SS-Politische Bereitschaften were formalised into the three Standarten (regiments) of the Verfügungstruppe (*Adolf Hitler*, *Deutschland* and *Germania*) to allow for more effective administration, and to further steps toward fulfilling Hitler's ambitions for the SS. As part of this restructuring, in October the Munich unit was amalgamated with two similar formations into Standarte 1 of the SS-Verfügungstruppe (SS 1.VT), becoming 1st Battalion (I./SS 1.VT). (Although it was originally to have been the 1st SS Regiment, Hitler later decreed that the *Leibstandarte Adolf Hitler* was not to be included in the numbering sequence for SS units, to emphasise that it was to remain instead his personal domain.)

An NCO cadre was selected around which the sub-units of Standarte 1 were organised along military lines. But although the newly formed regiment had all the bearing of a military unit, and nominal administration passed from the Nazi party to the 7th Infantry Division, it was not yet considered to be a regular Army unit. All the same it was stationed in regular barracks accommodation, with the battalion taking up residence in the quarters at Munich Freimann in which the regimental headquarters was established in 1939.

At the same time, the 4th Battalion, which to all intents and purposes was the renamed Politische Bereitschaft Württemberg, was formalised and quartered at Ellwangen barracks. The men were predominantly southern Germans from Nazi strongholds in Bavaria and Württemberg.

During the Reichsparteitag celebrations of 1934 Standarte 1. SS-VT was given the title *Deutschland* and the constituent battalions received colours. Later an honour cuff band bearing the same legend was awarded, and a 2nd Battalion taken on strength and quartered in Ingolstadt Landstrasse. This was comprised of the Hilfswerk Schleissheim, (a group of expatriate Austrian Nazi volunteers) which had been drafted into the SS-VT at the suggestion of Himmler to circumvent a diplomatic clash with the Italian dictator Mussolini over the secondment of foreign volunteers to the German forces. The 3rd Battalion was not formally established until July 1936 at the Munich Freimann barracks, around a cadre of volunteers and transferees from the 1st and the 4th Battalions, and recruits drawn mainly from Württemberg and Bavaria.

In October 1936 SS-Sturmbann N (Nürnberg) was formed around a cadre from SS-*Leibstandarte Adolf Hitler* and SS-Standarte *Deutschland*. It took part in the annexation of Austria as a part of SS-Standarte *Deutschland*. It was then converted into a motorcycle battalion in November 1938 and redesignated SS-Kradschützen-Bataillon N.

SS-Standarte 2. VT Germania, October 1934
3 x Sturmbann
1 x Trench mortar Sturm
1 x Motorcycle Sturm

as at February 1935
3 x SS-Sturmbann
each of 3 x Infantry Stürme,
 1 x Signals Platoon, 1 x MG-Sturm x 3
SS Motorcycle Sturm
SS Trench mortar Sturm
SS Band
3 x Motorised supply columns

REGIMENT *Germania*

The second of the two principal units of the future *Das Reich* was Regiment *Germania*, formed as SS-Standarte 3./VT in 1934. It was renamed SS-Standarte 2./VT when Hitler ordered that SS-*Leibstandarte Adolf Hitler* would not be included in the numbering sequence. In September 1936, SS-Standarte *Germania*, then stationed in Hamburg, received its colour standard at the Reichsparteitag in Nuremberg. It was organised formally as a regiment on 1 October of that year, with three infantry battalions and three heavy weapons companies. Although these units were administered together, they rarely coalesced and lacked both a common training schedule and true cohesion. Even so the regiment played a role in the annexation of Austria, was responsible for security during Mussolini's subsequent visit to Germany, and also took part in the annexation of Sudetenland under detachment to the Army. *Germania* later served as a guard regiment in Prague, as Wach-Regiment des Reichsprotektors von Böhmen und Mähren, until July 1939. For the invasion of Poland it was attached to Fourteenth Army and following that campaign formed part of the SS-Verfügungstruppe Division.

By the end of 1936 the two core units of the SS-VT – and thus *Das Reich* – had been established. At this time they had a combined nominal strength of 5,040. To these were later added further battalions of pioneer, artillery and signals troops and, after the annexation of Austria, the 3,500 men of the *Der Führer* Regiment (see below). Together with the separate wholly separate *Leibstandarte* Regiment (2,600 troops), and the concentration camp guards of the *Totenkopfverbände* (3,500 troops), these regiments comprised the armed strength of the SS.

Below: *Germania* march past led by the regimental band. Pre-war photograph taken in Hamburg.

REGIMENT *Der Führer*

Completing the triumvirate of SS-VT units was the SS-Standarte *Der Führer*. It was formed as SS-Standarte 3./VT in Vienna in March 1938, following the annexation of Austria, of Austrian volunteers around a cadre from SS-Standarte *Deutschland*. At the Reichsparteitag in Nuremberg in 1938, while still stationed in Vienna, it was renamed SS-Standarte *Der Führer* and received its colour standard. Command of this unit was temporarily transferred to the Army during the mobilisation in October 1938. It took part in the occupation of Czechoslovakia and later served as a guard regiment in Prague, as Wach-Regiment des Reichsprotektors von Böhmen und Mähren. There was no role for the regiment in the invasion of Poland, during which it was stationed on the West Wall.

READY FOR WAR

From the earliest days of the Third Reich, both Hitler and Reichsführer-SS Himmler gave voice to their shared desire to see the SS develop into a paramilitary force of 'soldier-policemen' that could take over responsibility for law enforcement from the established police force. Hitler believed that it should have sufficient military bearing to impress its authority on the public and that the right to such authority could only be won in combat, thus concluding that the SS-VT should undergo training to prepare it for military service in time of war. This was the rationale behind the creation of the SS-Verfügungstruppe, which in due course became the Waffen-SS, or 'armed SS'. One of the strongest indications of the military role that Hitler and Himmler envisaged for the SS-VT came with the issue of field grey service uniforms to the troops in 1935. The publicly stated role of the SS-VT was the protection of the Nazi 'revolution' but in 1935 Hitler admitted that it would be incorporated into the Army in time of war, and by the outbreak of hostilities it had been trained for a very different role than the one for which it was first conceived.

BELIEVE! OBEY! FIGHT!

This slogan was borrowed from the Italian Fascist call, *Credere! Obbedire! Combattere!* and adopted as the motto of the SS. It accurately sums up the ethic that pervaded the ranks of the SS-VT. There was a flood of applicants to join the party's elite corps, attracted by the boldness of such rhetoric, by the kudos that membership was thought to confer, and the absence of discrimination toward Germans outside the ruling classes. However, of these, only a small percentage were deemed fit to wear the SS uniform. Earning the right to wear the SS-Verfügungstruppe insignia was far from easy. Recruits had to pass a stringent selection, including a physical examination, with measurements of 'racial features' like the shape of the skull, nose and ears, the distance between the eyes and other such criteria, and a detailed investigation into their family lineage. In 1931 Himmler, who was obsessed with such matters of race, introduced the rule that each SS man had to be able to trace his Aryan ancestry back to 1750, with no Jewish, Slav or other 'extraneous' blood. If he wanted to marry, his future wife was subjected to rigorous mental and physical vetting by SS doctors. Interestingly, although the physical standards for entry to the SS-VT were much higher than for the Army, intellectual standards were somewhat lower. This stands in contrast to the other branches of the SS, the ranks of which were swelled by an influx of middle-class German professionals.

TRAINING CENTRES

Deutschland recruits, and those of the other SS-VT regiments, underwent training at a number of purpose-built infantry schools, the so-called Junkerschulen, and at Army facilities. Junkerschule (Officer Candidate School) Bad Tolz and, to a lesser extent, the Officer Candidate School Brunswick (Braunschweig) were the premier Waffen-SS training

Below: IIIrd Battalion of *Deutschland* returning to quarters after training. The column is snaking through Soltau, on the edge of the Lüneberger Heide, an area well-known to British servicemen who served in the postwar BAOR.

centres for officers in the 1930s and during World War II. By 1937 the SS schools were graduating over 400 officers a year, in two sets of classes. The spirited aggressiveness taught at the school was not without cost – by 1942, nearly 700 Waffen-SS officers had been killed in action, including almost all of the 60 graduates of the 1934–35 Bad Tolz class. In addition to the two SS Junkerschulen, there were many other training grounds, schools and assembly areas.

Although the basic tenets of the training philosophy matched those of the Army, with weapon handling and drill as its foundations, SS-VT training differed radically, at least equalling and in some cases exceeding the standard required by the Army. Because of its status as an elite corps, with a prominent public image, the SS-VT training initially emphasised parade ground drilling. But in addition, certainly under the influence of Felix Steiner, and later Paul Hausser, the training had a very serious military purpose that was to pay untold dividends in battle. While serving during the Great War, Steiner had commanded a detachment of Stormtroopers from whom the post-war Freikorps, and later the SS, drew so much of their inspiration. These were small, select groups of heavily armed but mobile assault infantry tasked with using fire and movement to make small penetrations of the enemy lines to create a larger breakthrough. They had achieved considerable success in Germany's 1918 spring offensive and impressed upon a generation of German veterans the effectiveness of such tactics.

Not least among these veterans was Paul Hausser, upon whose appointment to the command of the Inspectorate of SS-VT troops on 1 October 1936 the SS gained a capable and influential leader. Hausser, a former Stahlhelm volunteer and Sturmbannführer in the SA, and until 1932 an officer of the Reichswehr, was formerly commander of the SS officer training school at Brunswick before promotion to Brigadeführer when the responsibility for training the SS-VT was handed to him. Furthermore, Hausser introduced a more open and flexible command structure. During the war he proved to be among the finest of SS officers.

From the late summer of 1935 Felix Steiner was commander of the 4th Battalion *Deutschland* Regiment, barracked at Ellwangen, and from the following July, regimental commander. Steiner broke with traditional, inflexible methods of training in an attempt to create a fighting soldier who was at once a superb marksman and athlete, and who excelled in fieldcraft and could think for himself on the battlefield. With such skills as these, he rightly surmised, the soldier stood a better chance of surviving, and the slaughter that had been witnessed during the Great War could be avoided.

Steiner's *Deutschland* Regiment, in particular, emphasised the benefits of physical fitness to the combat soldier. The commander believed, and was later proved correct, that a physically fit soldier could function in conditions of greater deprivation and hardship. Stamina and endurance were honed by long marches carrying weapons in full combat dress, at the end of which the soldiers were expected to be capable of functioning in the field. Hausser implemented the methods that Steiner had pioneered with the 4th Battalion throughout the entire Waffen-SS establishment as well as introducing his own. These drills have since been adopted by almost every regular Army, testimony to Steiner's visionary approach to combat training.

However, the importance of physical fitness was not the only one of Steiner's tenets; of equal importance was a soldier's ability to function as a leader should his own be incapacitated. And instead of the old, unwieldy field units his men were divided into small detachments, again similar to the stormtrooper battalions of the Great War.

These may not sound particularly revolutionary ideas today, but introduced as they were at a time when Western armies were practising infantry tactics that had seen little advancement since 1918, and maintaining the rigid hierarchies of their command structures, they represented a major advance. Throughout the war, there were countless

Above: Paul Hausser would end the war as an SS-Oberstgruppenführer und Generaloberst der Waffen-SS. 'Papa' Hausser (as his men called him) lost an eye on the Eastern Front and sported a black eyepatch thereafter. His military prowess is undeniable: his best-known exploits being the retaking of Kharkov in February 1943 and his leadership during the Falaise Pocket battle in Normandy in 1944. See biography page 84.

SS-Standarte Germania, September 1939

Regiment Staff
1st, 2nd, 3rd Infantry Battalions (motorised)
13th Infantry Gun Company (motorised)
14th Anti-tank Company (motorised)
15th Motorcycle Company
Intelligence Platoon
Motorcycle Platoon
Band

SS-Standarte Deutschland
Order of Battle identical to *Germania*

SS-Standarte Der Führer
Order of Battle identical to *Germania*

episodes in which SS troops demonstrated extraordinary soldiering skills, pointing to the effectiveness of the methods Steiner pioneered with the *Deutschland* Regiment. Furthermore, the training was continuously adapted to take account of the changing nature of combat – when Sturmbannführer Stadler took over the Panzer school in August 1944, he updated its methods based on his experience during the Normandy Campaign

Basic training lasted three weeks, although after 1942 all parade ground drilling was eliminated. Unlike in most modern armies, the SS recruit was immediately placed in his branch of service at the beginning of his basic training. However, he was also exposed to an above-average amount of multi-disciplinary training – meaning that artillerymen would learn how to use radios, signals troops would learn how to fire machine guns and so on. The Waffen-SS was also open to new ideas and innovations – by way of example, panzer crews of the 12th SS Panzer Division *Hitler Jugend* were required as part of their training to spend a week working on the assembly line at the MAN tank factory in Nuremberg.

Typically, the early morning reveille would be followed by ablutions and breakfast, a brisk period of exercise and drilling followed by a hearty lunch. The troops then proceeded to the ranges for practice in fieldcraft and weapon handling. Sports activities, particularly those such as boxing that involved physical contact (to imbue a toughness in the men), played a major part in the programme, and unarmed and close combat techniques, with bayonet and knife, were practised with instructors. Steiner's vision of the *Deutschland* at the spearhead of rapier-like thrusts into the enemy line ensured that speed in the attack, which had been a key aspect of the stormtrooper tactics, was constantly emphasised by the instructors.

Lectures on political matters were another regular feature of the curriculum – what one might today call indoctrination – which impressed upon recruits the idea that they were elite warriors in a race war, a war that would make Germany the great power that she had once been. The supposed heroes of those times – Frederick the Great and Barbarossa, for example – were co-opted for Nazism, and lauded along with latter-day Nazi figures as Horst Wessel. Other topics were the philosophy of Nietzsche, reinterpreted and taken out of context by Nazi theoreticians, and the ideology of race theorists such as Houston Stewart Chamberlain and the Comte de Gobineau. Furthermore, every recruit was required to read Walter Darre's (the head of the SS Race and Resettlement Office) *Blut und Boden*, and *The Myth of the 20th Century*, an anti-Semitic diatribe penned by the influential Nazi 'philosopher' Alfred Rosenberg that came as close to a Nazi Bible as existed.

The courses to indoctrinate Waffen-SS troops with Nazi ideology were not as successful as the hierarchy hoped. Far more productive in this role were the informal *Kameradschaftsabend* – SS 'comrade evenings' – in which unit members would gather together to eat, drink, sing traditional folk songs or patriotic and Nazi anthems and receive ideological instruction. Officers and men addressed each other as '*Kamerad*'. These evenings were a frequent feature of the pre-war Allgemeine-SS, but the tradition seems to have been carried on into the Waffen-SS as well.

In contrast to the *Leibstandarte* Regiment, the SS-VT regiments actually enjoyed good pre-war relations with the Army. Because of the lack of combat experience within the SS-VT ranks, the training staff were initially drawn from the ranks of the regular Army, and this helped to dispel some of the hostility that had sprung up between the two forces. But a certain contempt remained. The accusation most often levelled at the SS-VT by the Army was that it was merely a parade ground force, and its members were derided as 'asphalt soldiers'. The accusation rankled, particularly with Himmler, who determined to silence some of the critics. Although the critics were still vocal even after the Polish campaign, a perfect opportunity presented itself at the annual spring manoeuvres in 1938. At these the SS-VT was to have the opportunity to show off its finely honed battle skills. In front of a clutch of high-ranking observers, in the final stages of an attack the regimental assault detachment skirmished up to, attacked, and overran the enemy trenches, to the evident delight of the onlookers. Hitler had an opportunity to see for himself the effectiveness of the training at manoeuvres in May, 1939, when he observed a *Deutschland* assault under live fire.

THE *BLUMENKRIEG* (FLOWER WAR)

Of course all this was not without purpose and even as these manoeuvres were taking place Germany was advancing headlong on the course to war. Behind the scenes political machinations by Hitler and the Austrian Nazi movement (which been outlawed for murdering Chancellor Dolfuss in 1934) had destabilised the Austrian government while Nazi calls for *Anschluss* (union) of the two countries became increasingly strident. After the resignation of Chancellor Schuschnigg his replacement, the puppet leader, Artur Seyss-Inquart, requested the German Army to intervene, ostensibly to restore order. The *Deutschland* Regiment was among the units that crossed the border on 12 March 1938, to a rapturous welcome.

Hitler then began demanding the transfer to Germany of the Sudetenland region of Czechoslovakia, and in a speech on 26 September 1938 claimed this would be his last territorial claim in Europe. At the Munich conference shortly thereafter the Sudetenland was duly ceded to Germany, and occupied by the Army with the SS-VT in support. 'Not bullets but flowers greet our soldiers', said Propaganda Minister, Goebbels. The next spring Hitler moved to occupy all of Czechoslovakia (Fall Grün), and the newly created *Der Führer* Regiment moved to take up occupation duties in Prague, where it remained until the outbreak of war.

Below: A long way from the flowers and garlands that they received in 1938, these battle-hardened Panzergrenadiers of *Das Reich* are taking part in the battle of Kharkov, 1943. The unit's 'wolf's hook' symbol is faintly visible on the rear of the vehicle.

IN ACTION

POLAND

The war for which the SS-VT had been so rigorously preparing began in the east, against Poland. According to Nazi ideology, the independent status of Poland stood directly in the way of legitimate German expansion into the areas currently occupied by the 'subhuman Slavs'. 'The bleeding frontiers of the east', a reference to the loss of Prussian territory brought about by the Treaty of Versailles, were stressed in Nazi propaganda from the earliest days of the movement, and from the early 1930s Nazi leaders began to use the metaphor *Polnische Wirtschaft* ('Polish Business') to suggest a state of chaos in Poland and prepare the population for war, as part of the projected drive east.

In 1934 Hitler temporarily adjusted difficulties with Poland by concluding a ten-year military and commercial pact, but five years later the pact was broken when he insisted upon the annexation of Danzig and the creation of a roadway between Germany and the separate German province of East Prussia. Great Britain and France guaranteed the independence of Poland and assured Hitler that aggression would be met with force. Nonetheless, on 3 April 1939, Hitler issued a general directive to Field Marshal Keitel, chief of staff of the OKW (Oberkommando der Wehrmacht – High Command of the Armed Forces), on preparations for war. Annexed to the directive was a document containing details of Fall Weiss, the plan for a projected attack on Poland.

Below: Troops of *Deutschland* during the Polish campaign – as part of Panzer Group Kempf, the first pairing of Army and Waffen-SS units. The regiment performed efficiently and without the problems that *Leibstandarte* experienced.

The Armies

The Polish Army, with a potential strength of 1,800,000 men, was hardly an insignificant force, well regarded in Europe and reputed to have the continent's finest cavalry. The infantry were skilled in the arts of anti-tank warfare and heavy German losses of armour during the campaign would point this out. In a man-to-man infantry fight it was clear that the Germans had no advantage over the Poles, whose tactical style was based upon their experiences in the Russian-Polish War and emphasised manoeuvre and the use of combined arms. But this combined arms doctrine looked back to the First World War, and since the Polish Army moved on foot or horseback, speed of manoeuvre was limited to the pace of the slowest horse. Another critical weakness was the complete lack of modern communications equipment even at the highest command levels. In other areas, a German signal battalion had twice as many trucks as an entire Polish infantry division, most of the weaponry was of First World

War vintage, and although the Poles possessed about 1,000 armoured vehicles, three-quarters of them were small tankettes of questionable value. Two brigades of 7TP light tanks comprised the bulk of the force. While they were to prove superior to the Panzer I and Panzer II and were a near match for the Panzer III, the Poles were hopelessly outclassed in the tactical use of armour. Most crucially, the General Staff had chosen to disperse this force along the frontier, rather than concentrate it at the most gravely threatened points.

Germany's forces were by comparison larger (for the campaign they employed some 2,600 tanks and over 2,000 aircraft of all types), more modern and well balanced. As well as a numerical superiority in weapons they had modern communications equipment, and were expert in the doctrine of combined arms.

Panzer Group Kempf

It will be remembered that after the bloodless Anschluss, the *Deutschland* Regiment participated in the occupation of Bohemia and Moravia during March 1939. Hitler ordered that the regiment should be expanded to a division, but as the war loomed nearer, this event had to be postponed.

In July, the OKH (Oberkommando des Heeres – Army High Command) decided to create a unique unit in preparation for the assault on Poland, which duly formed in the summer of 1939 from a mix of Army and SS-Verfügungstruppe units in East Prussia. The OKH remained highly sceptical of SS abilities away from the parade ground, but had little option but to acquiesce with Hitler's wishes for the SS to be included. On 25 July 1939, units of the SS-Verfügungstruppe arrived by rail and sea at Stettin and Königsberg. Independent of the SS-VT units, the 7th Panzer Regiment (which had previously been part of the 4th Panzer Brigade) was transferred by freighters to Königsberg and proceeded to its assembly area near Zinten.

Officially this sudden movement of troops was a part of the preparations for the upcoming Tannenberg celebrations, being staged to commemorate the German victory over the Russians won there by Hindenburg in 1914 (a large memorial had been constructed at the battle site in which were entombed the remains of Hindenburg and his wife).

The new unit was designated as the Kampfgruppe 'Panzer-Verbände Ostpreussen' (East Prussian Tank Units) and command was given to Generalmajor Werner Kempf, the former commander of the 4th Panzer Brigade. Under his charge, the unit was referred to as Panzer Group *Kempf*. Along with Kempf, other members of the 4th Panzer Brigade (which was subsequently disbanded) formed the core of the new divisional staff. As a part of this formation, during the invasion of Poland, SS Regiment *Deutschland* was first blooded, fighting at Mlava, Rozan, Lomza, Kliczym and Modlin.

The staff set up headquarters at the Stablak Training area, south of Königsberg, East Prussia and made preparations for the remaining units of the division to arrive. Recognising the potential for further expansion of the Waffen-SS, Gruppenführer Paul Hausser accompanied the unit as an observer for the duration of its operations in Poland.

Panzer Division *Kempf* was unique, in that it was the first Army division to be composed of both Army and Waffen-SS units. Despite the fact that Panzer Group *Kempf* was structured as a regular Army panzer division, in material strength it amounted to little more than a reinforced panzer brigade. There was only one motorised infantry regiment as opposed to the authorised strength of two regiments and additionally, except for the 7th Panzer Regiment and the SS Reconnaissance Battalion, the unit was severely lacking in vehicles with cross-country capability. Notwithstanding the shortfalls, the experiment was to prove a success, and serve as the precursor of the first SS division.

Throughout the month of August, the soldiers of Panzer Group *Kempf* engaged in manoeuvres while some diversion was found in assisting the local population with the

Above: Motorcycles were used extensively during the war by all sides. This is a captured Soviet motorcycle that is being brought back into service by a Waffen-SS soldier. In the background is a captured Soviet 76.2mm ZIS-3 dual purpose field gun, one of the most successful Soviet artillery designs, and a most desirable piece of booty. Slightly modified, captured guns of this type made excellent anti-tank weapons and were widely used mounted on various German tank chassis. The machine gun lying next to it is the standard Russian 7.62mm StP Maksima Mod. 1910 on a typical Russian wheeled carriage complete with armour plate that afforded some protection for the gunner.

Panzer Group Kempf, September 1939

7. Panzer Regiment
SS-Regiment *Deutschland*
SS-Artillery Regiment
SS Signal Battalion
SS Reconnaissance Battalion
II./47. Heavy Artillery Battalion
2./SS Anti-Aircraft MG Battalion
505. Pioneer Battalion
Field post detachment
171. Admin Service Unit
Transport Column 502
Supply services
Medical services

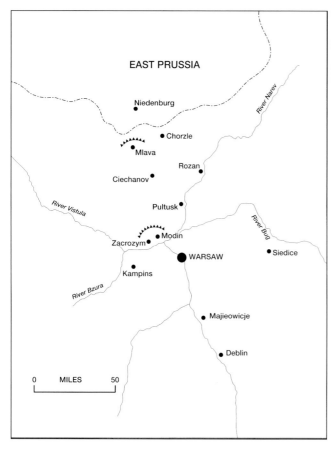

EAST PRUSSIA

Niedenburg

Chorzle

Mlava

Rozan

Ciechanov

River Vistula

Pultusk

River Narev

River Bug

Zacrozym • Modin

WARSAW

Siedice

Kampins

River Bzura

Majieowicje

Deblin

0   MILES   50

Above: The operational area in Poland, autumn 1939.

harvest. Preparations for the Tannenberg celebrations continued apace, disguising the true purpose of the military build-up. To help authenticate the ruse, veterans of the Great War from all over Germany gathered in the area.

On 19 August Panzer Group *Kempf* and the 61st and 11th Infantry Divisions, were assigned to the I Army Corps, and were subsequently moved closer to the border with Poland. Here, as the diplomatic crisis between Germany and Poland deepened, the units of the division continued to practice for the parade planned for the Tannenberg celebrations. The parade, scheduled for 24 August, never took place. Instead the division was moved further south to Kommusin Forest near Neidenburg, well within sight of the Polish border. From here the various regimental and battalion commanders and their adjutants made regular reconnaissance trips, scouting out possible assembly areas for the division.

On 25 August the protracted negotiations between Germany and Poland collapsed, and, in a last minute attempt to intimidate Hitler, the British announced that they had entered into a full military alliance with Poland. It was to no avail. Kempf's group was ordered to move forward to the I Army Corps assembly area. Notice arrived soon after that the attack would begin the next morning at 06.00. Using the tactics of Blitzkrieg, the OKH planned to use maximum surprise in the attack, code-named Fall Weiss. Throughout July and during early August some 98 Wehrmacht divisions had been mobilised and moved quietly into positions east, on the Polish border, and west, to meet the expected counter-attack by the British and French. The plan called for an attack in the north from Pomerania by General Fedor von Bock's Fourth Army while his Third Army (together constituting Army Group North), advanced from East Prussia to complete a pincer movement. To the south Generaloberst Gerd von Rundstedt's Eighth (Blaskowitz) and Tenth (Reichenau) Armies were to strike from Silesia toward Warsaw, and the Fourteenth (List) to move on Krakow in the south-west to cut off any Polish retreat.

Panzer Group *Kempf* (attached to I Corps, Fourth Army) had orders to occupy the southernmost position in East Prussia, directly in front of a strong Polish bunker system known as the 'Mlava position'. As part of this movement, under the cloak of darkness, sub-units of *Deutschland* deployed along the border, while the divisional artillery emplaced the gun batteries that would support the morning assault.

At daybreak on the 26th, barely minutes before the attack was due to commence, came an order to postpone. But poor communications, hampered by a poor road network made worse by a recent rain storm, ensured that the message was not passed to all elements of *Deutschland* in time. A reconnaissance patrol from 9./*Deutschland* advanced several miles across the border and, although there was no contact with the enemy, it required considerable effort to disseminate the belated order. Nearly three hours had passed before all units had been recalled to their assembly points, a somewhat ignominious start to the campaign. However, there were some useful lessons to learn from this apparent bungle. Prime among them was the suggestion that Polish forces would not engage the division at the border, and that the first point of resistance would most likely be encountered in front of the Mlava position.

Negotiations began once more in earnest. I Army Corps was withdrawn from the Polish frontier, and reassembled at the former divisional command post at Neidenburg. Four days later, on 30 August, the talks broke down again, and once again the troops of Panzer Division *Kempf* were mustered.

Their officers were called to a briefing at the divisional HQ at Neidenburg for the commanders of I Army Corps regiments. At the meeting Generalmajor Kempf, to the evident amazement of the officers assembled, ordered the division 'back into their old foxholes'. This was an extraordinary order considering one of the basic tenets of war is never to reoccupy assembly positions if they have been made known to the enemy. Despite this, the men of SS Regiment *Deutschland* moved into their old positions and waited for the coming events.

The attack was set for 04.45 on 1 September, and this time no halt order arrived to arrest the invasion. On the night of the 30th, SS units staged incidents along the border including a hoax Polish raid on the German radio station at Gleiwitz (Operation Himmler). Shortly before 01.00 on 1 September some 37 German divisions began to move from their start points toward the German–Polish border, and began to cross at dawn. Preceded by an artillery bombardment and attacks by dive-bombers, Panzer Group *Kempf*, which had been entrenched near Neidenburg, moved from its start lines against the positions in front of Mlava. *Deutschland* troops had as their first objective the small villages of Dvierznis, on the right flank of the line of advance, and Zavadski, on the left. The 1st and 3rd Battalions, respectively, were charged with capturing them, and then the high ground beyond. Moving south down the Mlava road the regiment initially met little resistance and took the villages, but at the base of the bare ridge lying behind, on which the Poles had sited strong defences, the attackers came under heavy fire and were halted.

At 15.00 the attack began anew, with a frontal assault by the SS on a hill designated Point 192. On this sector the defences were strong; the supporting armour of 1st Panzer Battalion was soon ensnared in the steel traps, providing Polish gunners with easy pickings until the mounting losses forced the panzer commander to break off the attack. The order left the infantrymen, who had worked their way through the barbed wire barricades and at one point advanced to within 150 metres of the enemy, exposed on the ridge. Here they stayed under a rain of Polish fire until nightfall, when they withdrew back to the main defence line under cover of darkness.

Rozan

The following day *Deutschland* was pulled out of the line at Mlava and redeployed to the east, to the area around Chorzele, where a breakthrough had been achieved. Marching south-east with the 7th Panzer, the regiment ran up against the Polish defenders in the Tsarist-era forts at Rozan on the River Narev. Initial attempts to seize the town were met with fierce fire, halted, and then repulsed by counter-attacking Polish cavalry. Forced temporarily onto the defensive, the division was regrouped and successfully invested the town, then carried the advance south-east, behind the capital Warsaw, to Loriza, Czervin and Hadbory, all the time fighting in high summer heat through cloying soil that sapped the energies of the exhausted soldiers and ravaged their arms and machines.

Below: A captured Polish officer is taken to HQ for interrogation.

Warsaw

Within five days Bock's Army Group North had overrun the Danzig corridor, and by 7 September elements of Reichenau's Tenth Army

Division name

As it expanded *Das Reich* underwent a number of name changes, which are detailed below.

SS Division Verfügungstruppe (mot) (10 October 1939–1 April 1940)

SS-V Division (1 April 1940–2 December 1940)

SS Division *Deutschland* (3 December 1940–27 January 1941)

SS Division (mot) *Reich* (28 January 1941–May 1942)

SS Division *Das Reich* (May 1942–9 November 1942)

SS Panzergrenadier Division *Das Reich* (9 November 1942–January 1944)

SS Kampfgruppe *Das Reich*** (17 December 1943–27 April 1944)

2nd SS Panzer Division *Das Reich* (January 1944–May 1945)

**While the majority of *Das Reich* returned to France for refit, portions of the division remained behind to fight as an independent battle group

(Army Group South) had advanced from Silesia north-east to within 50km of Warsaw, in the first move of a double pincer envelopment, and succeeded in cutting off Polish forces before they could retreat behind the Vistula. That same day the Eighth Army succeeded in taking Lodz, 120km south-east of Warsaw.

With the route to Warsaw now wide open, Tenth Army turned its axis of advance north and advanced toward the capital from the south-west, while the Fourth Army closed from the north. Instead of withdrawing east to escape the pincer movement, on 10 September the Polish commander, Marshal Rydz-Smigly, ordered a retreat to south-east Poland. On the day of the Polish withdrawal *Deutschland* crossed the River Bug at Brok, attempting to link up with the southern arm of the pincer and intercept the retreating Poles.

With their defensive perimeter considerably diminished, the Poles now had the advantage of concentrating their forces, and the resistance thickened. They struck south at the Eighth Army, protecting the northern flanks of the Tenth Army, and caught the Germans temporarily off balance, but without air cover, much of which had been destroyed in the first days of the war, the Poles faced an untenable position. In the ensuing week Guderian's armoured corps advanced from the north-west, linked up with Kleist's armour moving from the south at Brest-Litovsk on the 14th, and effectively cut off any potential escape route for the encircled armies. *Deutschland* had by this time advanced as far as Siedlice, and now swung to the south-west towards Majieowicje as the great battle in the Bzura bend destroyed the last credible Polish opposition.

The final prize, the capital Warsaw, was as yet untaken. On the north-western fringe of the city lay the towns of Modlin and Zakroczym and it was at these that the regiment was ordered to strike, and the forts to west and north-east of Modlin.

Investing them proved to be a formidable challenge that engaged the regiment for the better part of nine days. The first preparatory assault went in on 22 September, with the pioneer battalion clearing paths for the main attack. In the interim the Luftwaffe sent droves of bombers to weaken the defences, until finally, at 05.30 on the 29th, *Deutschland* troops began crawling through the breaches in the wire and formed up for the assault. At 06.15 artillery opened up on the town of Zakroczym and the No.1 Fort. Following in the wake of the barrage came the infantry. In a little over an hour and a half the town was taken, and a concentrated bombardment forced the men holed up in the No.1 Fort to capitulate in the early afternoon.

Although scattered resistance continued until 10 October, the capture of Warsaw and its forts effectively brought an end to the campaign. It marked, too, the end of Panzer Group *Kempf*, which was shortly disbanded. The campaign had lasted less than two months and ended in the destruction of the Polish Army and the Fourth Partition of Poland. German losses were surprisingly heavy considering the brevity of the campaign. The casualty total was some 48,000 men of whom 16,000 had been killed. Fully a quarter of the tanks the German committed to battle were lost to Polish anti-tank guns. The Luftwaffe was forced to write off some 550 aircraft. Despite the losses, the stunning success of Fall Weiss confirmed to the German commanders that the military machine that they had built was indeed the best in the world and worthy of their confidence.

THE WESTERN OFFENSIVE

On the day that Warsaw fell Hitler notified the OKH to begin planning an attack in the west, to take place as soon as possible. Code-named Fall Gelb, as first outlined on 19 October this was limited in scope to taking ground in Belgium for air bases and ports on the North Sea. A week later, Hitler proposed an attack directly into France avoiding Belgium, and then at the end of the month, he suggested an attack through the Ardennes.

Right: The Western Campaign, 1940. A Waffen-SS NCO from SS Regiment *Germania* (note the cuff title) discusses the next move with members of his reconnaissance patrol. Note the lack of the usual Waffen-SS camouflage jackets and the SS collar patches normally worn on the tunics. The soldier on the left, holding a P08 pistol, is carrying, slung on his back, a tripod for an MG 34.

The enormous complexity of the preparations, and the need to rest and re-equip the armies forced several delays. Over the winter, Fall Gelb was scheduled and cancelled four times. At a conference of 180 top German commanders staged on 23 November Hitler, aware that every day gave the Allies further time to prepare, tried to instill some urgency. Finally, Fall Gelb was set to be ready for 17 January 1940, but a week prior to the scheduled attack, a communications aircraft ferrying a German staff officer, with highly classified documents outlining the attack plan, crashed in Belgium, and despite his attempts to destroy the documents, portions of Fall Gelb were soon in the hands of the Belgian and the Dutch commands. Both gave the order to mobilise. Learning of the disclosure, the German military attaché in Holland notified Berlin, forcing Hitler to cancel Fall Gelb the day before the attack.

Orders were given for the OKH to come up with a new plan. Of the numerous proposals the most radical was that of Rundstedt's chief of staff, General Erich von Manstein. Through good connections he was granted an audience with Hitler, and on 17 February spent the entire day presenting the 'Manstein Plan'. Hitler was favourably impressed with the plan and thereafter over-rode any objections. A draft, code-named 'Sichelschnitt' (Sickle Stroke), had been produced by 24 February and formed the basis for the Western offensive.

Below: The Western Campaign, 1940. A Waffen-SS NCO catches up on some sleep after hectic action.

It was typical of the bold, mobile warfare favoured by the forward thinking staff officers of the time, of whom Manstein was perhaps the most brilliant. His plan, the Manstein Plan (which was in fact a variation on the original OKH plan), was central amongst the advantages that the German forces enjoyed during the Western campaign. These were certainly not numerical, for the French Army was considered to be the finest in Europe at this time and in pure numbers outweighed the Germans in key areas. Rather, it was the deployment of the forces that was crucial.

The plan relied on deep strategic penetration by independently operating armoured forces, with tactical air support, a technique which had proved so devastatingly successful in Poland. The offensive was to have three parts: the first an attack on Holland to provide a base from which to attack Belgium and France; a subsequent attack upon the Belgian defences; and finally a coordinated thrust from points north and east into France. For the offensive three Army groups, A, B, and C, under Rundstedt, Bock and Leeb were created. Army Group B, which included the Eighteenth (Küchler) and Sixth (Reichenau) Armies were to aim at Holland and Belgium respectively. The key tank units, including the 5th and 7th Panzers under Rommel, the Kleist Armoured Group (with the XIX Corps under Guderian) and the 6th and 8th Panzers under Reinhardt were attached to Rundstedt's group. It was charged with the most daring element of the plan, a drive through the ravined and forested Ardennes region behind the main concentration of Allied forces, thus bypassing the formidable French Maginot defensive line, and a race to the undefended

Left: The war in Poland was effectively over by the end of the second week. Warsaw held out until 27 September and Modlin (illustrated here) capitulated on 28 September. The last organised resistance ended on 6 October. In the campaign the Germans took 694,000 prisoners, and an estimated 100,000 men escaped across the borders into Lithuania, Hungary, and Romania. The Germans lost some 16,000 killed of around 48,000 casualties; Polish losses will probably never be known.

Channel coast, before turning to complete the encirclement. Bock's attack on Belgium, where the Belgian Army was concentrated on a defensive line on the Albert Canal and Meuse River lines aimed at diverting attention from this, and at seizing the strategically important fortress at Eben Emael.

In contrast to this highly mobile concept of warfare, the orthodoxy of French and British military thinking still favoured static deployments with armoured support. The Anglo-French Plan D, formulated by the Allied commander-in-chief General Maurice Gamelin and approved by the Allied Supreme War Council, demonstrated a total failure to grasp the nature of Blitzkrieg and left the Allies unprepared for the attack that fell upon them.

THE SS-V DIVISION

After the fall of Poland *Deutschland*, with the SS-VT *Germania* and *Der Führer* Regiments, moved into barracks at Pilsen, Czechoslovakia. Here on 19 October the separate Standarten were combined into a designated SS-V Division, with an artillery regiment, battalions of signals, reconnaissance, pioneers, anti-tank and anti-aircraft gunners, under the command of Paul Hausser. With the British and French forces strung out along the Maginot Line, and little activity in the west to speak of (called the *Sitzkrieg* or 'sit-down war' by the German soldier), the division underwent a six-month period of training to prepare it for the coming battles.

In December, with planning for Fall Gelb already well advanced, the SS-V Division received preliminary orders under which it was revealed that various sub-units were to be parcelled out to the Army. *Der Führer* and a battalion of the artillery regiment plus a pioneer company and the transport column were placed under the command of the 20th Infantry Division and the divisional reconnaissance battalion together with a platoon of *Deutschland*'s armoured cars were seconded to the 254th Infantry Division. The remainder of the division was placed under the command of the Eighteenth Army (Küchler). Army Group B had as one of its objectives an envelopment of the southern flank of the densely populated 'Fortress Holland', a region formed by rivers and canals around the five major Dutch cities – Amsterdam, Rotterdam, Utrecht, Leiden and Den Haag. The most important of the Dutch defences were the Ijssel–Maas river line, the

Grebbe line in the north and the Peel line in the south and from the Zuider Zee to Maastricht. Inside of them the 400,000-man conscripted Dutch Army had concentrated.

It was also likely that the Dutch would open their dikes and flood the land, and create another obstacle to the invasion force. To counter such a move, it was essential to capture bridges intact, and for this objective the SS-V Division received thorough training in waterborne assault during the spring of 1940.

In February the threat of a British invasion of Norway forced a temporary diversion and further delays to the opening of the western offensive. After further postponements because of the weather, the assault finally began before daylight on 10 May, with extensive air attacks on the Dutch and Belgian airfields and the seizure of vital river crossings by paratroops at Moerdijk and Rotterdam. At dawn Küchler's Eighteenth Army, on the northern flank of Bock's group and including the 9th Panzer Division, drove into Holland. In the van were *Der Führer* and the recce battalion; the latter with an Army battalion and artillery unit formed the 'Grave group', and attacked in five detachments the bridges over the Waal at Nijmegen, and at Neersbosch, Hatert, Malden and Heuman. Of these two were taken, at Heuman and Hatert, albeit for heavy loss. With a vital bridgehead secured by the end of the first day, the recce battalion rejoined the division. *Der Führer*, also in the first wave, assaulted across the River Ijssel and captured Westervoort and Arnhem by mid-afternoon. Bivouacking at Renkum, on the next day the regiment attacked the second line of Dutch defences (the Grebbe line) and broke through at Rhenen on the 12th. With the Dutch Army now forced back to the cities of Amsterdam, Rotterdam and Utrecht, and with the Dutch air force reduced to just a single bomber, the *Deutschland* Regiment spearheaded the drive to Amsterdam, and finally halted at Zandvoort on the North Sea.

The remainder of the division had by contrast seen little fighting thus far, having spent the opening two days moving west as part of the vast column of men and matériel pouring across the Rhine. The Maas was crossed and, meeting only light opposition, the SS units advanced toward Hilvarenbek to the north of Antwerp. Their task was to protect the left flank of the Eighteenth Army to guard against a predicted strike by Gort's British Expeditionary Force, Blanchard's First Army, and the Belgian Army in northern Belgium, but when this failed to materialise, the division was instead ordered to intercept the French Seventh Army, which General Giraud had marched north to Breda, to threaten the extended German left flank. Running headlong into the 9th Panzer, the French column was at first stymied, and then pushed back onto the Dyle–Breda line.

Moving on the choked road network proved no simple feat, and only with some difficulty was the division regrouped at the objective. No sooner was this achieved than orders came to move west again, this time past Antwerp. The details of this operation required the SS division to take Walcheren and Beveland to the north-west of Antwerp. Both are approached across a narrow neck of land, which then opens out into south Beveland. In May 1940 the Dutch had inundated much of this area; at the western end a bottleneck traversed by a strongly defended dam guarded the entrance to Walcheren, and now this formed a formidable barricade to the island behind the flood waters.

By 13 May the advance column of German forces striking toward Rotterdam had brought the bulk of the Dutch Army to its knees and was halted at the outskirts of the city. Refusing to countenance delays Hitler issued an ultimatum to the Dutch – capitulate or Rotterdam would be destroyed. Negotiations began, but at 14.00 on 14 May the Luftwaffe attacked, killing over 900 and destroying much of the old city.

However, south of Rotterdam, the Allies were determined to resist the German advance into the network of islands and waterways of the Scheldt. Attacking in two main battle groups on 16 May, led by the 1st Battalion (Witt) and 3rd Battalion (Kleinheisterkamp) of the *Deutschland* Regiment, the division advanced through the first bottleneck along a narrow thrust-line under heavy Allied artillery and naval gunfire, fanning out west of Kapelle and across flooded, heavily mined ground onto the Walcheren Dam. Here the resistance was predictably tough, and when it finally pulled out on 17 May the division had paid a heavy cost for victory.

In the centre of the German attack, Rundstedt's Army Group A advanced with such speed as to cause discord bordering on panic among the Allied armies. His main tank force, under Kleist, went through the Ardennes, over the Meuse and swept around behind the French First Army. By the evening of 17 May, the French were back on the Oise, and a large salient was forming between the Allied forces in northern France and Flanders and those that were being driven back onto the Somme River line. To strengthen the walls of the salient, the SS-V Division, reassigned to XLI Corps command with 6th and 8th Panzer Divisions, was ordered to drive to Calais without halt, leaving only a token force of the Eighteenth Army to hold positions in the Netherlands.

On the night of the 22nd the division was halted in dispersed positions between Divion and Aire on the corps' right flank, as part of a holding action to prevent a possible British breakout to the south across the La Bassée canal. Against these positions the French launched powerful armoured and infantry thrusts, seeking to find weak spots in the line through which to escape the encirclement. In a night of confused fighting, the French assaults drove the *Der Führer* Regiment back to St. Hilaire, threatening a breakthrough in that sector. With daylight some semblance of order was regained; the regimental anti-tank guns were turned on the enemy armour and a potential crisis narrowly averted. Having flung the enemy back, the division then launched powerful counter-attacks that carried it across the La Bassée canal and secured vital bridgeheads, which it had to fight hard to protect from British 2nd Infantry Division.

On the 26th the SS-V was handed the difficult task of clearing well-constructed positions in the Forest of Nieppe north-east of Aire of British troops, among them the men of the first-rate Queen's Own Royal West Kent Regiment. The grenadiers of the *Germania* and *Der Führer* Regiments, with the recce battalion, began to sweep through the forest at 08.30 on the 27th. On the right *Germania* soon ran into the Queen's Own, which delayed it with excellent marksmanship until overwhelmed and forced into retreat by the material superiority of the attackers. By nightfall *Germania* was drawn up against Haverskerque, while on the left flank elements of *Der Führer* had reached the banks of the Nieppe Canal.

The *Deutschland* Regiment had been seconded to the 3rd Panzer Division for an attack on British units on the Lys Canal near

Below: The Western Campaign, 1940. A cheerful Waffen-SS soldier takes a break during an action. This close-up shows to advantage the camouflage patterning on his steel helmet cover and jacket.

Merville. Having forced a bridgehead over the waterway, the regiment was struck by a British armoured counter-attack and, lacking heavy weapons, the grenadiers were checked and then driven back. But excepting such local reverses in fortune, the BEF was now in a precarious position – trapped in a pocket surrounding Dunkirk, its only remaining port, pressed by Army Group A from the south along the fragile canal line and from the east by Army Group B through Belgium, where the Belgians appeared on the brink of collapse.

Aware of the need to conclude operations in the forest of Nieppe, the corps command ordered further attacks for the 28th. But with the announcement of the general surrender of Belgian forces the British flank was suddenly exposed, and this hastened their retreat from a now indefensible position into the cordon around Dunkirk, from where an evacuation had been under way since the 27th.

At this juncture the corps HQ, acknowledging that the strain of two weeks fighting was beginning to gnaw, ordered the division to rest. It was soon on the march again, though, pursuing the British as they fought in retreat from the shrinking Dunkirk perimeter to the beachhead. At hilltop vantage points at Cassel men of the *Der Führer* Regiment watched the drama unfold.

On 1 June, with the bulk of the British Expeditionary Force returned to England, 2,000 fresh troops were brought in to replace those lost from the division, and at full strength it moved on Bapaume, where a tenacious Allied garrison was still holding out. Three days later the last ship left Dunkirk, laden with French soldiers but stranding 30,000 more on the beaches.

With this the division, by then resting as part of the Army Group Reserve, was free to take its role in the next stage of the offensive, the conquest of France, starting on 28 May. Code-named Fall Rot, this was to be an attack on a scale hitherto unseen in warfare. Two army groups were ranged along a 360km line stretching from the Channel to Montmédy on the Franco-German frontier, with a third poised over the Rhine. In the west Army Group B was to open the attack on a front extending east to Reims, and force a breakthrough across the Seine. The main body of troops, in Army Group A, would then attack from the Aisne to the frontier, and while holding them the French Army of the East would then face the strike of Army Group C on the Maginot Line from the east. In matériel terms, the French could still field 60 divisions south of the Somme River line, deployed in tight clusters around existing obstacles – an arrangement known as quadrillage, or chequerboard – in an attempt to establish a defence in depth and prevent the rapid breakthroughs achieved in May. Together these formed the Weygand Line, a static line of defence on the Somme and Aisne Rivers in which the French placed great faith. Hitler had some 140 divisions at his disposal, and in the air, fast establishing itself the decisive battleground in this modern form of warfare, the Luftwaffe had by now achieved almost total dominance.

The attack, scheduled for 5 June, placed the SS-V Division with the *Leibstandarte* and the 9th and 10th Panzer under XIV Corps, Panzer Group Kleist, which was to march on Paris at the spearhead of Army Group B. By the second day the division was across the Somme River, meeting only light opposition. On the 7th the lead units were pinned down by a concerted artillery barrage from French units around the River Aire and, although the division was able to force several bridgeheads across the river, resistance quickly stiffened. In the ensuing actions Kleist lost 30 per cent of his armour and was ordered to withdraw before redeploying to the east to the Aisne, where a breakthrough had been made. After this, on the 9th, the SS-V Division was pulled back to positions behind the Somme.

On 14 June Paris fell, signalling to all effects the end of France. With the French Third, Fifth and Eighth Armies trapped to the east in the Maginot Line, facing imminent

Right: Forward! Somewhere on the Eastern Front. The face of the German soldier – a Waffen-SS soldier pauses next to a pontoon carrier.

collapse, and such other pockets as remained in dire threat of encirclement, little hope was left of resisting the German forces sweeping south. SS-V rejoined Panzer Group Kleist, which had been strengthened by the secondment of both *Totenkopf* and *Leibstandarte*, and marched towards Dijon to cut off French troops trying to escape to the south-west, netting some 30,000 prisoners on 17 June before redeploying to Bordeaux on the Atlantic coast. It was here on 22 June that the troops heard news of the French cease-fire, followed two days later by the formal surrender.

For his part in the stunning success of the Western Offensive, Paul Hausser was summoned to Berlin by a jubilant Hitler, and was among three SS commanders (Sepp Dietrich and Georg Keppler were the others) to receive the Knight's Cross at the Führer's victory celebration in the Reichstag.

Until the Yugoslavian campaign, the division was detailed for occupation duties in conquered territories. After a brief interlude in southern France SS-V travelled to Holland, to assist in the disarmament of the Dutch Army, and then from September to November 1940 was engaged on occupation duty at Visoul in France. In August, as the Battle of Britain reached its height, the division was stationed near the Bay of Biscay, refitting and training in the amphibious assault techniques that would be required for Operation Seelöwe – Hitler's proposed seaborne invasion of England. However, by early December, with the renamed SS Division *Deutschland* at Visoul, this operation had been postponed indefinitely.

During this period major reorganisation and expansion of the SS was undertaken, under which on 15 August Himmler ordered all reserve SS-V units into the Waffen-SS. SS-V Division lost some members of its NCO cadre, who were posted to the *Leibstandarte* to assist in its expansion. Others from the *Germania* Regiment, and the respected commander of the *Deutschland* Regiment, Felix Steiner, went to raise the new SS Division *Wiking*. Within the SS-V Division itself, the infantry units were restructured, and additional artillery battalions, a self-propelled battery, a motorcycle battalion and men of 11th SS Infantry Regiment *Totenkopf* were brought in to fill gaps. In December Himmler ordered a name change to SS Division *Deutschland*, which at the end of the following month became SS Division *Reich* (mot.), with its own tactical sign.

OPERATION MARITA – YUGOSLAVIA

In the early spring of 1941, events in the Balkans conspired to bring about the invasion of Yugoslavia and Greece by German forces. During February, the diplomatic crisis prompted by Hitler's demands upon the Yugoslav government deepened, and speculation over a German campaign in the Balkans grew. The Soviet Union, still Germany's ally at the time, tore up its non-aggression and friendship pacts with those two countries on 5 April and the next day German forces invaded.

SS Division *Reich* was engaged on manoeuvres in southern France when it was ordered to make the long road journey to Temesvar in Romania, where it joined XLI Corps of List's Twelfth Army in preparation for the invasion of Greece and Yugoslavia.

The Attack on Belgrade – Operation Punishment

In the early morning hours of 6 April the Luftwaffe opened its assault on Belgrade with a saturation bombing raid, directing the main effort against the centre of the city, where the principal government buildings were located. The weak Yugoslav Air Force and the

Below: Map of the area around Belgrade.

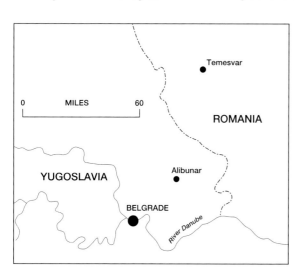

inadequate flak defences were wiped out, and virtually all means of communication between the Yugoslav high command and the forces in the field were destroyed.

Belgrade then became the focus for three separate German thrusts (Operation Punishment), which converged on the capital from points south and east. Early in the morning of 8 April, First Panzer Group jumped off from its assembly area north-west of Sofia. Crossing the frontier near Pirot, the XIV Panzer Corps advanced in a north-westerly direction toward Nis, and broke through the enemy lines on the first day of the attack. On 9 April the lead tanks rumbled into Nis and immediately continued their drive toward Belgrade. From Nis north-westward the terrain became more favourable, allowing the armoured columns to follow the Morava valley all the way to the Yugoslav capital. By 10 April XIV Panzer Corps' forces were swiftly advancing through the Morava Valley in close pursuit of enemy units retreating toward their capital and, on the evening of 12 April, First Panzer Group tanks stood less than 65km south-east of Belgrade.

Timed to coincide with the armoured thrust of the XIV Panzer Corps from the south-east, the XLI Panzer Corps drive led across the south-eastern part of the Banat and toward the Yugoslav capital. Spearheading the attack were the Infantry Regiment *Gross Deutschland* closely followed by SS Division *Reich*. Their primary objective was the bridges over the Danube, but to reach these the corps first had to gain the highway leading from Alibunar west to the banks of the river. All efforts were thus directed at reaching this objective, as the first unit on the road had been promised priority of movement. Hausser was determined that his SS division would be the first into Belgrade but, faced with the difficulties of an advance across difficult ground the chances of achieving this appeared slim. After the division crossed the frontier north of Vrsac on 11 April, these fears were soon confirmed as vehicles became mired in the swampy ground. By determination and guile advance elements of the motorcycle battalion were able to force a way along railway embankments and dykes, entering Pancevo that same day. The remainder of the division reached Alibunar by 17.30, thus ensuring right of passage on the highway. Having meanwhile advanced to within about 70km north of Belgrade, the main body of XLI Panzer Corps met with only isolated resistance as it rolled toward the enemy capital.

As the three separate attack forces converged on Belgrade simultaneously, the advance to Belgrade developed into a headlong race. Despite advancing over the most difficult terrain, on the evening of 12 April Second Army and OKH were briefed that, of the three converging armoured forces, XLI Panzer Corps was reported closest to the capital, having reached Pancevo on the east bank of the Danube about 15km east of the city. South of Belgrade resistance had stiffened as the 11th Panzer Division, spearheading the First Panzer Group forces, closed in.

The Fall of Belgrade

Toward early evening of 12 April began one of the most celebrated of *Das Reich* actions, one that made a national hero of Hauptsturmführer Klingenberg, commander of No.2 Company of the Motorcycle Battalion. That morning Klingenberg and members of his motorcycle assault company had approached Belgrade from Pancevo along the bank of the Danube. Klingenberg was anxious to enter the city but the swollen river and lack of any usable bridges prevented a direct assault, and the motorcycle assault company had no bridging equipment or

Below: On 14 May 1941 Fritz Klingenberg received the Knight's Cross for his role in the Yugoslavian campaign (see over page). At the time he was an SS-Hauptsturmführer (as shown here) and commanding officer of the 2nd Company, SS Motorcycle Battalion, (SS-Kradschützen-Btl.) from SS Division *Das Reich*, part of XXXXIst Army Corps of the Twelfth Army operating in the Balkans.

rafts. After commandeering a motor launch discovered on the north bank of the river, Klingenberg crossed over with one of his platoon leaders, two sergeants and five privates. On reaching the other side, Klingenberg sent two men back for reinforcements and proceeded with the remaining six men into Belgrade. Soon after Klingenberg encountered a group of 20 Yugoslavian soldiers and without firing a shot took them captive. Further on, a group of military vehicles approached Klingenberg's men, and after a short battle, the Germans captured those, too. The assault group, now fully mobile, headed towards the Yugoslavian War Ministry, but arrived to find the building abandoned. Since there was no military command left in Belgrade, Klingenberg and his men proceeded to the German embassy, which remained open, and at 17.00 they unfurled a large swastika and raised it atop the legation to declare the capture of the city. The mayor of the city was then summoned and, persuaded that Klingenberg was in fact the commander of a large force and that failure to surrender would bring down another Luftwaffe attack, at about 19.00 he surrendered the city to Klingenberg and a representative of the German Foreign Minister, previously interned by the Yugoslavs. It was not until the next day that a sizeable German force arrived to secure the city. For this feat SS Hauptsturmführer Fritz Klingenberg was awarded the Knight's Cross, and henceforth was known as the 'man who captured Belgrade'.

The Final Drive on Sarajevo

After the collapse of their border defence system and the fall of Belgrade the Yugoslav Army leaders hoped to withdraw to a mountain redoubt in the interior of Serbia, where they intended to offer prolonged resistance. Fully aware of the Yugoslav intentions, General Weichs, the Second Army commander, launched a vigorous pursuit of the enemy forces withdrawing in the general direction of Sarajevo. Speed was of the essence since the OKH intended to pull out and redeploy the motorised and armoured divisions as soon as practicable as these had to be refitted for the coming Russian campaign.

Below: Otto Weidinger, SS-Sturmbannführer and Commanding Officer of the Reconnaissance Battalion (SS-Aufklärungs-Abteilung) from 2.SS Panzer Division *Das Reich* seen here (in field-grey uniform) standing on his command vehicle.

Armistice Negotiations

Recognising the hopelessness of the situation, the Yugoslav command requested an armistice. During the afternoon of 15 April General Weichs and his staff arrived in Belgrade and drew up conditions for an armistice based on the unconditional surrender of all Yugoslav forces. The armistice was concluded and signed on 17 April. Ten days later, the surrender of the last British troops in Greece signalled the end of the Balkan campaign. Its mission complete, the division returned to Temesvar and then to rest and refit in Austria.

OPERATION BARBAROSSA

The actions in the Western and Balkans campaigns laid the foundations for the military reputation of the 2nd SS Division, but it was on the Eastern Front, over nearly four years of bitter fighting, that this reputation was cemented. Thus far the division had been on the sidelines, used piecemeal by Army commanders to bolster up the flanks or guard the rear of its own divisions, yet in the east, within a short time, its true capabilities were thrown into relief by the unstinting severity of the fighting. Such were the early triumphs that Hitler began to develop a wildly exaggerated confidence in the Waffen-SS and, seeking to emulate the qualities of its premier formations, he authorised a ten-fold expansion in the number of divisions by the end of the war. Such qualities were not so easily duplicated.

As the ideological and political background to the Eastern campaign is widely understood and documented, I have foresworn a detailed description of the general events of the offensive, preferring instead to focus on the actions of *Das Reich*. It should be emphasised at the start, however, that the war in the east was vastly different in kind from any of the campaigns involving the Western Allies. The scale of the territory over which *Das Reich* operated, the extremes in climate the soldiers endured, the spartan yet vital transport infrastructure on which the fighting necessarily focused, and the sheer volume and tenacity of forces that faced them, all these were in marked contrast to the situation in any of the campaigns in the west.

Aufbau Ost

Stemming from Order 21 issued by Hitler on 18 December 1940, Aufbau Ost – the military build up of the infrastructure in the occupied part of Poland – began in January 1941. Preparations for Barbarossa finally concluded by 15 May. In advance of the planned start date of 22 June, *Reich* moved by train from Salzburg, where it was resting, to Lublin and then positions on the bank of the River Bug, were it joined XXIV (Motorised) Corps in Guderian's Second Panzer Group, on the central sector of Bock's Army Group Centre. From here the troops watched the Red Army opposite preparing their defences.

At 12.05 on the 21st came the order for the attack to commence, and the division formed up on its start lines. At 04.15, just before dawn, on 22 June a mighty artillery barrage commenced, and the first German troops began crossing the river. For *Das Reich*, this was the start of a year of almost continuous combat in the east.

For the initial attack the Second Panzer Group advanced on a line that took it east from around Brest-Litovsk, and in the opening days XXIV Motorised Corps had the task of regulating the vast transport column moving along this line. When the division was finally called up to the front, vehicular access on the one useable highway was denied, and so the grenadiers were forced to march instead. Arriving in the battle zone, they were given the objective of forcing a river crossing between Citva and Dukora, while a detached battle group was to move along the No.1 Highway at Sluck. The latter force,

Above: The battle for Taganrog has ended. A captured Red Army soldier unstraps his equipment and weapons while his Waffen-SS captor carefully checks the prisoner's jacket lapel.

Right: *Das Reich* operational area on Eastern Front.

Below right: Eastern Front, May 1944. "Done! The hotly fought-over height is finally in our hands. The Soviets were taken completely by surprise by the well-planned and pre-pared German offensive and they could not hold out against the assault of the Waffen-SS grenadiers. The photograph shows one of the victorious Waffen-SS grenadiers enjoying his pipe while keeping his eyes on the enemy. Several destroyed Soviet T-34/76 tanks are visible in the background."

SS Division Reich (1941–42)
Division strength: 19,000
SS Infantry Regiment *Deutschland*
  1st Battalion
    1st–4th Companies
  2nd Battalion
    5th–8th Companies
  3rd Battalion
    9th–16th Companies
  Light Infantry Detachment
SS Infantry Regiment *Der Führer*
  as *Deutschland*
11th SS Infantry Regiment *Totenkopf*
  as *Deutschland*
Artillery Regiment
  1st Battalion
    1st–3rd Batteries
  2nd Battalion
    4th–6th Batteries
  3rd Battalion
    7th–9th Batteries
  4th Battalion
    13th–15th Batteries
Assault Gun Battery
Ranging Battery
Motorcycle Battalion
  1st–5th Companies
Reconnaissance Battalion
  1st–3rd Companies
Light Reconnaissance Detachment
Tank Hunter Battalion
  1st–3rd Companies
Pioneer Battalion
  1st–3rd Companies
  Bridging Section
  Light Pioneer Detachment
Intelligence Battalion
  1st & 2nd Companies
  Light Intelligence Detachment
Economics Unit
Ration Supply Depot
Bakery Company
Butchery Company
Supply Services
  15 x Motorised columns
  Supply Company
Repair Services
  3 x Workshop companies
  Spares column
Medical Units
  Field Hospital
  2 x Medical companies
  3 x Motorised ambulance platoons

comprising the motorcycle battalion, the recce battalion, flak and pioneer detachments, soon ran into trouble at Starzyca and had to be saved from encirclement by the mobile artillery and the 3rd Battalion.

From here the division began the advance through the great Pripet Marshes, and by 2 July had reached Beresivo. Moving on to Moghilev, and all along the way hampered by poor roads and harassed by forces that struck and then melted ghost-like into the vast forests, the division was ordered to protect the northern flank of the advance along the Minsk–Smolensk highway to Yelnya. Smolensk was only captured after dogged resistance.

Yelnya

On 14 July, after three weeks in Russia, the division was at Gorki. A week after began the first of its major actions on the Eastern Front – a month of heavy fighting at Yelnya on the Desna River. Yelnya would appear to be of no greater significance than any of the other countless small towns in Western Russia, but was accorded great strategic value by the fact that it straddled a crossroads of the Moscow highway. Furthermore, to the east lies high ground which dominates the surrounding steppe and the highway. Hitler thus focused much attention on Yelnya. So, too, did Konev's West Front of the Red Army, which had constructed an elaborate and well-sited trench system in front of the high ground there.

The attack on these lines opened on 22 July, *Deutschland* Regiment advancing with support from 10th Panzer, and *Der Führer* on the right. Since the attackers lacked adequate supplies of shells, no effective artillery support could be given; the grenadiers nevertheless carried the advance swiftly up the slope through a fusillade of fire and by nightfall were on the crest of the first ridge. On the right *Der Führer* crossed its start lines somewhat later, advanced determinedly through a ferocious hail of shot and shell, and had breached the main defensive line by the late evening.

Exhausted by a day of fighting uphill in the pitiless summer heat, the division was hit the next morning by a Soviet counter-attack, spearheaded by fresh troops brought into the line during the night. Fighting in the trenches and across the coverless, parched upland east of Yelnya continued throughout the day. In the thick of the heaviest action, *Das Reich*'s anti-tank gunners held off repeated tank attacks that threatened to overrun the divisional artillery positions. Some detachments, including part of the motorcycle battalion, were virtually destroyed and the remnants had to be taken out of the line. The reward for their sacrifices during another day of intense fighting was a temporary victory; by evening the Russians were in retreat off the slopes.

Soviet attacks now followed with monotonous regularity, as Konev threw more and more of his reserve units into the battle. These were not the poorly-led, sparsely equipped conscripts that German troops often faced, but elite troops imbued with seemingly suicidal bravery. On the battlefield, criss-crossed with static defences, the fighting took on the characteristics of the Western Front in World War I, neither German nor Russian able to make a decisive breakthrough.

Thus, with the SS division held at Yelnya, the farthest point east to which any German Army unit had penetrated, the drive to Moscow, still some 300km distant, was halted. The cost to the Red Army was enormous, and also to Army Group Centre, but the manpower reserves of the latter were far more finite, and already stretched. A particularly heavy toll was exacted on *Reich*, which fought at Yelnya until 8 August, by which point losses had become so severe that the division was withdrawn to the area of Smolensk and given three weeks for rest and refitting.

The Kiev Encirclement

Hitler then paused to consider his next move. He deliberated and, temporarily abandoning the drive on Moscow, favoured the tactical advantages offered by an attack on the great salient centred at its western point on Kiev, which had been formed between Army Group Centre and South by the great Pripet Marshes during the advance east. Within this the bulk of five Soviet armies was concentrated.

The Kiev encirclement was planned as a classic pincer movement, with two vast forces attacking from points north and south to close the mouth of the salient while another held the enemy at the western end. *Reich* was attached to the XXIV Panzer Corps of Guderian's Second Panzer Army which, with the Second Army on its inner flank, was to strike south to meet the drive of the Seventeenth Army and First Panzer Group coming up from the south-east of Kiev. *Reich*'s specific orders were to move south-west, penetrate the Russian line, and move round to the rear and thus encircle the Russian forces to the front of the left wing of the Second Army.

The attack was launched on 6 September; at first progress was rapid, but at Sosnitsa on the River Desna Guderian was halted for want of a crossing point. The capture of a railway bridge discovered as yet intact at Makoshim appeared to be the only chance to retain the momentum,

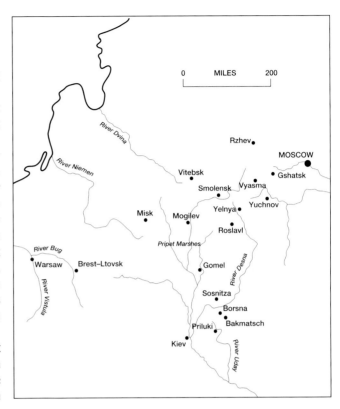

and Guderian called on the *Reich* divisional motorcycle battalion to storm it. They did so in spectacular fashion, driving at headlong pace along the length of the bridge, while the sidecar machine gunners raked the Russians on the south bank with fire. Crashing through the barriers, the SS troops quickly set up a perimeter. At this point the promised close support from the Luftwaffe, which had failed to materialise at the given time, appeared overhead to rain bombs on the positions now held by the motorcycle battalion, killing ten and injuring many more. But the positions were held and, after the engineers had secured the demolition charges, the rest of the division was able to cross. Guderian had his bridgehead, out of which the *Reich* Division struck south in the second week of the battle along the railway line towards the River Uday, first to the junction at Bakhmach, and on to the northern river bank. Throughout the advance to the river the troops were hindered by the pitiful state of the roads and the minefields sown in their path, yet crossed on the 16th under heavy fire to the south bank at Priluki (*Der Führer*) and east at Brosna (11th SS Regiment).

With the establishment of a secure bridgehead at Priluki by the 18th the immediate objectives of the division were met. Already the Kiev encirclement had almost been completed, and Bock's HQ was moved to issue a letter praising the 'achievements of the commanders and men of SS Division *Reich*'. Pockets of resistance within the tightening noose fought on; at Putivl the motorcycle battalion faced a suicidal charge by cadets of the Kharkov military academy, all of whom were killed, but on the 24th, assured of victory, the division was taken out of the line for rest.

With the collapse of the last resistance in Kiev and the formal surrender there on 26 September, huge numbers of Soviet troops passed into captivity. Including those killed or wounded, Soviet losses are estimated at 660,000 men. It was a huge defeat for the Red Army – five armies were completely destroyed and two nearly so, half of its current active strength. But although it was undeniably one of the greatest German victories of the war, a country with the manpower resources of the Soviet Union was able to absorb such losses. The cost was to prove greater for the Germans, who had fatally delayed their attack on Moscow, and to which they could only now return, ominously, as the winter set in.

Typhoon

The Führer handed the task of implementing his plans, given the code-name Typhoon, to Bock's Army Group Centre. Strengthened by Höpner's Panzer Group, which had been sent from Leningrad, it was to drive east toward Moscow on three axes of advance; this accomplished, the northern and southern arms were then to turn inward to close the jaws of the pincer. The concept, though admirably simple, was short-sighted in its failure to provide for the Russian winter.

It did stress the need for a quick victory. On the day that Kiev fell 4th Army and 4th Panzer Group, to which *Reich* was attached, was ordered to return with all haste to the north for their role in the attack on Moscow, and although Guderian tried to win much-needed time for repairs to his tanks, Hitler refused. Thus, only the minimum could be achieved. For its part, *Reich* Division had a brief period of rest to count the cost of three months in Russia. Of the men who had marched east, 1,500 of each of the *Deutschland* and *Der Führer* Regiments had been killed, while other units had suffered comparable losses, though prior to the opening of Typhoon, these deficiencies at least were made good with men from the reserve battalions.

Above: A half-naked, and still shocked, Soviet armoured car crewman, who was lucky to escape with his life, looking helplessly up at a Waffen-SS soldier, while his BA-10 three-axled armoured car is burning close by. The hapless Russian's chances of further survival were slim: the percentage of PoWs who died through starvation, fatigue and maltreatment at the hands of their captors was significant.

Bock began his three-pronged advance on 2 October. On the northern spearhead, Guderian placed the Army's elite *Grossdeutschland* Division, a motorised division, three panzer divisions and the reinforced *Reich* Division, which positioned for an attack east of Roslavl on Krichev and Ladishino with 10th Panzer Division.

Initially there was spectacular progress. Both objectives were taken and the division was ordered to move north-west to Yukhnov, gain the area between Gzhatsk (later called Gagarin) and Vyazma, despite the threat of an open right flank that this presented, and widen the fractures that the rapid advance had rent in the Soviet lines. Prime among the objectives was Gzhatsk, which held a commanding position on the Smolensk–Moscow highway. Its importance was not lost on the Red Army, ensuring that for three weeks the area was the focus of heavy fighting.

Komyenka was taken by 1st Battalion *Deutschland* on 7 October, and the Smolensk–Moscow highway cut by the 3rd Battalion in the early hours of the 8th. The following day these same two *Deutschland* battalions battled through mud on foot up the

highway. In the woods on the right flank, fierce fighting held up the progress of the 1st Battalion, but late in the day Gzhatsk was taken.

Above: Paul Hausser receiving his Knight's Cross on 8 August 1941, while still commander of SS Division *Das Reich*. It was part of the XXXXVIth Panzer Corps from the Fourth Panzer Army operating with Army Group 'Centre'. Hausser would hand over command of *Das Reich* to Willi Bittrich in October 1941.

Zhukov, who had recently assumed command of the Moscow defence, was not about to give up this most important town lightly. Reinforcements were rushed in and counter-attacks soon began to fall on the division. To try and disrupt these attacks, *Der Führer* was sent to the east, where it seized the high ground near Slovoda, and then succeeded in pushing through the Soviet lines and on to the highway beyond. The division now had a clear route up the road to Moscow, and victory seemed within its grasp. On the 13th, *Der Führer*'s 2nd and 3rd Battalions moved up the highway again, battling through the outer ring of defences manned by fanatical Siberian troops to the famous town of Borodino, scene of Napoleon's great battle, which was captured by *Der Führer* after fierce combat with 32nd Siberian Division on 15 October.

On the southern sector, Guderian had taken Orel in the first week. With Bryansk and Vyazma also encircled, 650,000 Soviet troops were trapped. The Soviet 3rd Army surrendered at Vyazma on 14 October and the 32nd at Bryansk six days later. But as yet more Soviet prisoners passed into captivity, the advance slowed to crawl as the autumn rains set in and the few roads became hopelessly clogged with traffic. Hitler's advantage was already running out. The temperature began to drop and around Moscow a citizen army marshalled by Soviet commissars was labouring to construct elaborate defensive works devised by Zhukov, who ordered a state of siege declared within the city. Furthermore, reinforcements were expected from the Far East, and most of the surviving Soviet warplanes were being concentrated around the city.

On 19 October *Der Führer* pushed up the highway from Istra to beyond the road junction at Mozhaysk, within 100km of the Russian capital. *Deutschland* troops moved north of the highway under a screeching Soviet rocket and shell bombardment at Mikhailovkoya and Pushkin; at Otyakova the troops fought hand-to-hand with tough Siberian and Mongolian troops manning the outer ring of defences.

Above: A Waffen-SS SdKfz 250/12 light survey/range plotting armoured half-track entering a burning Russian village.

The flanking attacks launched to the north and south of the capital by Guderian and Hoth had pierced the Soviet lines, but lack of ammunition and supplies, and worsening weather conditions, now brought a temporary stay to the advance. Most of the troops had reached the limit of their endurance; rations had been reduced to a pitiful level; vehicles and weapons were almost inoperative in the severe weather conditions and losses had been such that, on 22 October, 11th SS Infantry Regiment *Totenkopf* was broken up and its members sent as replacements to the *Der Führer* and *Deutschland* Regiments. Cumulatively the division had suffered 7,000 casualties – 60 per cent of its combat strength – since the start of campaign. Elsewhere within Army Group Centre losses were equally severe.

In November the weakened components 4th Panzer Group was attached to XXXX Corps. In mid-month the roads froze and the firmer ground allowed the offensive to be taken up again. XXXX Corps was ordered to attack on the 18th with a drive on Istra, and then a move to encircle the capital from the north. The advance crossed the River Istra on the 25th, and in the next two days Istra, and then Vyssovka were captured. A week later the most advanced group of the division, its motorcycle battalion, reached the terminus of the Moscow tramway system at Lenino.

The Soviet Counter-Attack

Bock's forces were by now exhausted and most commanders were calling for a halt in the offensive. Night-time temperatures had by now plummeted as low as -32 degrees, and everywhere men began to drop from frostbite. With other casualties, this meant that for the final attack planned for Moscow itself, both the *Deutschland* and *Der Führer* Regiments were reduced to two battalions, and supported by the seven tanks that were the full strength of 10th Panzer Division.

Sensing the weakness in his enemy as the offensive faltered, Zhukov chose 6 December to launch a major counter-attack on a 100km front with a million and a half men in 18 full strength divisions. Wave upon wave of attacking infantry were sent against the German lines, and under the sheer weight of the Soviet offensive, the German spearheads north and south of Moscow quickly crumbled. Soon, Soviet breakthroughs in the north and south threatened the encirclement of the entire Army Group Centre. On the 8th Hitler issued the momentous Directive 39 which, citing problems with the weather and logistics, ordered his troops to go on the defensive: 'thus to establish conditions suitable for a resumption of full-scale offensive operations in 1942.'

This order was met with little enthusiasm by the SS troops. Recrossing the River Istra, the division fell back in good order to the River Rusa as XXXX Corps' flanks threatened to give way. Hitler blankly refused to allow further retreat and demanded instead a solid defence. And so, although unprepared and poorly equipped to fight through a Russian winter, the troops moved into positions behind the Rusa, which they were to hold into the early new year.

THE CAMPAIGN OF 1942

A second wave of Russian attacks came crashing through the German line between Lake Ilmen and Lake Seliga on 7 January. The Sixteenth Army was threatened with encirclement and, despite the rapid despatch of *Totenkopf* reinforcements to the area, very soon a crisis developed, further compounded by Hitler's refusal to allow a withdrawal. By 20 January the Sixteenth Army was encircled in a pocket around Demyansk. Here it remained trapped for 73 days.

On 16 January the *Reich* Division was ordered to make a fighting withdrawal to the positions west of Gzhatsk that it had contested so bitterly the previous summer, and now fought to save from repeated Russian assaults. At Rzhev the Russians broke through and *Reich* was ordered to mount a counter-attack that succeeded, despite bitter cold and mounting losses, in sealing off the Russian penetration and trapping the 29th and 39th Soviet Armies. At the end of January, in an attempt to link-up with the encircled armies, the Soviets launched another mighty armoured attack. Their troops continued to batter the divisional lines throughout the first two weeks of February, achieving a breakthrough on the 17th that could only be stemmed by bringing the cooks, clerks and mechanics into the line.

A brief pause in the fighting ensued, allowing the widely scattered units to regroup. Counting the losses in the defensive fighting at Istra, Rusa, and Rzhev the *Reich* Division had suffered 4,000 casualties. Of the once 2,000-strong *Der Führer* Regiment, only 129 men remained, and as there were no longer any self-propelled guns, the unit was disbanded and the men re-allocated.

Placed on the reserve of Ninth Army, the shattered division (now in reality a battle group) was rebuilt to some level. *Der Führer* was reorganised as a panzer-grenadier regiment around the men who had survived the winter, a number of rehabilitated troops, and 3,000 new recruits. In March, the *Reich* battle group, still deficient in a host of areas, was shifted into positions in the bend of the Volga to meet an expected Russian assault over the great river. Preparatory attacks began on the 17th, and on the 25th the Soviets began a concerted effort on the 10km stretch of line held by *Reich*. Soviet tactics were again reliant on driving closely spaced waves of infantry one after the other headlong at the German lines. Cut down in droves by the German guns, their bodies lay strewn across the frozen battlefield. Following behind came more, and more. At some points troops began to experience ammunition shortages but the line was held and, by the middle of

Below: This young Volksdeutscher from Hungary, a volunteer serving in the Waffen-SS, has just received his mail from home.

April, the attacks had petered out as the spring thaw set in. May saw further defensive actions on the central sector.

Leaving behind two battalions of the division – Kampfgruppe *Ostendorff* – on 1 June the division left the Eastern Front for Germany, to rest and refit, and to be rebuilt as a panzer-grenadier division. It arrived on 10 June and was subsequently rejoined by Kampfgruppe *Ostendorff*. Renamed SS Division *Das Reich*, and then, at the Führer's behest, SS Panzergrenadier Division *Das Reich* (this title became active from November), under this reorganisation a battalion of Panzer III and IV tanks was added, and the 3rd Battalion of *Der Führer* and the recce unit were equipped with SPW. The latter was expanded to battalion strength and given the honour title *Langemarck*, but was disbanded in November. Late in the year, a final act of reorganisation was the raising of a self-propelled gun battalion.

VICHY FRANCE – OPERATION ANTON

This process was well under way by July when the *Der Führer* Regiment moved into France, followed later by the remainder of the division, where it undertook occupation duties, initially at Le Mans. In the aftermath of the Allied landings in North-West Africa, Hitler ordered the occupation of Vichy France – Operation Anton – and from 27 November the division was at Toulon to guard against an Allied invasion of southern France, should one have been planned. These duties, a world away from the horrors witnessed the previous winter, carried over into the new year of 1943.

That winter and the following spring saw a reversal in Germany's fortunes. In Africa, Rommel's Afrika Korps was decisively beaten and swept out of the continent forever. On the Eastern Front, the German offensives in the Caucasus (Operations Blücher and Braunschweig) failed, Army Group B's attack (Fischreiher) was halted in front of Stalingrad, and on 27 November the Soviet counter-attacks succeeded in encircling the entire German Sixth Army around the city. With the Sixth Army bottled up in Stalingrad, the Soviet South and Southwestern Fronts struck west toward the Dnieper in an effort to isolate Army Group A in the Caucasus, while the Bryansk and Voronezh Fronts drove into the German centre. Great breaches were made in the sectors held by Hungarian and Italian armies, and quickly exploited.

To avert the catastrophe unfolding on the Don Front, the newly organised SS Panzer Corps, which included the re-equipped 2nd SS Panzergrenadier Division *Das Reich*, and the *Leibstandarte* and *Totenkopf* Divisions, was sent back to Russia on 9 January 1943, with orders to rejoin Army Group South, halt the Soviet offensive, and then launch a counter-attack that would send them back east. The first units to arrive were immediately despatched as a battle group to Voroshilovgrad on the River Donets, to counter the Soviet effort in that sector against 6th Panzer Division.

In the last week of January the German Army reeled under another blow, as news of the surrender of the Sixth Army at Stalingrad was received. SS Panzer Corps was currently concentrating in the Kharkov area, which during the spring became the focus of intense fighting. To the west the Germans were holding on to a bridgehead over the River Oskol, through which the Italian Eighth Army was retreating, but to the north the Soviets had captured the transport hub of Kursk and everywhere breached the Army Group South line. In the final days of the month the division, still without the battle group fighting at Voroshilovgrad, moved into defensive positions on the River Oskol, battling against overwhelming odds to keep open the bridgehead there. On 1 February it was forced to withdraw back across the Oskol, and under concerted pressure fell back to the next natural barrier, the River Donets. The division's armour strength on 1 February was 66 Panzer IIIs, 60 Panzer IVs, and 4 Tigers.

It was now three months since the launch of the Soviet winter offensive. Lengthening lines were already creating supply problems and, as fatigue began to set in, the Soviet attacks began to lose impetus. Stalin was nonetheless determined to retain the initiative, despite the growing evidence that the momentum could not be sustained, and now grasped for the next prize, Kharkov.

With other centres like Novgorod, Rzhev, Vyazma, Bryansk, Orel, Kharkov and Taganrog, the city of Kharkov had proved crucial to the Germans in the winter defence of 1941/42, forming part of the system of fortified bastion towns known as the 'hedgehogs', which served as communications and logistics bases. Soviet forces, though able to regain territory around these bastions, had thus far been able unable to capture them.

An offensive launched at Kharkov by Timoshenko in May 1942 had penetrated to the west of the city, but Paulus' Sixth Army counter-attack succeeded on 19 May in cutting off the Russian advance, and left the route down the Donets corridor to Stalingrad open. Nine months later, after the defeat of the Sixth Army at Stalingrad, Army Group South was again on the defensive, and Kharkov had assumed strategic importance once more. So the premier formation – SS Panzer Corps under the command of Paul Hausser – was ordered to hold it.

Forced to relinquish their positions on the Donets by early February, the troops retreated into a perimeter east of the ruined city. Already the Soviets had thrust between gaps on the corps' northern and southern flank, and by the middle of the month the three divisions had almost been enveloped in the arms of the Soviet movement. On Hausser's right, troops forming the southern arm of the pincer were flooding through a 40km gap between *Leibstandarte* and the 320th Infantry Division. Seizing the opportunity to cut them off, and thus stabilise his line, Hausser created a temporary battle group with the *Der Führer* Regiment, a regiment of the *Leibstandarte* and the motorcycle battalions from each.

On 10 February the battle group moved into positions at Merefa for the attack. The following day, cloaked in a blinding snowstorm, it moved off, and within 48 hours had penetrated 50km to the Soviet rear. Enduring temperatures that dropped to -40 degrees at night, the SS troops made contact with the 320th Division on 16 February, cutting the southern pincer and destroying the elite 7th Guards Cavalry Corps. With this bold stroke Hausser stabilised his southern flank. However, in front of Kharkov the remainder of the corps was gradually withdrawing, though reinforced by the return of the battle group. Soviet forces now abandoned the attack on the southern flank and concentrated on delivering hammer blows from the north and east which, by the middle of the month, had taken Smiyev and Belgorod. Hausser requested permission for a tactical withdrawal, but this provoked a rebuke and the terse order from Hitler to 'hold at all costs!' In open defiance of the Führer's orders Hausser nonetheless withdrew the corps through a narrow corridor from Kharkov on 15 February, back into positions on the River Uday.

Here it was temporarily rested and reorganised to offset the enormous losses endured, while preparing for a planned counter-attack by Army Group South. Before that could be contemplated, Manstein moved to halt the drive of the South-West Front at Dniepropetrovsk. Then, on 19 February, the attack to retake Kharkov began.

One notable action took place on the southern flank. Just after 09.15 on the 22nd, 150km south of Kharkov, Hauptscharführer Karl Kloskowski in PzKpfw III 431 seized a bridge across the Woltschia River on the western outskirts of Pavlograd, in the process destroying three T-34s and a number of anti-tank guns. Soon, assisted by Unterscharführer Paul Egger's Tiger, the two panzers held the bridge until reinforcements arrived, allowing Das Reich panzergrenadiers to secure the town less than two hours later. Kloskowski was awarded the Knight's Cross in July 1943 for this action. Within five

Above: February 1943. Zenta, a message-carrying dog, sits calmly while her handler removes the message container from her collar.

Below: Another February 1943 photograph, this shows a foot patrol checking field telephone lines. Well-protected from the cold and armed with an MP40 sub-machine gun, this soldier examines a telephone wire that lay hidden beneath the deep snow.

Above: A German assault boat patrol on a wide river, somewhere in Russia. The Waffen-SS gunner responds to enemy fire directed at his vessel from the far bank with a MG34 mounted behind a forward-sloping armour plate. Note the 75-round saddle magazine fitted when this machine gun was used in a light portable mode.

Opposite, Above: A group of *Das Reich* soldiers pushing try to move an open-top staff car stuck in deep mud. The car is towing a 7.5cm leIG 18 light infantry gun. In the autumn and spring it was often more difficult to drive on Russian country roads than the fields next to them.

Opposite, Below: February 1943. Waffen-SS troops fire their 15cm sIG 33 heavy infantry gun into Soviet assembly positions spotted by a Luftwaffe tactical reconnaissance aircraft.

Left: A member of a Waffen-SS assault group in action with the 1941 model of the standard German flamethrower. This weapon incorporated a flash cartridge ignition system.

Above: April 1943. Two Waffen-SS *Essenträger* (meal carriers) take a pause to light their cigarettes behind the cover of a destroyed building.

days the division was at Pavlograd, where with 4th Panzer Division it halted the Soviet drive to the Dnieper. Wheeling around to the north-east, *Das Reich* and *Totenkopf* aimed next at Lozovaya, a railway junction of considerable importance held by the 1st Guards Tank Army, and after three days of bitter fighting had seized control.

The Soviet command, unaware of the strength of the counter-attacking forces, continued to commit divisions. Advancing on Yefremovka through pouring rain and mud in the early days of March, *Das Reich* unwittingly outflanked the 3rd Tank Army moving in the opposite direction. With *Leibstandarte* positioned on the opposite flank, Hausser seized the chance to envelop this mighty force, which included much of the Voronezh Front's strength, and closed the jaws west of Berefka. Turning inward on the pocket, in three days *Das Reich* had crushed the desperate Soviet attempts to escape, and helped to force a final halt in the Soviet winter offensive.

Kharkov

South of the River Donets, Popov's Bryansk Front had been all but annihilated, losing 100,000 men killed or captured. With this threat removed, SS Panzer Corps was free to begin the attack on Kharkov itself, although now only 11 Panzer IIIs remained combat fit, and began to move north on 5 March. By 10 March the division's two battle groups were in positions to the west and south-east of the city – Kampfgruppe *Deutschland*, on the western boundary of the corps' positions, and Kampfgruppe *Der Führer* to the south-east protecting the corps' right flank. At 08.00 the following morning, the troops moved across their start lines. On the northern flank, having started well, *Deutschland* was pinned down by strong anti-tank fire for most of the day. In the centre, Salyutine railway station was captured in mid-afternoon, and Kampfgruppe *Der Führer* succeeded in cutting the road to Merefa.

Das Reich then received fresh instructions to move through Kharkov and then south against the forces concentrated in the industrial quarter, a task much complicated by a yawning anti-tank ditch that had been dug at the city perimeter, and the presence of a strong Soviet garrison. Beginning in the early hours of 12 March, a pioneer detachment crossed under heavy fire, and quickly established itself on the far bank. Grenadiers of 3rd Battalion *Der Führer* followed, and self-propelled artillery was then brought up to provide cover as the perimeter was widened. By dawn the anti-tank ditch had been breached and the first panzers were across. At 14.00 on 14 March Hauptscharführer Karl-Heinz Worthmann in PzKpfw IV 631 raced ahead of Kampfgruppe *Harmel* to storm a hill near Vosychevo, 13km south-east of Kharkov. He destroyed 27 heavy anti-tank guns, 2 artillery pieces, and numerous MG nests, driving the Russians from a strong-point that was preventing the encirclement of the city.

Resistance in the city crumbled, and on 15 March, exactly four weeks after the SS Corps had retreated out of Kharkov, it was back in German hands. With Soviet forces retreating in disarray, Manstein determined to retain the initiative and carry the advance further east. With *Das Reich* at the spearhead, SS Panzer Corps retook Belgorod on 18 March. Thus, in spectacular style, the operation to stabilise Army Group South's front was concluded, and territory previously lost to the Soviet forces regained. During the campaign the division knocked out an estimated total of 292 tanks and assault guns, and itself lost only 77 tanks and assault guns.

In late March the spring thaw once again halted operations. From 22 April *Das Reich* moved into billets around Kharkov and during the relatively quiet period that preceded the summer campaign there was time for rest and relaxation. As the unit began training for the summer offensive, some necessary restructuring took place. The motorcycle battalion was reformed as a reconnaissance battalion, and officers were transferred to become the nucleus of the III SS Panzer Corps (Germanisches). In May Motorcycle Bataillon *Langemarck* transferred to SS Volunteer Brigade *Langemarck*, and in June SS Infantry Regiment *Langemarck* was removed. At corps level the SS Panzer Corps became II SS Panzer Corps on the formation of I SS Panzer Corps (from cadres drawn from *Leibstandarte*, and *Hitler Jugend*), under Sepp Dietrich.

For his leadership of the 2nd Battalion during this period, Sturmbannführer Tychsen received the Knight's Cross on 31 April, as did Karl-Heinz Worthmann. In April Obersturmbannführer Karl-Heinz Lorenz, winner of the German Cross in Gold as commander of 2nd Panzer Company, joined the 2nd Panzer Battalion staff, while Hauptsturmführer Herbert Zimmermann took over the Tiger company.

During this period also the majority of the 1st Battalion personnel travelled west to train on the new Panther tanks, and did not return to Russia until after Operation Citadel. Thus to bolster *Das Reich*'s lone remaining panzer battalion for Kursk, captured T-34 tanks were formed into a company (9th Company, 2nd Battalion). The 5th and 6th Companies had Panzer IVs for the upcoming battle, but the former's strength had to be filled out by a platoon of Panzer IIIs, mostly left over from the Kharkov battles.

ZITADELLE (CITADEL)

Among the officers of the OKH, and throughout the embattled Reich, there was considerable elation over the Kharkov triumph. Fuelled by this new optimism, an ambitious, but ultimately misconceived plan to regain the initiative on the Eastern Front was now hatched to eliminate the salient extending between Kharkov and Orel, which effectively extended the German front by some 400km. An Allied attack in the west appeared imminent, and the troops needed to defend this salient were much needed elsewhere. Further incentive was drawn from the fact that from the northern base, anchored on Maloarkangelsk, to the southern lip at Belgorod, the neck of the salient was only 110km wide.

Preparations for the proposed attack began at once, and over the ensuing three months some 900,000 men, supported by 2,700 tanks and 2,000 aircraft were brought up. OKH envisaged a double envelopment of the salient, with converging strikes on the northern flank by Ninth Army under General Kluge's Army Group Centre, and from the south by Group *Kempf*, comprising XI Corps, XLII Corps and III Panzer Corps, and the Fourth Panzer Army, comprising XLVIII Panzer Corps, LII Corps and II SS Panzer Corps, under the overall command of Manstein's Army Group South. Manstein planned a concerted attack in the centre toward Kursk by II SS Panzer Corps, supported by dual drives on its right flank by Kempf's III Panzer Corps (6th, 7th and 19th Panzer Divisions), and on the left by XLVIII Panzer Corps, which would then turn inward to meet Hausser's spearhead and trap a mass of Soviet forces.

The attack was originally scheduled for May, but there were many postponements as Hitler fretted over the minutiae of the operation, which he dreamed would 'shine like a beacon to the world' and avenge the crushing defeat at Stalingrad earlier in the year. But as he later privately revealed, he had considerable misgivings about the whole affair.

Those fears were well-founded. Pre-warned of the German intentions by intelligence sources, Zhukov used the delay to fortify the salient with eight concentric circles of defence, on a scale never seen before. Troops and 300,000 of the local civilian population worked on laying a massive array of tank traps, minefields, anti-tank guns and other defensive positions

Below: May 1943. The original caption to this photograph reads like something out of *Enemy at the Gates*: 'A duel between snipers! The moment when a Waffen-SS Unterscharführer silenced a Soviet sniper. The duel was witnessed by his platoon commander observing through his stereo-telescope.'

in anticipation of the German attack. The extensive minefields were specially designed to channel the armoured formations into killing grounds, where it was hoped that the German attack would founder. Armour and troop concentrations were also built up, and by the time the attack was launched the Soviets, with 1,300,000 men, 3,600 tanks, 20,000 artillery pieces and 2,400 aircraft, had a clear numerical superiority over the Germans.

The attack was in fact successively postponed from 4 May to 12 June by delays in the delivery of the new Panther and Elefant tanks, then for a further period by the collapse of the African front in Tunisia. Finally, on 29 June, the troops moved into their concentration areas. During 3 July *Das Reich* received orders to form-up for the attack in positions just to the south of the Belgorod–Tomarovka rail link. That night sappers began clearing paths through the minefields, and during the following day Stukas bombed the defences. As the dive bombers turned for home German artillery and Nebelwerfers opened up. To the east, Kempf's III Panzer Corps began to advance on Savidovka, Alekseyevka and Luchanino while on its sector II SS Panzer Corps launched preliminary attacks early on the 5th to secure observation posts on a 20km front between Beresov and Sadelnoye.

Das Reich had 48 Panzer IIIs, 30 Panzer IVs, 12 Tigers, 8 Panzer III command tanks, 18 T-34s, 33 StuGs, and 10 Marders combat ready, and was positioned on the right of the corps. During the night 3rd Battalion assault troops equipped with flamethrowers penetrated behind the outpost line and at 02.45 took the initial objective – Yakontov. At 03.00 *Deutschland*, occupying the inner wing, led off the attack, as the infiltrating 3rd Battalion assault troops began clearing bunkers. Ten minutes before the offensive proper was to begin the Soviet Central Front launched a pre-emptive artillery bombardment on the German positions, with 600 guns, mortars and Katyusha rocket launchers. German artillery responded and by 04.45 the artillery duel had grown in intensity, but as most of the German armour and infantry was still under cover, the barrage failed to disrupt the advance. Finally at 06.00 on the 5th, the main body of the division moved off, using a tactic known as *Panzerkeil*, a spearhead formation led by heavy Tiger I tanks with Panther, PzKpfw IV and PzKpfw III tanks in support. Russian positions in front of Beresov were quickly overrun and by 08.15 the division was in positions to the north, from where it assaulted the town. Late in the afternoon a second, successful attempt to secure Hill 233.3, 6km north of Beresov, was made by 3rd Battalion *Deutschland*, but heavy minefields prevented further progress.

On the 6th, *Der Führer* took up the attack, aiming at Prokhorovka, and the road towards Luchki, which would allow corps armour to exploit the breach and carry the fight to the high ground north of Prokhorovka and the Belenikhino railway line to the east. At 08.00 the division began an attack on Hill 243. Within an hour *Der Führer* had been halted, but with the weight of the divisional artillery brought to bear, by noon it was on the hill. By now the division had penetrated 32km, against increasingly heavy resistance and, despite suffering great losses, had torn a hole in the sector held by 6th Guards Army.

Early the next morning the Panzer Regiment formed up with the tanks of *Leibstandarte*, and started out from Teterevino to Prokhorovka. From positions north and north-west Russian armour moved to intercept, and for nearly five hours battled to drive off the attacks. Although rain now began to slow movement to a crawl, the speed of the opening attack had been such that on the corps' left, Kempf's 6th, 7th and 19th Panzer Divisions, which had been stalled by 7th Guards Army after crossing the River Donets, were now far behind and exposing Hausser to attack. As a temporary measure *Totenkopf* was moved to cover this flank while *Das Reich* and *Leibstandarte* continued north, engaging concentrations of the 6th Guards Army. Early on the 8th *Das Reich* and *Leibstandarte* moved out to attack north-west, and during the morning ran into a strong concentration of Russian armour south-east of Vesselyi, and at Teterevino, and at Kalinin.

Above: A group of Waffen-SS grenadiers rush out of their dugout for the camera. Note the bayonet..

Above right: July 1943. The original caption says, "Captured in his own trench! Completely flabbergasted by this unexpected turn of events, and still wearing his helmet, this Soviet prisoner is immediately interrogated."

Below right: July 1943. The original caption says, "Thorough preparations save losses. Well camouflaged, heavy machine guns have been brought into position at all the important sectors on the front. Their fire will protect the Waffen-SS infantry advancing towards the Soviets holding the higher ground." This MG34 is being used as a heavy machine gun mounted on a tripod and equipped with a telescopic sight for long-range fire.

By midday, the grenadiers had regrouped and were fighting in concert with *Leibstandarte* to capture Vesselyi and Hills 239.6/227.4 and, with these secured, they moved into defensive positions as heavy rain continued to fall. Here they came under massed assault by the forces sent from the north and north-east to halt the SS advance. Warned of a position made precarious by the rapid German advance and the collapsing 6th Guards Army, the Soviet high command ordered reinforcements from Konev's Steppe Front – 4th Guards, 4th Guards Tank, and 3rd Guards Mobile Army – to the Kursk area to block any German breakthrough. Soviet commanders realised that they would soon face the combined weight of the German armoured corps and, seeking a decisive encounter, had already sent the 5th Guards Tank Army with orders to concentrate east of Prokhorovka.

On the 9th, with *Das Reich* guarding his eastern flank, Hausser began a push toward Beregovoy, with orders from Fourth Panzer Army HQ to destroy the enemy to the north-east of that town and reach the eastern bank of the River Salotnika. Under concerted attack by 1st Tank Army, II SS Panzer Corps fought with XLVIII Corps through a sea of mud to reach the banks of the River Psel (the last natural obstacle before Kursk) west of Prokhorovka. On the eastern flank *Das Reich* blunted sustained assaults, and by late afternoon on 10 July was in position on the plain north of Prokhorovka to attack the 5th Guards Tank Army now gathering there.

Early on 12 July the II SS Panzer Corps divisions formed up for what was widely realised would be the decisive clash of Operation Citadel. Although some 700 of their tanks remained operational, Fourth Panzer Army troops were astonished to see the masses of Soviet armour ranged before them. Soviet commanders had concluded that their relatively under-gunned and under-armoured tanks would fare better at close range, where superiority in main armament and armour counted for little. They therefore concentrated the entire strength of 5th Guards Tank Army, some 850 tanks, into an area

Below: August 1943. "More than one hundred Soviet T-34 tanks are rolling towards the German lines and the tank destroyers have their hands full." The crew of this Waffen-SS 7.5cm PaK mounted on a PzKpfw 38 (t) chassis have just registered another 'kill'. With a sudden jet of flame and thick black smoke – there goes another T-34.

Left: Two Waffen-SS grenadiers interrogate a small party of newly captured Red Army soldiers. The first two men wearing dark uniforms would appear to be officers. Rank and file soldiers of the Red Army had their heads shaved on joining.

Below: SS-Hauptsturmführer Wolfgang Gast, photographed on 4 June 1944, just after he had received the Knight's Cross. At that time he was the Commanding Officer of the 1st Battalion, 2nd SS Artillery Regiment from *Das Reich*, part of Army Group 'D' operating on the Russian Front.

of only a few square miles. In this tiny area, through the heat and dust of the day and into the evening, one of the biggest tank battles of the war was fought.

At midday, south of Vinogradovka, the division repulsed a heavy attack by 40-plus tanks of the 2nd Tank Army. Another assault by more than 70 tanks was launched at a little after 14.00, this time from the east through Vinogradovka towards Yasnaya Polyana. Engagements were fought over short distances, and in many instances Soviet crews engaged German tanks by simply driving headlong into them. Fierce fighting raged through the day. When it was concluded a thick pall of smoke hung over the battlefield, now littered with the wreckage of hundreds of burning tanks. By 21.00 both sides were pulling back into defensive positions.

Hausser remained grimly determined to break through, and his staff issued orders for *Leibstandarte* and *Totenkopf* to destroy the enemy on the east and western flank of the River Psel, as well as those south of Petrovka. During the course of the following day, the attack switched to *Das Reich*'s right flank, where Hausser hoped to force a breach at Pravorot and, reinforced by III Panzer Corps, which had by now linked up with Fourth Panzer Army, drive north.

Early on the 14th, the 1st and 3rd Battalions of *Der Führer* attacked across minefields towards the high ground south west of Pravorot. Belenikhino was taken by nightfall and, during the night, with the advance slowed to a crawl in heavy rain, the panzer regiment succeeded in linking up with III Corps and trapped significant forces in a pocket around Gostischevo-Leski. This was to be the last success of the operation, for although II SS Panzer Corps had pushed upwards of 60km into the southern sector of the bulge, the loss of a 10,000 troops and 300 tanks (half of his armour) meant that Manstein now lacked the strength to continue the offensive. In the north, the Ninth Army had been able to penetrate a mere 10km and had lost 25,000 killed, 200 tanks, and 200 aircraft in so doing, and was still a long way north of Fourth Panzer Army.

Events elsewhere had already conspired to force Hitler's hand. On 10 July the first Allied troops had come ashore on Sicily and, however badly they were needed on the Eastern Front, he knew that units would have to be transferred to bolster the defences in Italy. Furthermore, the Soviet forces had already launched counter-attacks to the north and south of the Kursk salient. Kluge and Manstein were duly summoned to his headquarters. Manstein's argument that one final effort would be decisive persuaded the Führer to allow operations to continue in that sector, but since Hitler also withdrew II SS Panzer Corps from the battle he effectively brought the offensive to an end.

German losses for the period 5–13 July are put at 100,000 men killed or wounded, and overall casualties between 5 July and 22 August may have been as high as 500,000 men. The Soviet casualty figures were not released until the fall of the communist regime in the USSR and were recorded at 250,000 killed and 600,000 wounded for operations between the start of Zitadelle in July 1943 up to the final reconquest of Kharkov by the Red Army in August. They also lost 50 per cent of their tank strength during the Kursk offensive. From 5 to 16 July *Das Reich* accounted for 448 Russian tanks and assault guns, losing a total of 46 panzers and assault guns destroyed.

In the aftermath of the titanic battle the Germans withdrew to the partly prepared Hagen line at the base of the salient. On 13 July the counter-offensive by Rokossovsky's Central Front was launched against Orel and had in two weeks driven the Eleventh Army back to its start lines. To the south of Kursk the Russians re-grouped and on 3 August another offensive opened on both flanks of the Kursk salient. A 64km gap was torn between Fourth Panzer Army and Army Detachment *Kempf*, and on 5 August Orel and Belgorod were liberated.

On 28 July *Das Reich* was bolstered by the transfer of *Leibstandarte* armour before the men of that unit departed for Italy. Nine Tigers, 39 Panzer IVs and 4 Panzer IIIs, were added to the 33 Panzer IIIs, 17 Panzer IVs, 2 T-34s, and 2 Tigers that remained combat ready. The departure of *Leibstandarte* led to the dissolution of II SS Panzer Corps, and creation of another corps, III SS Panzer Corps, from *Das Reich*, *Totenkopf* and the Army's 3rd Panzer Division, which from 30 July transferred south to oppose another Russian counter-attack, this time across the Mius River. *Das Reich* grenadiers were in action at Stepanovka, and helped to recapture positions there, but with the fighting for the river lines still raging a new threat to Kharkov brought them back north.

At Kharkov, Soviet forces were attempting an encirclement, presaging the fourth and last battle for the city. On 18–19 August the division was in the city outskirts, battling grimly to hold the city won at such cost in the spring. A fresh crisis now arose to the west where on the 22nd around Starya-Lyubotin and Kommuna, the Panther battalion (see note at left) destroyed 53 Soviet tanks. On the next day, 12km west of Kharkov, it broke up a Russian tank assault.

In the mid-August Malinovsky's forces crossed the Donets, and soon the German front was penetrated in three places. With the advance of Tolbukhin's Southern Front threatening an envelopment of Army Group South, Manstein concluded that the Red Army could no longer be contained at Kharkov and abandoned the city, ordering his divisions to withdraw to the Dnieper. From here on the Germans would be fighting defensive battles all the way back to the frontiers of the Reich and into the Reich itself.

Pulled out of Kharkov, on 28 August the division was ordered to the south-west, toward the Dnieper. Fighting as it withdrew, by 13 September the division was in positions around Valki, some 60km west. Twenty kilometres west of the town a large detachment of T-34s attacked *Das Reich*'s reconnaissance battalion. From his position in the reserve, Hauptsturmführer Holzer led his company to the rescue, and in 40 minutes destroyed 28 Soviet tanks.

On the 15th came a fresh order to retreat to the west bank of the Dnieper. After crossing the only bridge over the Vorskla at Poltava on the 20th, in the last days of the month *Das Reich* was back on the great river, struggling to contain the Soviet forces at Michurin-Rog, near Kremenchug, where they had gained a bridgehead over the Dnieper in the sector held by First and Eighth Panzer Armies.

Note: I. Abteilung/SS Panzer Regiment 2 had not been operating with the division since 1 May 1943. It was at Mailly-le-Camp, France, converting to the PzKpfw V Panther. Returning to the front in the aftermath of Kursk, this battalion first saw combat on 22 August, around Starya-Lyubotin and Kommuna, knocking out 53 Soviet tanks. Panthers were first used in action on 5 July 1943, with Panther Abteilungen 51 and 52 of Panzer Regiment 39 (subordinated to Army Group South). The former was attached to *Grossdeutschland* for the Kursk battle, and Panzer Abteilung 52 to the 11th Panzer Division, and they had between them a total of 192 factory fresh and untested Panthers Ausf. D. By the evening of the first day of operations only 40 were still combat ready.

Below: July 1943. The end of the line for a Lend-Lease tank. Waffen-SS troops have made themselves comfortable in front of a disabled 39-ton British Churchill III infantry tank.

Throughout the withdrawal *Das Reich* Tigers continued to score heavily against Russian armour. On 23 September Untersturmführer Alois Kalls received the German Cross in Gold for his adept leadership of his Tiger platoon during the late summer. His assistant platoon leader, Hauptscharführer Johann Reinhardt was posthumously awarded the German Cross in Gold on the 25th. On the 24th, 6th Panzer Company, newly supplied with side-skirted Panzer IVs, battled 60 T-34s between Udy-Bogens and Orkan, just south-west of Kharkov. Twenty-nine of the 60 were destroyed. Both Untersturmführer Karl Meileck and Hauptsturmführer Kesten, 6th Panzer Company commander, were later awarded the Knight's Cross for these actions. In all, from 30 July to 21 August *Das Reich* destroyed a total of 391 tanks and assault guns. By 27 August it had 4 Panzer IIIs, 31 Panzer IVs, 6 Tigers, and 6 command tanks combat fit, plus one Panther company, as the others had been parcelled out to other divisions.

Above: August 1943. The task has been successfully completed. Despite the obstacles they had to overcome, the soldiers of the Waffen-SS are in a cheerful mood.

Defence on the Dnieper

By the end of September Army Group South was in a tenuous defensive position behind the Dnieper River, the strongest natural defensive line in western European Russia, but over which the Russians already had five bridgeheads. In two and a half months Army Groups Centre and South had been forced back for an average of 240km on a front over 1,000km long and in so doing lost the most valuable territory taken in past advances. The *Das Reich* Division was fighting in the Dnieper bend to recapture high ground lost to the enemy, so as to reduce his bridgehead. As part of the containment, on 30 September, *Der Führer* was sent to Grebeni, where the struggle continued to 5 October.

This first week of October was relatively quiet as the Russians regrouped and brought up new forces. Their numerical superiority allowed them to rest and refit their units in shifts, and they had accordingly reached the Dnieper with their offensive capability largely intact. On 15 October the full weight of the Second and Third Ukrainian Fronts was thrown against Army Group South, and soon a 320km wide bridgehead was forced between Cherkassy and Zaporozhe, while to the south the Third Ukrainian Front threatened important iron and manganese mining areas near Krivoi Rog and Nikopol. The German front line was pushed progressively westward.

Just after 05.00 on 29 October, just outside of Khodorov on the western bank of the Dnieper, some 75km south-east of Kiev, Soviet armour pierced *Das Reich*'s defence line. Quickly advancing to this dangerous breakthrough, a platoon of 5th Panzer Company knocked out 17 T-34s. On 1 November, as the Russians continued to consolidate their bridgehead over the Dnieper, 2nd Panzer Battalion, on the right flank of *Das Reich*'s position, drove off enemy tanks and infantry attempting to outflank them. That same day 8./Panzer Regiment *Das Reich* scored the 2,000th armour kill for the division in 1943. The Panzer Regiment, which had accounted for some 1,100 of these, had accumulated losses of over 250 tanks.

Above: The main line of resistance at Kharkov – a Waffen-SS Sturmmann, his face still marked with the strain of combat, uses a break after two days' continuous action, to change his position.

Right: A group of regimental officers from *Das Reich*, photographed in December 1943. Nearest the camera from left to right: SS-Gruppenführer und Generalleutnant Walter Krüger, Divisional Commander; Sorg, Commander of *Das Reich* Signals detachment; Sylvester Stadler, known by his nick-name 'Vestel' seen as SS-Sturmbannführer and Commander of SS Panzergrenadier Regiment *Der Führer*. Walter Kruger had taken over command of *Das Reich* in March 1943 and had received the Oakleaves to his Knight's Cross five months later on 31 August 1943.

Opposite, Above: September 1943. A successful tank crew sits astride the barrel of their hard-hitting gun. The tank is a PzKpfw IV Ausf.G (SdKfz 161/1).

Opposite, Below: A 7.5cm PaK 40 in action against Soviet tanks.

In the first week of November, the division fought near to Kiev but could not prevent it from being retaken by the First Ukrainian Front on the 7th. Subsequently, Fourth Panzer Army was pushed back to the west and south of the city, a setback which threatened to destroy the entire left flank of Army Group South. Until the end of the year *Das Reich* fought on in retreat, first with *Leibstandarte* under XLVIII Panzer Corps, and then XXIV Panzer Corps. During this time the division was refitted once again, and the name was changed to SS Panzer Division *Das Reich*.

Stories of stoicism in the face of adversity characterise the retreat from the Dnieper. One of them concerns Obersturmführer Karl-Heinz Boska, 2nd Panzer Battalion adjutant. On the morning of 13 November, near Bolshaya Grab, Soviet infantry assaulted the battalion headquarters. Although heavily outnumbered, Boska led five panzers in a counter-attack, and drove them off. That same day, the Panzer Regiment's commander Obersturmbannführer von Reitzenstein received the Knight's Cross for the efforts of his unit during the summer and autumn. Soon afterward, charged with the murder of a *Hiwi* (Russian mess volunteer), he committed suicide.

On 25 November *Das Reich* was ordered to an area east of Zhitomir, to counter a Soviet offensive in the area Korosten–Berdichev–Radomyshl. As it went on the attack just nine Panzer IVs, two Tigers, seven Panthers and two command tanks remained operational, and these were soon halted. Reduced to a pitiful level and seriously lacking in motorised transport for its infantry regiments, in mid-December the division was ordered to France to re-supply and re-train. What remained was reorganised into a battle group of 5,000 men, officially known as Kampfgruppe *Lammerding*, with a depleted panzer battalion of two companies. This remained behind to continue the fight against the revitalised Soviet winter offensive, initially in the area Radomyshl–Guta–Sabelozkaya under XLII Corps, and then back on the Tetrev River, east of Zhitomir.

After a failed counter-attack at Krasnopol, in mid-January the battle group occupied positions north of Mal–Bratalov–Grinovshky. In defensive fighting around Zhitomir, from 25 December through 18 January 1944, the panzer battalion destroyed 12 tanks, 14 assault guns, and 12 anti-tank guns, but the battle group lost more than 20 per cent of its soldiers. It was briefly pulled out of the line, then transferred to Isyaslavl, which was invested and captured in the face of a renewed Soviet offensive launched on 3 March. Three of the precious Tigers were knocked out on 4 March east of Semyalintzy, leaving only a handful of tanks to fight on. The fighting at Isyaslavl raged until mid-month, by which time the battle group had been surrounded and battered, but not broken. Withdrawn west, the 800 survivors reached the Fourth Panzer Army lines at Buszacz on 8 April.

PREPARING IN FRANCE

From there the battle group rejoined the division, which as part of LVIII Corps, Seventh Army, Army Group G, had moved to Montauban, 25 miles (40km) north from Toulouse, a location personally chosen by the Führer. He reasoned that here the division would be available to intervene on either the northern or southern coasts of France, when an Allied invasion occurred, and furthermore could also guarantee the lines of communication between Army Groups G and B, which were constantly threatened by French Resistance attacks.

With a core of seasoned troops to form the backbone, the ranks of the depleted division were filled out by 9,000 replacements, most of them boys of 17 and 18 years of age with no combat experience. Throughout April and May they trained in the countryside surrounding Montauban, although partisan actions caused considerable disruption, and considerable time and resources were lost in pursuing them. During May 20 soldiers were killed and in retaliation 41 civilians were executed at Figeac.

Below: December 1943. A group of Waffen-SS motorcycle riflemen enjoying the hot food waiting for them after action. The man nearest the camera has a signal torch attached to a button of his winter parka. The torch's adjustable two-coloured mica shields gave red or green light when they were depressed. It was a standard item of military equipment issued to all German troops who had to operate at night.

**SS Panzer Division Das Reich
(October 1943–May 1945)**

2. SS Panzer Regiment
  1st Battalion
    1st–3rd Companies
  2nd Battalion
    4th–6th Companies
  8. schwere Panzer-Abteilung 'Tiger'*
    1st–3rd Companies
Panzergrenadier Regiment *Deutschland*
  1st Battalion
    1st–4th Companies
  2nd Battalion
    5th–8th Companies
  3rd Battalion
    9th–13th Companies
SS Panzergrenadier Regiment *Der Führer*
  as *Deutschland*
2. SS Panzer Artillery Regiment
  1st Battalion
    1st–3rd Batteries
  2nd Battalion
    4th–6th Batteries
  3rd Battalion
    7th–9th Batteries
  4th Battalion
    10th–12th Batteries
2. SS Motorcycle Battalion
  1st–5th Companies
2. SS Assault Gun Battalion
  1st–3rd Batteries
2. SS Reconnaissance Battalion
  1st–3rd Companies
Light Reconnaissance Detachment

2. SS Tank Hunter Battalion
  1st–3rd Companies
2. SS Anti-aircraft Battalion
  1st–5th Batteries
Light Artillery Detachment
2. SS Panzer Pioneer Battalion
  1st–3rd Companies
Bridging Section
Light Pioneer Detachment
2. SS Intelligence Battalion
  1st & 2nd Companies
Light Intelligence Detachment
2. SS Economics Battalion
Ration Supply Depot
Bakery Company
Butchery Company
2. SS Supply Services
  15 x Motorised columns
  Supply Company
Weapons Workshop Company
2. SS Repair Services
  3 x Workshop companies
  Spares column
2. SS Medical Unit
  Field Hospital
  2 x Medical companies
  3 x Motorised ambulance platoons
Military Police troop
Field Post section
2. SS War reporting Platoon

* Established 15 November 1942, At Kursk it
was led by Hauptsturmführer Grader

Left: Organisation of *Das Reich* in the last years of
the war.

Below: July 1943. Another defensive battle in the East.
German Waffen-SS grenadiers take a rest in their
trench after days of heavy fighting. They are in
constant radio contact with their comrades.

In mid-May *Das Reich* received orders to begin a reconnaissance of the local railway and road systems in anticipation of a move northward. At this time new Panther tanks and Panzer IVs to bolster the tank regiment were delivered. In addition, the division had a full complement of assault guns and both panzergrenadier regiments were at full strength. These 209 tanks and assault guns formed fully one tenth of the German armoured forces in France, and would be relied upon to strike swiftly when the Allies landed on French soil. Most agreed the Allied invasion would target the northern French coastline, but with *Das Reich* now some 700km from there, Rommel and many leading staff officers feared the dispositions had been badly misjudged.

On the day that landings began in Normandy, *Das Reich* began its march, now steeped in infamy, from the Toulouse area in south-west France on a line of advance through the French Massif Central to the battleground. Because of the pressure on the transport network, and the constant dangers of attack by roving Allied aircraft, the division did not move as one, and individual units were committed piecemeal to the battle as and when they arrived.

Although a shorter and safer route to Normandy, along the coast road, was available, *Das Reich* had orders en route to suppress an uprising of French maquis undertaken in conjunction with the Allied invasion. These are Rundstedt's words: 'Limited success in such operations is useless... the most energetic measures must be taken in order to frighten the inhabitants of this infested region.'

Moving to Limoges, on the 8th, I./*Der Führer* skirmished with resistance fighters at Groslejac and Cressenac. The following day, a battle broke out near Bretenoux, leaving 23 Resistance fighters and seven Germans dead, and upon arrival at Tulle, there were nine *Das Reich* dead and 31 wounded. At Tulle, the German garrison was under siege by resistance fighters, and was promptly relieved by the reconnaissance troop. It then began rounding up civilians. Ninety-nine were hanged, and another 149 deported to Dachau, where 100 were subsequently murdered.

Oradour-sur-Glane

Meanwhile north of Limoges, III./*Der Führer* had shot several residents in Argenton-sur-Creuse, and executed 29 resistance fighters near Gueret. While pulling back to Limoges early on 10 June, III./*Der Führer* CO Sturmbannführer Kampfe and Obersturmführer Gerlach were captured by maquis. At this time 1st Battalion *Der Führer*, under Sturmbannführer Dickmann, was at St. Junien, a town to the west of Limoges. Dickmann, a close friend of Kampfe, was informed by two residents that a German officer was being held in a town called Oradour-sur-Glane, a short distance from St. Junien.

In the afternoon of 10 June 3rd Company of Dickmann's battalion surrounded the village. At the sound of the village drum the inhabitants gathered on the village green, and

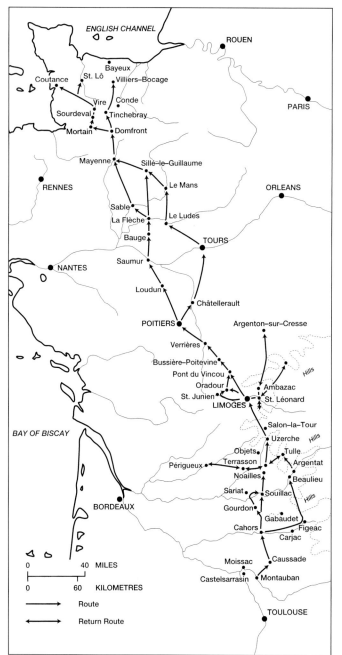
Below: The bloody march of *Das Reich* from southern France to Normandy.

any stragglers were rounded up, and were informed by the soldiers that they were conducting a search for weapons.

The women and children were separated from the men and led off to the church, after which Dickmann demanded hostages before making a search of the village. This completed, the men were divided into several smaller groups, and led into three barns, two garages, a warehouse and a hangar. Around 16.00 from inside the locked church, the women heard the rattle of machine guns and other small arms fire as the men were massacred almost simultaneously in their places of confinement. Survivors reported that *Das Reich* troops fired first at the men's legs, and continued to fire until nothing moved. Then, according to the few men who survived, the soldiers covered the bodies with straw, hay, wood and anything else that could be used for fuel to burn the corpses.

A small number of men managed to escape the bullets. According to their accounts, when the first volleys of machine-gun and rifle fire began they threw themselves to the ground and feigned death. Then, extricating themselves from the piles of bodies above them, they made their way to a corner of the barn and waited while the inferno that had been set by the Germans raged around them. When they could no longer stand the flames and smoke, they made a break for the countryside where they hid until nightfall. Meanwhile, at the church, troops tossed grenades among the 400 people packed inside, before barricading the doors and setting the building ablaze. Other residents who had not complied with the order to gather at the square were shot, and their houses and buildings burnt. Some 642 civilians, including 207 children, were massacred. Before they left the following morning, troops looted the village.

In the aftermath more senior German commanders considered instigating an enquiry into the events but Dickmann was killed in action before any proceedings could begin and the matter was allowed to drop. In 1953 a French military court sentenced a number of the surviving members of the SS detachment to death. None of the executions was carried out. The gutted, abandoned village has been left unreconstructed; its ruins are still a memorial to the victims. A new village, with a strikingly modern church, was built nearby.

The Normandy Battle

The first *Das Reich* units arrived at the concentration area near Domfront, as part of Army Group Reserve. Here they came under attack by Allied fighter-bombers. Other units arrived over the next week, but with concentration still incomplete (some units were still in Toulouse in mid-July), on 26 June orders came for a panzer and artillery battalion to move to the area north of Torigny-sur-Virein to support II.Fallschirmjäger Corps (see note at right), and for a battle group of the 1st Battalions of *Der Führer* and *Deutschland* to join 2nd Panzer Division at Caen. British VIII Corps intended to strike between Caen and Villers-Bocage, and then cross the River Orne as a preliminary to breaking out of the beachhead. To counter this II SS Panzer Corps, to which the battle group was subordinated, was to attack into the enemy flank along the Villers-Bocage–Caen road.

Beginning on the 29th, the advance through the treacherous *bocage* was met by a storm of fire which cost *Der Führer* fully 60 per cent of its front-line troops, but succeeded by nightfall on 30 June in halting the British offensive and preventing a breakthrough to the River Orne. The battle group was then pulled back and on 2 July reverted to *Das Reich* control.

Above: The Atlantic Wall, April 1944. Generalfeldmarschall Gerd von Rundstedt (far left) inspects reserve formations stationed along the Atlantic Wall. The details of a tank exercise are explained to him by SS-Gruppenführer Sepp Dietrich (gesturing).

Note: The actions of II.Fallschirmjäger Corps (General der Fallschirmjäger Eugen Meindl) are well-documented. The corps comprised 3.Fallschirmjäger Division (Genlt Richard Schimpf) and 5.Fallschirmjäger Division (Genlt Gustav Wilke). II.Fallschirmjäger Corps was part of the Seventh Army entrusted with the defence of the Cotentin Peninsula. In January 1944, 3.Fallschirmjäger Division was moved from Reims to Mont d'Arrée, 30km east of Brest. On 7 June, D-Day+1, the division moved to Avranches, with only a spearhead made up of Kampfgruppe *Alpers*, the rest of the division had to follow on foot. Between 17–18 June the division took up positions to the north of St Lô. 5.Fallschirmjäger Division was in Reims from March 1944, and at the end of May moved to Rennes in Brittany. In early June 1944, the division moved to Mont Saint Michel to prevent any Allied landings. Its neighbouring units were 17th SS Panzergrenadier Division *Götz von Berlichingen* on the left and the Panzer Lehr Division on the right. Divisional HQ was 4km SE of Dinan near Tressaint.

There were other actions before the division could concentrate as a single unit. On 4 July, now under LXXXIV Corps, such units as were available were formed into three battle groups, one under 353rd Division at La Haye-du-Puits, the second – including the 5th and 7th Panzer Companies of the 2nd Panzer Battalion – were attached to the 17th SS Panzergrenadier Division *Götz von Berlichingen* and positioned near to Sainteny, north-west of St. Lô, for a planned counter-attack. The 6th Panzer Company was attached to I./*Deutschland*, also under 17th SS, to form the third and moved to positions south of Sainteny.

On 7 July the US 9th and 30th Divisions began pushing across the Vire River at Le Dezert. The 5th and 7th Panzer Companies, which had formed a defensive line running from Les Landes to Lemonderie, were attacked by the US 83rd Infantry Division. On the next day, along a road near Le Dezert, a company of the US 743rd Tank Battalion in pursuit of two Panzer IVs was ambushed from the flank by Obersturmbannführer Kloskowski's 7th Panzer Company, and in 15 minutes, nine Shermans were destroyed, and three so damaged that they had to be abandoned.

While the 5th Panzer Company engaged near Bois Grimot, trying to contain the breakthrough over the Rivers Vire and Taute, Seventh Army moved 3rd and 4th Panzer Companies north-east toward Sainteny. West of Château d'Auxais, they ran into the US 3rd Armored Division. The counter-attack broke down and was then brought to a complete halt by a massive artillery bombardment, and by the 9th the Germans were back on the defensive. Although ultimately a failure, this operation played a crucial role in delaying the 14 divisions of Bradley's First Army now positioned in the Périers–St. Lô sector.

Into the second month of the Allied offensive, the *Das Reich* battle groups fought in a series of desperate local counter-attacks and defensive actions to plug breaches in the line. On 15 July, near St. Denis, Fritz Langanke single-handedly destroyed five Shermans. A month later, for this and other actions, Langanke was awarded the Knight's Cross.

The previous day, under tremendous pressure, the Germans had been forced to give up St. Lô. The ruined town was key to the operation which Bradley now envisaged – Operation Cobra – a strike by VII Corps to take St. Lô and smash the German positions between the Rivers Vire and Louzon. Patton's Third Army would then drive south to the base of the Cotentin Peninsula. Preceded by a devastating artillery and aerial barrage Cobra began on 25 July. The sector held by *Das Reich* battle groups west of St. Lô was the focus of the heaviest attacks; during the day no less than 13 separate infantry and armoured assaults were repulsed, before LXXXIV Corps command issued a series of vaguely-worded orders to pull back.

In the confusion that followed the US 1st Infantry Division (*see Spearhead 6*) and the 3rd Armored Division struck at Marigny, against the badly-battered *Das Reich* units and the 353rd Infantry Division. To counter them *Das Reich*'s Panzer Regiment had but eight command tanks, 35 Panzer IVs and 35 Panthers combat ready. Of these one was commanded by Unterscharführer Ernst Barkmann. On the morning of the 27th, north-east of Coutances, Barkmann's now famous action took place. Driving his Panther straight from the workshop along the road to St. Lô in order to intercept a force of Shermans, he parked in the shade of an oak tree near a crossroads at Le Leroy. As the first tank came into view Barkmann's gunner opened fire and in the mêlée that followed, though under attack by fighter-bombers, Barkmann and his men knocked out nine of them, and stalled the advance of an entire armoured column, before withdrawing in the badly damaged Panther.

After two days of heavy fighting the division was holding a line north of the St. Gilles–Coutances road and Coutances was still in German hands. But on *Das Reich*'s right flank, the First Army made significant inroads, and almost encircled the entire LXXXIV Corps. US aircraft and artillery poured bombs and shells into the pocket and,

under a withering rain of fire, a battle group comprising *Das Reich* and 17th SS Division withdrew from Coutances on the 28th, and broke out to the south-east to Percy. During this withdrawal each unit experienced losses of between 30 and 90 per cent.

Operation Liege – Avranches

The US First Army under Hodges now struck down the coast, peeling the German line away from Avranches, at the base of the Cotentin Peninsula. Avranches fell on the 30th, and in a fatally miscalculated attempt to form a cohesive line, Dollman's Seventh Army command ordered LXXXIV Corps to withdraw south-east, thus widening the breach and compromising the German southern flank. The Allied command was quick to exploit the situation, and Patton turned part of his force east from his drive into Brittany to advance inland from the base of the Cotentin Peninsula.

At this point Hitler finally allowed the divisions being held in reserve in the Pas De Calais area to be released for an attack towards Avranches on the deep but narrow Allied spearhead, believing that if the city could be taken, the entire US Third Army under Patton would be cut off from Bradley's command. He then envisaged a drive up the peninsula to smash the American lodgement on the Normandy beaches.

Briefly rested and re-equipped, and formed into three battle groups, *Das Reich* was transferred to the command of XLVII Corps. The main effort was to be made by the 1st and 2nd SS Panzer with 116th Panzer and a 17th SS Panzer Division battle group – Kampfgruppe *Fick*. Of the three *Das Reich* battle groups, *Der Führer* on the right was to take heights to the north-west of Mortain; on the central sector Kampfgruppe *Fick* aimed at Point 317; and to the south *Deutschland* with SS Panzer Reconnaissance Battalion 2 was tasked with recapturing Mortain itself, and defeating US units to the south of the town. The panzer regiment was ordered to follow behind *Deutschland* and exploit any breakthroughs in the American defences, with Avranches some 35km to the west as the ultimate objective.

Below: Normandy, 1944. In American hands. An assorted group of captured Waffen-SS and Fallschirmjäger officers await their interrogation.

Just after midnight on 7 August, the Avranches counter-attack began. On the right heavy traffic on the roads soon bogged down *Der Führer*'s advance, and although the grenadiers quickly overcame several roadblocks and scattered units of 2/120th Infantry Regiment, 30th US Infantry Division, it was dawn before the regiment was able to fan out into its battle formations. There was another surprise, for although intelligence had predicted only light resistance, on approaching the crossroads of L'Abbaye Blanche just to the north of Mortain in heavy fog 3rd Battalion came under heavy fire. Allied air strikes were called in, and until the afternoon the regiment was pinned down. Taking up the advance, 9th Company engaged 1st Platoon of Company A/823rd Tank Destroyer Battalion and took heavy losses. Nine vehicles, including six of the precious SdKfz 251s, were destroyed.

On the left by mid-morning 3./*Deutschland* was able to report that it had taken Mortain after a fierce fight with C/120th Infantry, although scattered resistance continued in the town for the remainder of the afternoon. The panzers now struck west, and

Above: Normandy, June 1944. A Waffen-SS Hauptscharführer points out the two direct hits that disabled this American M4 Sherman tank.

south-west toward St. Hilaire. The 2nd Battalion *Deutschland* soon gained its initial objectives near Romagny, just south-west of Mortain, but further attacks on C/197th Field Artillery positions were beaten off for several hours.

Allied commanders now began to come alive to the surprise attack, and heavy fire began falling on the *Der Führer* positions north of Mortain. A brief lull in the shelling allowed the *Der Führer* and *Deutschland* Regiments to link up on the hills immediately to the west of the town, but *Der Führer* had as yet been unable to establish contact with *Leibstandarte* to the north. In the centre of the *Das Reich* sector, Kampfgruppe *Fick* had surrounded the 2/120th Infantry atop Hill 314 just east of Mortain, but proved unable to reduce that position despite a heavy artillery preparation.

At 08.15 on the 8th, Kampfgruppe *Ullrich*, consisting of an infantry battalion from 17th SS Panzergrenadier Division and a troop of Panzer IVs from Panzer Regiment *Das Reich*, launched an abortive assault on the positions of B/120th Infantry on Hill 285 located just to the north-west of Mortain. A dismounted attack by the battle group further to the north was more successful and forced A/120th Infantry to pull back. *Der Führer*, arrayed north of Mortain, had by now linked up with *Leibstandarte* above the US roadblock at L'Abbaye Blanche, held by elements of Coys. A/823rd TD and F/120th Infantry, but an attack against these positions during the night had been repulsed.

With the two *Deutschland* battalions defending Mortain and to the south Romagny, and the Panzer Reconnaissance Battalion screening the southern flank, in mid-morning Seventh Army commander Hausser visited the division command post with the news that the attack would continue after the XLVII Panzer Corps received additional tanks.

During the night of 8/9 August, however, *Das Reich* received orders to go on the defensive. At sun-up Allied fighter bombers once more became active, and artillery observers were able to direct heavy fire on the division's front. In the late morning, US troops began an attack from the direction of Juvigny against the *Der Führer* positions. Several other American attacks, supported by tanks, came in from the north and north-west and, although they were brought to a halt, casualties were heavy, the right flank of *Der Führer* was threatened, and the link with *Leibstandarte* severed. Hill 285, north-west of Mortain, was briefly re-occupied by the Americans, but recaptured in a swift counter-attack.

Right: Normandy, 1944. American troops examine wrecked German tanks and equipment from *Das Reich* strewn along the roadside near the Normandy village of Roncey captured by the Americans on 30 July 1944. The armoured fighting vehicle on the left of the photograph has a 15cm Schw. Panzerhaubitze mounted on a PzKpfw III/IV tank chassis (SdKfz 165).

Below right: Normandy, 1944. A mixed batch of recently captured young Waffen-SS soldier stands inside an improvised PoW cage. It is interesting to note the mix of different styles of camouflage clothing being worn by these four prisoners.

Below: Normandy, July 1944. British soldiers, captured during a Waffen-SS reconnaissance sortie, are brought back on a ground-to-air communications vehicle, a modification of the SdKfz 250 light armoured troop carrier complete with a frame aerial.

In the evening another armoured thrust came against Romagny, but was abandoned in the face of a counter-attack by 2nd Battalion *Deutschland*. Then, to counter the advance of the US 35th Infantry Division, the battalion hurriedly took up defensive positions along the Mortain–La Houberte–Bion line. These positions and those of 1st Battalion were assaulted without success the following afternoon. Meanwhile, in the sector held by *Der Führer*, tanks of the US 3rd Armored Division were repulsed, although casualties were again very heavy.

It was clear that the attack had lost all hope of success. Allied movements on the south of Mortain toward Falaise and on the north toward the Seine now threatened an encirclement of both the Fifth and Seventh German Armies. At 18.00 on 10 August, transferred from XLVII Panzer Corps to LVIII Reserve Panzer Corps, the scattered *Das Reich* units were ordered to pull back to a line to just east of Mortain. Despite the terrain and heavy artillery fire, by nightfall the last stragglers were back.

FALAISE

Meanwhile, Patton's drive to the Seine and a co-ordinated thrust from the coast was threatening another encirclement, this time of the entire Fifth and Seventh Armies. During the second week of August the division pulled ever backward toward Falaise, around which the noose was tightening, countering aggressive and well-led armoured thrusts and all the time harassed from the air. On 16 August the division was ordered to join II SS Panzer Corps at Vimoutiers, 20 miles east of Falaise. Should the Allies succeed in closing the pocket OKH intended to use II SS Panzer Corps to crack it open. On 18 August the Polish Armoured Division began to move on Chambois, aiming to link with Canadian forces approaching Trun and cut off the escape route to Vimoutiers. The next day Trun fell, sealing the pocket, and Field Marshal Model at once ordered attacks by II SS Panzer Corps to break gaps in the ring.

The Polish Armoured Division was now positioned on Mont Ormel ridge, straddling the Chambois–Vimoutiers road, from where it aimed to block any escape. On 20 August *Das Reich* began a three-pronged advance through Champosoult and across Mont Ormel at the Falaise pocket, assaulting up the steep-sided ridge under a hail of fire from the Polish tanks on the crest. By mid-morning, 3rd Battalion *Der Führer* was in contact with forces inside the ring, and these now began to stream east through the breach. At mid-day having driven the Polish tanks off the vital high ground and widened the escape route, the battalion was ordered to continue the advance to Coudehard and Chambois. But with Allied forces now alive to the attack, and launching powerful counter-strikes on all sides, this was an unrealistic hope.

On the left *Deutschland* moved on St. Pierre-la-Rivière, through heavy woodland that slowed the advance to a crawl. Polish armour that turned to block them was brushed aside, nonetheless, and by mid-afternoon the regiment had also forced a way into the pocket. During the remaining hours of the 20th and through much of the 21st the battle groups fought off dozens of determined attacks on the narrow corridor. Through this passed 20,000 German troops, among them the former commander, Hausser, snatched from the jaws of defeat by the men of *Das Reich*.

Retreat

From Falaise began an inexorable retreat toward the German border. On 25 August the division was back at Vimoutiers, as Paris was liberated. During seven weeks of combat in France, the regiment destroyed over 200 Allied tanks, but the cost had been enormous. On 1 September, *Der Führer* Regiment was down to 120 men and the division as a whole could muster only 450 men and 15 tanks.

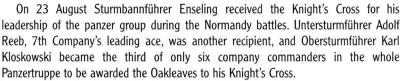

Right: Normandy, August 1944. Waffen-SS Panzergrenadiers carefully unload their wounded comrades at a casualty clearing station.

Below right: Captured during September 1944, the Battle of the Bulge lost the Germans at least 100,000 men killed, wounded and captured.

Below: Otto Kumm (saluting) photographed at the funeral at Sarajevo of Michael Reiser, July 1944. At this time Otto Kumm was commanding the 4th SS Panzergrenadier Regiment *Der Führer* from *Das Reich* operating on the Eastern Front.

On 23 August Sturmbannführer Enseling received the Knight's Cross for his leadership of the panzer group during the Normandy battles. Untersturmführer Adolf Reeb, 7th Company's leading ace, was another recipient, and Obersturmführer Karl Kloskowski became the third of only six company commanders in the whole Panzertruppe to be awarded the Oakleaves to his Knight's Cross.

In late August the division moved back over the Seine at Elbeuf, and over the Maas on 7 September. Halting temporarily at Rousen and St. Vith, and in the dense woodlands of the Schnee Eifel, on 11 September the division pulled back behind the German border into positions on the Siegfried Line between Brandsheid and Liedenborn in western Germany. Hitler ordered that these defences, though considered inadequate for the task by the field commanders, were to be held to the last man, and strengthened the 63 depleted divisions manning them with such units as could be mustered. Thus the *Das Reich* troops found themselves fighting alongside Luftwaffe and Kriegsmarine men for whom this was a wholly new type of fighting, and one for which they were ill-prepared.

Although there was now a significant loss of momentum from the Allied attack, there was little respite for the troops in the line, which was battered by continual assaults as the Allies tried to break through to the Rhine. In mid-October, after enduring nearly a month of these attacks, *Das Reich* was relieved and ordered to the Sauerland, and throughout October and November was rebuilt for the final effort Hitler planned for the winter.

THE ARDENNES BATTLE

During the autumn, although still badly in need of replacement tanks, troops and supplies, Hitler decided on an ambitious counter-attack, code-named Wacht am Rhein (Watch on the Rhine), involving a westward drive by four armies through the Ardennes region of Belgium, with the ultimate objective of splitting the British and American forces and capturing their main supply port of Antwerp. Correctly assessing that the Allies had outrun their supply lines, Hitler believed that the panic and confusion caused by a rapid thrust would allow him to transfer some of his troops to the Eastern Front and deliver a similar strike on the Soviets. Rundstedt and Model, both horrified at the patently unrealistic plans, argued without success for more restricted objectives.

For the offensive an entire new army was created under the command of the highly experienced Oberführer Josef 'Sepp' Dietrich. This Sixth Panzer Army consisted of: I SS Panzer Corps, incorporating the *Leibstandarte* and *Hitler Jugend* Divisions as well as the Army's 12th and 277th Volksgrenadier Divisions and the Luftwaffe's 3rd Paratroop Division; II SS Panzer Corps under Obergruppenführer Wilhelm Bittrich, comprising the *Das Reich* and *Hohenstaufen* divisions; and LXVII Corps under Generalleutnant Otto Hitzfeld, comprising 272nd and 326th Volksgrenadier Divisions, as well as a number of independent assault gun, Tiger, Jagdpanther, combat engineer, artillery and other units. These formations were split up into several different battle groups. Also available for the attack were General Hasso von Manteuffel's Fifth Panzer Army and two other Armies, the Seventh and Fifteenth. In reserve there were one Panzergrenadier division and two Volksgrenadier divisions.

The area earmarked for the advance was defended by only four divisions of inexperienced American troops, covering a front of 135km. On the northern flank, with I SS Panzer Corps spearheading the advance, the main thrust was to be made by Sixth Panzer Army on a narrow front between Monschau and Losheim and then on to the Meuse River between Liège and Huy. All this was to be accomplished in a matter of four days. II SS Panzer Corps was to be held in reserve and used to exploit any significant breakthroughs.

Early on 16 December the offensive began with a massed artillery barrage that hit American positions all along the front. But after crossing its start lines I SS Panzer Corps was quickly stalled by spirited defence, and by the delays caused by traffic jams as the SS Corps, 12th Volksgrenadier Division and 3rd Paratroop Division moved on towards Losheim. The US troops did not fold as predicted, disrupting the tight schedule to which I SS Panzer Corps had to adhere, and at the end of the first day it had still to make a decisive breakthrough. At the spearhead of the corps, Battle Group *Peiper's* advance began to stutter, and Field Marshal Model decided to shift responsibility for the main thrust of the attack to Fifth Panzer Army, with Sixth SS Panzer Army supporting the northern flank.

On 18 December II SS Panzer Corps was ordered to move from its assembly area east of Schliede to support the southern flank of I SS Panzer Corps' drive, west of Amblève. But with the roads hopelessly clogged with traffic, and lacking sufficient reserves of fuel, the movement was badly delayed. On the 20th Bittrich ordered *Das Reich* to capture the vital Baraque de Fraiture crossroads, then move north-west at Manhay and on to the River Ourthe, but again they were forced to wait for fuel. Finally on 23 December, 7th Panzer Company was attached to II. *Der Führer* and an assault gun company to III. *Der Führer*, and given the task of seizing the crossroads. A platoon of Shermans from the US 3rd Armored Division held the position, but just after 16.20 a detachment under Obersturmführer Gresiak attacked and had overrun the junction by 18.00. Gresiak's company claimed a total of 17 armour kills for the day. Seriously wounded the next morning, he received the Knight's Cross a month later. By around 22.00, 7th Armored Division was retreating north-west of Baraque de Fraiture to Malempre. After slipping unnoticed into the American column, just south of town Hauptscharführer Frauscher and another Panther of his platoon swung out of line and opened fire, scattering the American armour in confusion. Nine Shermans were destroyed.

By nightfall on the 23rd *Deutschland* had captured the village of Odeigne and was preparing to advance on the road from Manhay at Grandmenil. On Christmas Day, in freezing conditions and under attack by fighter-bombers that had previously been grounded by fog, 3rd Battalion wrested Manhay and Grandmenil from US troops. The next day *Das Reich* attempted to renew the advance from Grandmenil, but the two-pronged attack was met head on by US troops. The first thrust was eventually halted on the Grandmenil–Erezee road; the other, though advancing through heavily wooded terrain along narrow winding roads, made good progress – until the route was blocked by felled trees. Halting to clear the obstacle, the armoured column came under a heavy artillery bombardment and was forced to retire.

That same day the Americans stepped up their efforts to recapture both Manhay and Grandmenil, launching air-strikes and artillery bombardments on both towns. Under the sheer intensity of American firepower *Das Reich* was forced onto the back foot. At Grandmenil *Deutschland* was surrounded and only by a skillful withdrawal was it extricated. By 27 December both towns were back in American hands, and the division in retreat back to the crossroads at Fraiture.

In the last days of the month 3rd Battalion *Der Führer* was detached to serve with 9th SS Panzer Division *Hohenstaufen*. Advancing towards St Vith, *Hohenstaufen* was stalled by the US 82nd Airborne Division at Villettes and Bra, and then turned south towards Bastogne to support *Leibstandarte* and *Hitler Jugend* in their battle to take that town from the US 101st Airborne. Many of the *Hitler Jugend* units, including the artillery, had been left stranded en route due to lack of fuel, and *Das Reich's* Panzer Reconnaissance Battalion, an artillery battalion and two infantry companies were sent to help the attack. But despite these reinforcements, and the unflagging morale within the ranks, in their weakened state the defences of Bastogne proved too strong for the SS, and attempts to take the town came to nothing.

In early January 1945 the other of *Der Führer's* battalions were in woodland north of Magoster, while on their left 9./*Deutschland* grenadiers held the northern end of the village. Resisting stubbornly until ammunition was all but exhausted, those few that survived the battles to hold Magoster were forced back to Beffe. Appraised of the now woefully weakened state of the division, on 4 January Bittrich put the units of the division into reserve, and ordered them to withdraw from their dispersed positions along the front.

It was already apparent that the offensive had been a failure. With a major Soviet offensive opening in the East, Hitler ordered his SS panzer divisions to be transferred back to that front. By 10 February all of the German units committed to the offensive were back on the east bank of the Rhine. The Allies had lost 75,000 men dead, captured or wounded, the Germans slightly fewer. The Germans had lost 600 tanks destroyed or abandoned by their crews when they ran out of fuel, the Allies around 800. In retrospect, the only achievement of the offensive was to waste precious German reserves of manpower and equipment, and thereby bring the war to a quicker conclusion.

LAST BATTLES IN THE EAST

In the east, following the conquest of Romania in 1944, Soviet forces under Malinovsky entered Hungary via Arad in late September. Advancing north to the outskirts of the capital, Budapest, a co-ordinated thrust by Tolbukhin's Third Ukrainian Front to Lake Balaton surrounded the city by 4 December. The embattled garrison in Budapest was ordered to defend the capital and the Balaton oil fields at all costs, but the desperate situation inside the city and the annihilation of 16,000 troops who tried to retreat to German lines resulted in the surrender of the city on the following day.

In mid-February with the Third Ukrainian Front threatening the Balaton oil fields, and Hitler desperate to retain them, Sixth Panzer Army began transferring in from the Ardennes to secure them. *Leibstandarte* and *Hitler Jugend* were quickly thrown in to the battle, and smashed 7th Guards Army's bridgehead over the Danube at Gran. With Gran relieved and a threat on Vienna averted, Hitler gave orders for a larger operation to destroy the Red Army between the Danube, Lake Balaton and the Drava, and establish a line east of the oil fields.

Immense secrecy surrounded the operation, code-named Frühlingserwachen (Spring Awakening). Sturmbannführer Otto Günsche, Hitler's adjutant, briefed Sixth Panzer Army commander Dietrich orally, and no reconnaissance was permitted. However, the secrecy was to no avail as, appraised of the plan by British intelligence, Tolbukhin, commander of Third Ukrainian Front, had ordered extensive defences to be laid where the main thrust would come between Lakes Balaton and Velencei.

Dietrich's Sixth SS Panzer Army, including the I and II SS Panzer Corps, two cavalry divisions and IV SS Panzer Corps (*Wiking* and *Totenkopf*), was ordered to attack south, on either bank of the Sarviz Canal. For the thrust Dietrich placed *Leibstandarte* at the spearhead, with II SS Panzer Corps (*Das Reich* and *Hohenstaufen*) to the left and I Cavalry Corps to the right. To retain the element of surprise, troops were held 20km from their assembly areas until the last minute and the long, tiring march to their start lines through clinging mud left them exhausted and in need of rest before the battle even began. They quickly learnt that Hitler's plan had not taken into account the appalling conditions created by an early thaw, in which normally frozen ground became heavily waterlogged. Not even tracked vehicles could operate off the paved roads, and these inevitably became badly clogged with traffic. Furthermore, there were shortages of ammunition.

In these miserable conditions *Das Reich* advanced on a line to the north-east of Lake Balaton on 5 March and on the following day engaged in combat south-west of

Left: Transylvania, October 1944. Guided by a fire-controller, Waffen-SS infantry guns prepare to deliver supporting fire for their comrades. The gunners are all wearing full camouflage suits complete with camouflage service caps. Their weapon is a standard 7.5cm leIG 18 light infantry gun.

Below left: Somewhere on the Western Front. Trophy time! American soldiers search another batch of captured Waffen-SS grenadiers.

Below: SS-Sturmbannführer Hans Hauser photographed before he was awarded the Knight's Cross of the Iron Cross. This was bestowed upon him on 6 May 1945 just two days before the end of the war in Europe. He received the Knight's Cross when commander of 1st Battalion in Regiment *Der Führer* from *Das Reich*. It was an immediate award authorised by 'Sepp' Dietrich, commander of the Sixth Panzer Army.

Budapest at Stuhlweissenburg. By 9 March *Totenkopf* had advanced 20 miles, and *Das Reich* panzers, reinforced by III./*Der Führer* overran Hill 159. Throughout the next three days fierce combat raged in the Kulso, Puskop and Myr areas, and *Der Führer* advanced with what remained of the division's panzers to Heinrich Major. On 13 March the advance ground to a halt in the face of overwhelming Soviet resistance, and within three days the Soviet counter-attack began, trapping the over-extended Sixth SS Panzer Army. *Das Reich* fought and held open a narrowing pocket through which the trapped divisions escaped, but with Hungarian formations deserting en masse, the full weight of the Russian Second and Third Ukrainian Fronts was brought to bear on the SS formations. Little more than a week after they had launched the attack, the two Ukrainian Fronts had broken through on either side of Lake Balaton and by the end of the month had crossed the border into Austria.

With the spectre of defeat looming ominously, a fighting retreat back to Austria began, where General Lothar Rendulic, recently appointed as commander of Army Group South, was told to hold Vienna and the Alpine passes. During the third week of March *Das Reich* was driven back south of Komorn, and then to positions in Austria.

Vienna

In Vienna an operation to evacuate the city was already in full swing. Sixth SS Panzer Army did what it could with what little it had to defend the approaches but, as their strength diminished, Hitler's demands to hold the city became wishful in the extreme. On the 28th, as it retreated north-west toward the Austrian capital, *Das Reich*'s Panzer Regiment had just 5 Panzer IVs, 2 Panthers, and 5 Jagdpanthers combat fit. On 6 April the Red Army was on the outskirts of the city and by the middle of the month was approaching the centre, while to the north and south of the city the Soviets were closing in.

On 11 and 12 April, *Das Reich* battled to keep open the small, but vital bridgehead at the Florisdorf Bridge, one of only two bridges across the Danube that had not been blown. On 13 April, *Das Reich* fought its last significant tank action in Vienna. As Soviet forces edged in on the southern end of the bridge, the CO, Obersturmführer Karl-Heinz Boska, rounded up three Panthers and tried to lead them over the bridge toward the dwindling bridgehead. Halfway across the bridge Boska's machine was hit, and the others were pulled back. That night the bridgehead was evacuated, and Vienna fell to the Russians the next day.

Already, on 1 April the Red Army had launched its last great offensive of the war and, with the Ruhr already encircled and Silesia gone, tank, artillery and ammunition production at a mere ebb, and fuel in hopelessly short supply, the fate of the Third Reich was sealed. On 16 April on the Oder–Niesse line the First Belorussian and First Ukrainian Fronts broke through toward Berlin. On 21 April Zhukov's First Belorussian Front reached Berlin, and with Konev's First Ukrainian Front moving up from the south-east, by 24 April the city was encircled.

The widely dispersed and tattered units of *Das Reich* were pulled back from the Danube across the Bisamberg River to concentration areas around Melk and St. Pölten. From here the bulk of division was ordered back to Dresden, and *Deutschland* to Passau where during the final days of the war it fought to contain the advance of American troops. Moving by rail and on foot, via Krems, Zwettl, Budweis and Prague, there were

Above: Vincenz Kaiser, seen here as an SS-Obersturmbannführer, photographed sometime late 1942. He had been awarded four Tank Destruction badges (shown here worn on the right upper arm) each for his single-handed destruction of an enemy tank without the aid of an anti-tank weapon. On 19 April 1945 he received the Oakleaves to his Knight's Cross (awarded on 6 April 1943) when he was commanding a battle group of the 17th SS Panzergrenadier Division *Götz von Berlichingen*. During the 1945 retreat from Southern Germany he was reported missing somewhere in the vicinity of Nuremberg. His body has never been found.

minor but inconsequential skirmishes with American units before, on 8 May, orders were received to lay down arms. *Deutschland* held a final parade where decorations were presented to the men. This done, they crossed over the Enns bridge to surrender to the American Army, and into uncertain captivity.

Der Führer's final act of the war was a somewhat unlikely mercy mission. On 30 April Obersturmbannführer Otto Weidinger, CO of the *Der Führer* Regiment, led the regiment into Prague, where he organised the evacuation by a convoy of 1,000 vehicles of wounded German soldiers and civilians. On 6 May, in the face of Soviet attacks and Czech civilian reprisals, this column reached the American lines at Rokizany.

Above: Surrender at the Elbe. A Waffen-SS general, possibly Jürgen Wagner, listens intently to his interpreter while being interrogated by an American colonel. SS-Gruppenführer und Generalleutnant der Waffen-SS Wagner joined *Leibstandarte* in 1933 and transferred to *Deutschland* in 1939. He commanded the Regiment *Germania*, and then the *Wiking* and *Nederland* divisions. It was while fighting Tito's partisans with *Nederland* that he was awarded the Oakleaves to the Knight's Cross. He surrendered to US forces on 1 May 1945 and was extradited to Yugoslavia for trial. Found guilty, he was executed in 1947.

Left: *Das Reich*'s war at a glance.

DETAILS OF THE LOCATION AND ASSIGNMENT OF Das Reich 1941–45

Date	Corps	Army	Army Group	Area
1–3.41	XXXXI	First Army	D	France
4.41	XXXXI	Twelfth Army	-	Yugoslavia
5–6.41	Refreshing	BdE – Wehrkreis XVII		
7–9.41	XXXXVI	Second Panzer Group	Centre	Smolensk, Kiev
10.41	LXVII	Fourth Panzer Group	Centre	Vyazma
11–12.41	XXXX	Fourth Panzer Group	Centre	Moscow
1.42	XXXXVI	Fourth Panzer Army	Centre	Mozhaisk
2.42	VI	Ninth Army	Centre	Rzhev
3–4.42	XXXXVI	Ninth Army	Centre	Rzhev
5.42	XXVII	Ninth Army	Centre	Rzhev
6–8.42	Reserve	Ninth Army	Centre	Rzhev
9–11.42	SS Panzer Corps	Fifteenth Army	D	Rennes
12.42–1.43	Reserve	-	D	Rennes
2.43	Reserve	OKH	B	South Russia
3.43	SS Panzer Corps	Fourth Panzer Army	South	Kharkov
4.43	Reserve	Kempf	South	Kharkov
5–6.43	Refitting	-	South	Kharkov
7.43	II SS	Kharkov	South	Belgorod
8.43 Reserve	Fourth Panzer Army	South	Stalino	
9.43	III	Eighth Army	South	Poltava
10.43	XXIV	Eighth Army	South	Dnieper
11.43	XXXXVIII	Fourth Panzer Army	South	Kiev
12.43	XXXXII	Fourth Panzer Army	South	Zhitomir
1.44*	XXXXVIII	Fourth Panzer Army	South	Vinniza
2–3.44*	LXXXVI	First Army	D	Toulouse
4.44	I SS	refreshing	D	Toulouse
5–6.44	Reserve	Seventh Army	D	Toulouse
7.44	LXXXIV	Fifth Panzer Army	B	Normandy
8.44	II SS	Seventh Army	B	Normandy
9.44	I SS	Seventh Army	B	Eifel
10.44	LXVI	Sixth Panzer Army	B	Eifel
11.44	Refitting BdE	Sixth Panzer Army	-	Paderborn
12.44	Reserve	Sixth Panzer Army	B	West Ardennes
1.45	II SS	Fourth Panzer Army	B	Ardennes
2–3.45	Reserve	BdE	South	Hungary
4.45	II SS	-	South	Hungary
5.45	-	-	Centre	Bohemia

* When the division was transferred to France a battle group (Kampfgruppe) remained in Russia in February and March. Its assignments were:

2.44	XXXXVIII	Fourth Panzer Army	South	Vinniza
3.44	LIX	First Panzer Army	South	Hube pocket

INSIGNIA, CLOTHING & EQUIPMENT

Right: Captain Tom Carothers (right) tries on the tunic of an officer from *Das Reich* during the September 1944 offensive in Normandy. Note the cuff title (see pages 163,164).

Below: From top to bottom – white gnome as used by Tiger company; symbol found on Sturmgeschütz Abteilung equipment in 1943; symbol seen on Das Reich vehicles around Operation Citadel (some months before and after).

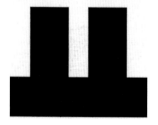

UNIFORMS

The divisional emblem (used on its standard, vehicles and some personal insignia) was based on the 'wolf's hook' or 'wolf's angel', a Nordic rune said to possess the power to ward off wolves. It was adopted in the 15th century by peasants in their revolt against the mercenaries employed by the German princes, and henceforth became a symbol of liberty and independence. During the Thirty Years' War, it was known as the Zeichen der Willkür or 'badge of wanton tyranny' and subsequently became a heraldic symbol representing a wolf trap. As such it appeared, and still features, on the coat-of-arms of the city of Wolfstein.

SS INSIGNIA

The SS in general wore the national emblem (*Hoheitszeichen*), an eagle clutching a *Hakenkreuz* (swastika), mounted either on the top front of an officer's cap, above the cap band, on the front or left side of soft crush caps, or more unusually on the upper left arm of the combat, service and walking-out dress; also the *Totenkopf* (Death's Head) symbol, whose origins lay in the Prussian and Imperial German Army, worn on the front of an officer's cap, in the centre of the headband, or on the top front of soft crush caps. SS men also wore *Siegrunen* (SS Runes), representative of a double lightning bolt, which were adapted for the SS for their right collar insignia from an ancient Norse symbol for Thor, the god of thunder.

Rank Insignia

The Waffen-SS used a system of rank insignia that differed from that of the Army, and with the development of the camouflage uniform, some difficulties arose with identifying rank in the field. Therefore in May 1940 a ranking system was devised that incorporated a system of lace or cloth strips to identify the wearer's rank. Although collar patches with rank insignia were worn in some cases, on many types of uniform sleeve insignia were worn. These were embroidered in artificial silk on a rectangular black cloth background and worn on the left sleeve, to the following colour scheme.

Generals of the Waffen-SS	Golden Yellow
Officers up to the rank of Oberführer	Bright Green
NCOs	Bright Green

Other ranks wore a series of either mouse grey chevrons or a pip (for an Oberschütze). The badge for the rank of Oberstgruppenführer was three mouse grey embroidered pips on a yellow stripe. Panzerobergrenadiers wore a black wool or felt circle containing a white or silver embroidered diamond on the left sleeve.

Above: Three versions of the 'wolf's hook' – the Nordic rune used as a divisional symbol. Note its use on vehicles as illustrated on pages 169 and 172.

Left: Three collar patches, from left to right – SS-Standarte *Deutschland* (1934–40); *Germania* Regiment (1938–41); *Der Führer* (1939–41). After these dates the usual SS collar patches were used.

Waffen-SS Collar Tresse

SS collar *Tresse* were of the diamond Wehrmacht pattern and were required to be worn on all tunics (with the exception of camouflage tunics) and optionally also on overcoats. Before the war SS collar patches in many cases denoted the rank, branch of service and formation of the wearer. With the introduction within the system of cyphers, numbers and letters on the shoulder strap and the introduction of cuff titles, the SS collar patch was redesigned. A certain amount of confusion arose and an order dated 10 May 1940 rendered all SS-VT collar patches with numerals obsolete for security reasons. From then on collar patches with runes or death's head became standard insignia for the Waffen-SS. Ranks from Schütze to Obersturmbannführer had the SS-runes on the right collar-patch and the rank insignia on the left. Standartenführer to Oberstgruppenführer had rank insignia on both sides. Some Waffen-SS units had the unit emblem on the right collar patch instead of the SS-runes.

Left: Probably a family photograph. A young, blond-haired German woman is posing between two officers – the Army officer on the left is probably her father or father-in-law and the Waffen-SS Sturmbannführer from Regiment *Das Reich* her fiancé or husband. Both men are wearing walking-out uniforms.

Right and Below: The re-enctment photos in this section show men from a New England-based group that portrays the 9th Company of the 3rd Battalion of *Das Reich*'s 3rd Regiment – *Deutschland*. At right, in greatcoat and woollen toque this man carries a Mauser 98k and typical field equipment: note water bottle and gas mask container. In the lower photograph, set at a roadblock, note the *mittlere Schützenpanzerwagen* SdKfz251/9 (7.5cm) in the background.

Left: Gunther Müller stands next to the 'Blood Banner' in barracks. He's wearing the *Dienstmütze* or *Schirmmütze* (service dress cap). Note the Totenkopf badge and the aluminium officer's cords.

Right: Two men from the unit take a cigarette break. In the foreground the man is wearing a *Feldmütze* (also nicknamed the *Schiffchen* – little ship) cap. His camouflage smock is of the second, later, machine-printed oakleaf-pattern type (note the loops at the shoulder for camouflage foliage) with the green (summer) side out. Behind him, his colleague carries a belt of machine gun ammunition. Note, too, the camouflaged cover to his helmet.

Below right: Cuff title of the *Deutschland* Regiment. This honour title was awarded its in 1935.

Below: MP40 gunner. Note the SS runes on his M35/40 helmet and the brown (autumn side) to his later-type smock.

Deutschland

The *Tresse* were made of a piece of buckram (or metal in some cases) covered in black badge cloth or felt for all ranks up to and including the rank of Obersturmbannführer From the rank of Standartenführer to Oberstgruppenführer black velvet was used. In most cases it was sewn to the collar of the tunic, greatcoat or shirt. In some cases metal insignia was used and was screwed to the collar patch.

Before the war patches were often piped around the edges with aluminium twist cord but during the war this was often omitted from the patches on the field uniform. Officer's collar *Tresse* were outlined with a thin white or aluminium border. All ranks up to the rank of Obersturmbannführer were identified by 12mm silver pips and intermediate ranks had additional stripes of 6mm wide aluminium lace. Ranks above Obersturmbannführer had oakleaves and pips of hand-embroidered aluminium wire. Metal pips were never worn by general officers.

Shoulder Insignia

Until July 1935 members of the SS-VT wore the standard Allgemeine-SS shoulder cord, at which time Army style shoulder straps were adopted for the earth-grey field uniform. At first manufactured in earth grey cloth, then later from black cloth with rounded ends and black and white aluminium twisted cord, they did not identify the wearer's rank.

From March 1938 NCOs wore aluminium lace and white metal stars on two patterns of shoulder strap, which were secured to the shoulder by a loop at the shoulder seam and a button near the uniform collar. The first pattern was made from black wool material was rounded at the button end and had black and aluminium twisted cord piping. The second was made of coarser quality black cloth with pointed ends and no piping. In December 1939 black rounded shoulder straps with Army style *Waffenfarben* were made standard issue for soldiers of the Waffen-SS and remained in use until the end of the war.

Officers wore shoulder straps corresponding to their rank with appropriate pips and metal monograms. Non-commissioned officer's shoulder straps were trimmed with *Tresse* and also displayed the appropriate pips. Depending on the unit, shoulder boards were trimmed with various colours – white for infantry, yellow for reconnaissance, pink for panzer troops and so on.

Camouflaged rank insignia were worn on camouflage tunics and smocks.

Honour Title Cuff Bands

Cuff bands bearing unit 'honour titles' were worn by at least 50 elite German Army and Luftwaffe formations during the war. The actual cuff title was a strip of woven black tape 28mm wide and 490mm in length and was worn on the left-hand sleeve of the greatcoat or tunic. The lettering and precise design of the *Das Reich* cuff band were frequently changed during the war. Regimental as well as divisional titles were issued and worn but there were strict criteria for the award of these titles. *Deutschland* was awarded its honour title in 1935, *Germania* in 1936, *Der Führer* in 1938, and *Das Reich* in 1942.

Above: Squad drill re-enactment. The majority of the squad are wearing camouflage uniforms, the officer with his back to the camera pairing camouflage trousers with a field grey uniform jacket. The distinctive Waffen-SS camouflage uniforms led to friendly fire problems for the US Army when it introduced its M1942 two-piece camouflage suit to 2nd Armored Division in June 1944. While in close-up the uniforms are very different, in the bocage of Normandy they were too similar and the US troops quickly stopped wearing their camouflage uniforms.

Right: The most interesting item of clothing shown in this re-enactment photograph is the *Kradmantel* – the waterproof motorcyclist's coat that was made from rubber-coated twill. While it was certainly sought-after for its waterproof qualities, it was not sufficiently hard-wearing for infantry use.

Left: This photograph provides a good example of the first type camouflage smock being worn autumn side out, showing off the plane-tree pattern. Note the SS enlisted man's belt buckle: Waffen-SS officers had a distinctive, if not very efficient, round belt buckle which was often swapped for an army open-style buckle (see photograph on page 177.

VEHICLE INSIGNIA

All *Das Reich* vehicles were identified by the 'wolf's hook' or 'wolf's angel', and some by tactical designations. The divisional symbol – sometimes enclosed in a shield – was usually small, and painted in yellow or white on the hull of AFVs usually on or near the driver's plate (see page 67). Prior to Operation Citadel (the Kursk offensive) *Das Reich* adopted a temporary divisional symbol to confuse Allied intelligence. This symbol (a horizontal bar with two vertical bars) was seen on *Das Reich* vehicles several months before and after the Kursk offensive.

A tactical marking was also usually carried on most *Das Reich* AFVs although more often omitted on armoured cars and half-tracks. The number was usually in black, outlined in white, or sometimes in white or white outline only. The system or allocating these numbers was usually according to normal German Army markings, although there were exceptions to the general rule:

R 11 – Regimental Commander
R 12 – Regimental Adjutant
R 13 – Ordnance or Signals Officer
R 14, etc. – Regimental staff
A 11 – Commander of 1st battalion
A 12 – Adjutant of 1st battalion
A 13 – Ordnance officer of 1st battalion
A 14, etc. – Staff of 1st battalion

Left: A section of Waffen-SS grenadiers march in column along a Russian village street. The leading NCO is carrying an MP40 slung on his right shoulder with three spare ammunition magazines carried in a holder on his chest.

Below: An advance party from the *Das Reich* reconnaissance detachment has encountered another Soviet defensive position. The men dismount from their vehicles to move forward in open formation. Note the tactical signs on the rear left of the truck – a unit sign and the 'wolf's hook' divisional symbol.

Above and left: Excellently preserved BMW R71 sidecar combo with machine gun. Note the carrying panniers on the sidecar body, SS numberplate, and 7.92mm MG34 machine gun. 3,458 R71s were built by BMW between 1938 and 1941, until it was superseded by the R75. The R71 had a 750cc side-valve engine that developed 22hp for a top speed of 125 km/h, a four-speed gearbox and weighed 187kg. It was an impressive machine, particularly when teamed up with the standard military sidecar – so much so that it was imitated all over the world. In the United States, the U.S. Army asked Harley-Davidson to produce a motorcycle as good as the R71. Harley copied it, converting metric measurements to inches, and produced the shaft-drive 750cc 1942 Harley-Davidson XA (experimental army). The Russians, too, produced an identical copy named the M72 (with an identical copy of the Wehrmacht sidecar). The official history says that this was reverse-engineered from five copies smuggled out of Sweden, but it seems more likely that BMW supplied the necessary information as part of the transfer of technology between the two countries fostered by the Molotov-von Ribbentrop Pact.

Far left: SS-Untersturmführer Gunther Müller. Note *Deutschland* cuff title and his war badges (*Kriegsabzeichen*) – the infantry assault breast badge (for having taken part in three or more infantry assaults) and the close combat clasp in bronze that was issued for 15 days' hand-to-hand fighting..

Right: The division's Pioneer company ferries a despatch rider and his sidecar companion across the River Beresina in July 1941 on a standard service pontoon float. Note the 'wolf's hook' symbol on the rear mudguard.

Below: July 1944. A Waffen-SS assault detachment discusses an attack. An Obersturmführer familiarises the commander of the detachment, a Waffen-SS Hauptscharführer, with the details.

Opposite, Below left: A Waffen-SS grenadier with two Panzerfaust 30 single-shot anti-tank missiles – the hollow-charge warheads could penetrate up to 200mm of solid armour plate at a 30° angle of impact. The main drawbacks were short range (in this case just 30m) and the long backblast of flame.

Opposite, Below right: Otto Kumm in summer 1943 when he was CO of the Regiment *Der Führer*. He received the Oakleaves to his Knight's Cross on 8 April 1943.

101 – Officer commanding 1st company, 1st battalion
102 – 2nd-in-command, 1st company, 1st battalion
111 – Leader, 1st platoon, 1st company, 1st battalion
112 – 2nd vehicle, 1st platoon, 1st company, 1st battalion
133 – 3rd vehicle, 3rd platoon, 1st company, 1st battalion
201 – Officer commanding 2nd company, 1st battalion
301 – Officer commanding 3rd company, 1st battalion
B 11 – Commander of 2nd battalion
401 – Officer commanding 4th company (2nd battalion)

Tiger Company

The Tiger company used a sequential series of numbers from 801 until 1943, when it changed the first digit from an 8 to an S for *schwere* (heavy), followed by a two digit tank number denoting platoon and vehicle. The 'gnome' emblem (see page 66) often seen was actually known as the *Springender Teufel* (springing demon). Reportedly this was based on a figure found by a panzer crewman in the streets of Kharkov. He was transferred to the Tiger Company in April 1943, at which time the emblem was adopted by that unit.

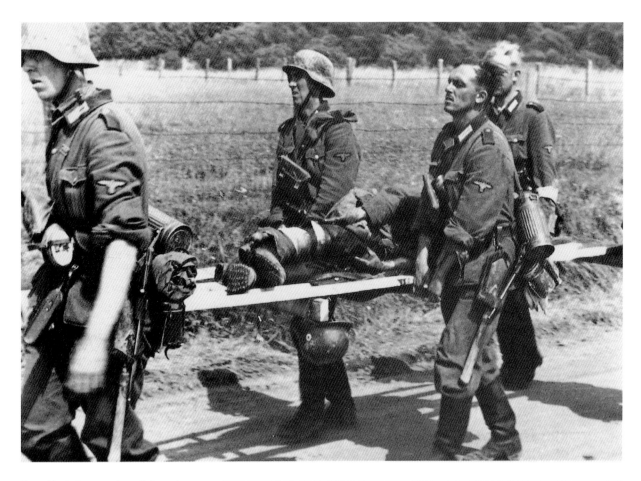

Above: 'That's what comrades are for!' says the original caption as a wounded man is carried to safety on a makeshift stretcher, accompanied by a medical orderly. The photograph gives a good snapshot of personal equipment including entrenching tool, gasmask container, etc. Note the forage cap tucked into the central man's shoulder strap.

Right: A Waffen-SS soldier crouches in his icy foxhole. The armband worn around his left sleeve and held in position by a single button was worn as a recognition mark to distinguish German troops from Soviet forces. When troops of both sides wore white snow camouflage it was difficult to identify who was who. The Germans adopted a simple system of red or green coloured arm bands to distinguish their troops. The colour of their bands was randomly altered in the same way as passwords were issued and used. Note the helmet cover.

Above left: December 1943, between Zhitomir and Kiev. The photograph shows part of the battlefield, with several burning Soviet T-34 tanks outside a recaptured village. A young Waffen-SS NCO signals his men to close up.

Above: The battle for Kharkov. The commander of a Waffen-SS motorcycle platoon gives the order to move out. Note the parka worn under his snow camouflage and the SS officer's cap with the death's head device.

Left: Belgium, December 1944. Members of the Waffen-SS, captured during the battle of the Bulge, are transported to the rear in an American truck. The lad on the left of this photographs appears to be very young.

PEOPLE

THE COMMANDERS

Obergruppenführer Paul Hausser (1880–1972)

Hausser served in the First World War, was decorated for action, and in 1920–32 served with various Army units, eventually reaching the rank of Generalleutnant. After retiring from the Army, he joined the Stahlhelm, which was later absorbed into the SA and served as an SA-Standartenführer. In November 1934 Hausser transferred to the SS-Verfügungstruppe and was assigned to SS-Junkerschule Braunschweig. In 1935 he became inspector of the SS-Junkerschule and was promoted to Brigadeführer in 1936. In Poland he was an observer with Panzer Division *Kempf* and, when SS-VT was formed as a division in October 1939, Hausser was given the command. He led the division through the battles in the west and during Barbarossa. During his command of *Reich* in Russia, Hausser was awarded the Knight's Cross and was severely wounded, losing an eye. After convalescing he commanded II SS Panzer Corps at Kharkov and led *Das Reich, Leibstandarte Adolf Hitler* and *Totenkopf* during Kursk. Promoted to command Seventh Army during the Falaise encirclement, Hausser risked capture to ensure the escape of as many men as possible. He ended the war on Feldmarschall Albert Kesselring's staff.

Brigadeführer Wilhelm Bittrich (1894–1979)

Wilhelm Bittrich began his military career as a fighter pilot in the First World War. He joined the SS in 1932 with SS Fliegerstaffel 'Ost' (SS Flying Echelon 'East') and later took command of 74. Standarte before leaving the Allgemeine-SS in August 1934. When Himmler re-established the Politische Bereitschaft in 1934, Bittrich was made commander. When this unit was expanded, and renamed Regiment *Germania*, Bittrich became 2nd Company Commander. In October 1936 he transferred to Regiment *Deutschland* as CO of 2nd Battalion and remained there until the spring of 1938. When the Austria-based Regiment *Der Führer* was created, Bittrich led I./*Der Führer*. He moved to the *Leibstandarte* on 1 June 1939, serving as Sepp Dietrich's HQ adjutant throughout the Polish campaign, before transfer to the replacement section of the SS-VT in early February 1940. He returned to the 2nd SS as commander of the *Deutschland* Regiment on 14 December 1940, and while in this post was awarded the Knight's Cross. As senior regimental commander, Bittrich replaced Hausser when the latter was wounded, serving until the end of December 1941, when he fell ill and had to step down. After he had recovered, Bittrich was assigned as CO of the SS Cavalry Brigade on 1 May 1942. Bittrich oversaw the expansion of that unit until it reached division strength, and then on 15 February took command of the 9th SS Panzer Division *Hohenstaufen*. When Hausser took command of Seventh Army, Bittrich was tasked as his replacement as II SS Panzer Corps commander and he retained this command till the end of the war.

Brigadeführer Matthias Kleinheisterkamp (1893–1945)

Matthias Kleinheisterkamp served in various units in World War I, during which time he was awarded both classes of the Iron Cross. After the war he served in both the infantry and the cavalry until 1934 when he joined the SS. He transferred to the SS-VT in 1938, taught at the SS-Führerschule Braunschweig as an infantry instructor and joined Hausser's Inspectorate as a senior staff officer. On 1 December 1938 he became commander of III./*Deutschland*, where he remained until the summer of 1940, when he was appointed CO of 11.SS Infantry Regiment *Totenkopf*. After this posting Kleinheisterkamp was transferred to take Bittrich's place as *Das Reich* commander, and was later awarded the Knight's Cross. After *Das Reich* he held various senior postings, ending the war as XI SS Army Corps commander.

Above: Walter Krüger awarding Knight's Crosses and other decorations after the Battle of Kharkov. The recipients are from left to right:
SS-Obersturmbannführer Otto Kumm,
SS-Sturmbannführer Christian Tychsen,
SS-Untersturmführer Karl Heinz Worthmann,
SS-Sturmbannführer Sylvester Stadler,
SS-Sturmbannführer Vincenz Kaiser and
SS- Sturmbannführer Hans Weiss. This photo is believed to have been taken on 6 April 1943.

Standartenführer Kurt Brasack (1892–1978)

Kurt Brasack was commissioned with the Allgemeine-SS in October 1931 with 21. Standarte. He commanded 91. Standarte from May 1934 to January 1937. He was promoted to Oberführer on 30 January 1938, and led SS-Abschnitte (Sections) XI and XXX. He served with the *Totenkopf* Division as CO of the 1st Artillery Battalion from October 1939 to March 1941, and was then reassigned to *Wiking*. He became CO of the *Wiking* Regiment in January 1942, and was acting divisional CO of *Das Reich* in March and April. He remained with *Das Reich* until June 1943. Brasack ended the war as the Arko (Artilleriekommandeur) of IV SS Panzer Corps when it absorbed VII SS Panzer Corps.

Above left: Paul Hausser (saluting) seen as an SS-Brigadeführer und Generalmajor der Waffen-SS on the occasion of a parade held to award the Knight's Cross to SS-Sturmbannführer Fritz Vogt, 4 September 1940.

Gruppenführer Walter Krüger (1890–1945)

Walter Krüger was wounded twice in the First World War and awarded the Iron Cross, First and Second Class. Afterwards Krüger served with various units and joined the Austrian SA. He transferred to the SS in 1935 and served as an instructor at Bad Tölz in 1937. In October, he took command of IV./*Deutschland* and from November was regimental commander of the Regiment z.b.V. *Ellwangen*. Krüger was assigned to the Polizei Division as a staff officer in January–October 1940, after which he was on the main SS staff as Inspector of Infantry. The following August he rejoined the Polizei Division and won the Knight's Cross for his leadership during the battles around Leningrad. After a brief return to the SS general staff, Krüger became commander of *Das Reich*, won his Oakleaves at Kursk, and left command of the division in October 1943. After holding a number of posts, he took command of VI SS Army Corps (Latvian), and was awarded the Swords for his actions during the battles in Kurland. Krüger committed suicide to avoid capture by the Russians.

Left: Wilhelm 'Willi' Bittrich. As this photo does not show him wearing his Oakleaves (awarded 23 August 1944) it is safe to assume it was taken sometime during the first half of 1944 when he held the rank of SS-Gruppenführer und Generalleutnant der Waffen-SS and before 22 August 1944. He had previously been awarded the Knight's Cross on 14 December 1941.

Brigadeführer Heinz Lammerding (1905–71)

An early Nazi supporter, Lammerding joined the SA as director of the engineering school, and worked in various capacities until 1935 when he joined the SS, and soon achieved the rank of Hauptsturmführer. On the staff of various pioneer battalions in the SS-VT Division from November 1940 to August 1942, he then commanded an infantry regiment, was on an armoured corps staff, and became chief of staff to General Erich von der Bach-Zelewski. At the end of 1943 he assumed command of *Das Reich* units operating against Soviet partisans, and was division commander from 23 October 1944 to 20 January 1945. In 1945 he was chief of staff of Himmler's Army Group Vistula. Other appointments included service as chief of staff to Eicke in the *Totenkopf* Division. After the war he and other higher ranking officers escaped prosecution for actions in France, though various junior personnel from the division were convicted and served minor sentences. He survived the war, prospering as an engineer in Düsseldorf until his death.

Standartenführer Christian Tychsen (1910–44)

Tychsen joined the SS in December 1931 with 50. SS-Standarte, transferred to 1. Sturm (*Germania*) in October 1934, and was a platoon leader in Bataillon 'N' from October 1936 until his appointment in December 1938 as CO of 1st Company. After 'N' was dissolved he led 1. Kradschützen-Ersatz Kompanie, which became 3./Reconnaissance Battalion in April 1940. In January 1942 Tychsen assumed overall command of the Motorcycle Battalion, but was wounded soon after and taught at Brunswick during recovery until May 1942. On his return to duty, he was given command of II./*Langemarck*, which became II./Panzer Regiment in October 1942. He was Panzer Regiment commander from 30 November 1943 until ordered to stand in as temporary CO of *Das Reich*. Wounded at least nine times, he was killed in Normandy while deputy divisional CO.

Standartenführer Otto Baum (1911–98)

Baum graduated with SS-Junkerschule Braunschweig's first class in 1935, and was posted as a platoon commander with 5./*Germania*. In 1938 he transferred to Regiment *Der Führer* as a platoon commander with 12th Company, and later moved to the *Leibstandarte* as 7th Company CO. In March 1941 he transferred to *Totenkopf* Division as a battalion commander and in this post won both the German Cross in Gold and the Knight's Cross. In 1943 he was promoted, and took command of Panzergrenadier-Regiment 5 *Totenkopf*. During battles in February and March he was awarded the Oakleaves. In June 1944 he commanded 17th SS Panzergrenadier-Division *Götz von Berlichingen*. He took command of *Das Reich* during the Normandy battles and led the division until replaced by Lammerding. For his leadership during the Falaise encirclement, Swords to his Knight's Cross were presented. He ended the war as commander of 16th SS Panzergrenadier Division *Reichsführer SS*.

Gruppenführer Werner Ostendorff (1903–45)

Ostendorff began his military career in 1925 with Jäger Regiment 1, remaining with the unit until enlisting in the Luftwaffe in March 1934. He qualified as a pilot and subsequently served in Russia under a technical exchange programme. After entering the SS as a commissioned officer on 1 October 1935, he was posted to Bad Tölz. After graduating Ostendorff took command of 4./*Der Führer* in April 1938, and led the company until appointed CO of the Anti-aircraft Machine Gun Battalion at its formation in June 1939. He remained with this unit until the Polish campaign when he acted as a staff observer with Panzer Group *Kempf*. Ostendorff was later appointed *Das Reich* chief of staff, and served in this capacity until 20 June 1942, during which time he was awarded the German Cross in Gold. In mid-1942, he became the chief of staff to the SS Panzer Corps and served with this unit at Kharkov and Kursk. On 23 November 1943 he was given command of the newly formed 17th SS Panzergrenadier Division *Götz von Berlichingen*. Wounded during the Normandy campaign, he recovered and returned to this command in October 1944, only to be wounded again in November. On 29 January he was appointed to command *Das Reich* and took up his post officially on 10 February . Wounded for a third time in Austria, he died in a field hospital on 1 May 1945.

Above: Werner Ostendorff received his Knight's Cross on 13 September 1941 as an SS-Obersturmbannführer and 1st Staff Officer from *Das Reich*, then operating as part of Army Group Centre, on the Russian Front. He is shown here as an SS-Oberführer.

Standartenführer Rudolf Lehmann (1914–83)

In April 1935 Rudolf Lehmann entered the officers' school in Bad Tölz, and upon graduation was assigned to *Germania*. During his service with *Germania* Lehmann was the commander of the armoured car platoon, and in April 1940 company commander of 14./*Germania*. After transferring to *Leibstandarte* in October 1940, Lehmann served as an ordnance officer until hospitalised in August 1941. A period of convalescence followed, then more training and a return to service in early June 1942 as chief operations' officer to *Leibstandarte*. After another stint in hospital, Lehmann was recommended for the Knight's Cross for his leadership of a battle group in the Zhitomir area during December 1943. In late 1944 Lehmann became chief of staff for I SS Panzer Corps. Here he remained until March 1945, when he assumed command of *Das Reich*, and subsequently won his Oakleaves. Also wounded during the fighting in Austria, Lehmann spent the remainder of the war recovering from his injuries.

OTHER NOTABLES

Oberscharführer Ernst Barkmann (1919–)

Barkmann joined the SS-VT in April 1939 with 9./*Germania* and served there until joining the Panzer Battalion. Wounded in Russia on 23 July 1941 near Dniepropetrovsk, he recovered with the replacement unit of *Wiking* (5th SS Panzer Division) then transferred to 2nd Company of the Panzer Regiment in 1942 and in January 1943 to 4th Company, where he remained until war's end. Promoted Oberscharführer on 1 August 1944, he was wounded in action five times and awarded the Gold Wound Badge and the '50' Tank Combat Badge.

Oberführer Fritz Klingenberg (1912–45)

Fritz Klingenberg joined SS-VT in 1934 and after graduating from the new SS-Junkerschule at Bad Tölz was promoted to Untersturmführer. He was first assigned to SS-Standarte *Germania*, then became one of the inspectors of the SS-VT. After the campaigns in the Low Countries, Klingenberg commanded a motorcycle company and it was during this command that he gained fame for the capture of Belgrade. Klingenberg lead the 2nd Company, Motorcycle Battalion, until 1942 when he transferred to the staff at Bad Tölz. In January 1945 Klingenberg assumed command of the 17th SS Panzergrenadier Division *Götz von Berlichingen*. He was killed near Herxheim while leading it.

Obersturmführer Karl Kloskowski (1917–45)

Kloskowski joined SS-VT with 3./*Germania* in December 1936. Later he served with 4./11. SS-Standarte until transferred back to the division in 1941 with 3./Reconnaissance Battalion. That unit became 3./Motorcycle Battalion and he stayed there until wounded on 16 November 1941. He was promoted to Hauptscharführer on 10 January 1943, and was later a platoon leader with 4./Panzer Regiment, and then regimental ordnance officer. He won the Knight's Cross for single-handedly preventing the destruction of an important bridge.

Obersturmführer Horst Gresiak (1920–)

Horst Gresiak joined the *Totenkopf* Standarte in September 1940 as a grenadier. After attending SS-Junkerschule Braunschweig (November 41 to April 42) he joined the *Das Reich* Panzer Battalion as a tank commander and later a platoon leader with 3rd Company. Later Gresiak moved to 7th Company as commander, and in this post was recommended for the Knight's Cross for actions around Baraque de Fraiture during the Battle of the Bulge.

DAS REICH SENIOR PERSONNEL

Commanding Officers
Oberstgruppenführer Paul Hausser (19 October 1939–14 October 1941)
Obergruppenführer Wilhelm Bittrich (14 October–31 December 1941)
Obergruppenführer Matthias Kleinheisterkamp (31 December 1941–19 April 1942)
Obergruppenführer Georg Keppler (19 April 1942–10 February 1943)
Brigadeführer Hebert-Ernst Vahl (10 February–18 March 1943)
Oberführer Kurt Brasack (18 March–3 April 1943)
Obergruppenführer Walter Krüger (3 April 1943–23 October 1943)
Gruppenführer Heinz Lammerding (23 October 1943–24 July 1944)
Standartenführer Christian Tychsen (24 July 1944–28 July 1944)
Brigadeführer Otto Baum (28 July 1944–23 October 1944)
Gruppenführer Heinz Lammerding (23 October 1944–20 January 1945)
Standartenführer Karl Kreutz (20 January 1945–29 January 1945)
Gruppenführer Werner Ostendorff (29 January 1945–9 March 1945)
Standartenführer Rudolf Lehmann (9 March 1945–13 April 1945)
Standartenführer Karl Kreutz (13 April 1945–8 May 1945)

Chiefs of Staff
Standartenführer Werner Ostendorff (1 April 1940–31 May 1942)
Obersturmbannführer Max Schultz (31 May 1942–22 May 1943)
Obersturmbannführer Georg Maier (23 May–? June 1943)
Obersturmbannführer Peter Sommer (20 June 1943–17 January 1944)
Obersturmbannführer Albert Stückler (18 January 1944–? Feb 1945)
Sturmbannführer Reinhardt Wörner (1 March–? March 1945)
Sturmbannführer Ralf Riemann (? March–30 April 1945)
Major Joachim Schiller (1–8 May 1945)

Quartermasters
Sturmbannführer Günther Ecke (1 April–30 November 1940)
Hauptsturmführer Eugen Kunstmann (1 December–21 December 1940)
Standartenführer Heinz Fansau (21 December 1940–? January 1941)
Hauptsturmführer Eugen Kunstmann (? January 1941–? 1942)
Sturmbannführer Alfred Jantseh (1 March–10 August 1942)
Hauptsturmführer Fritz Steinbeck (9 November 1942–? 1943)
Sturmbannführer Heino von Goldacker (31 July 1943–1 March 1945)

Emil Seibold (1907–90)

Emil Seibold entered the SS in April 1940 as an infantryman with the *Totenkopf* Standarte. In November 1940 he was transferred to *Das Reich* and joined the 3./Tank Destroyer Battalion, serving the company first as a motorcycle driver and later as a gun commander. In March 1943 the remnants of the battalion were given T-34s, with which Seibold scored many kills and went on to become one of the division's most successful tank aces. He was awarded one of the last Knight's Crosses of *Das Reich* after scoring his 65th kill.

Obersturmführer Fritz Langanke (1919–)

Fritz Langanke served *Germania* from 1937, first as an infantryman with 10th Company, in 1938 as a radio operator with the armoured reconnaissance platoon, and later a vehicle commander. In 1942 he moved to the Panzer Battalion and was a tank commander in the reconnaissance platoon. When the division was reformed in late 1943 Langanke was assigned to the 1st Battalion as an ordnance officer. He took command of 2nd Company on 25 December 1944, and remained at this post till the end of the war.

Hauptsturmführer Karl-Heinz Boska (1920–)

Boska joined *Das Reich* in June 1940, after six months with 1st Company of Kradschützen-Ersatz-Bataillon *Ellwangen*. During the western campaigns he was a motorcycle rider with 3./Reconnaissance Battalion, and gained promotion to Sturmmann on 1 November 1940. He stayed with 3rd Company when it was absorbed by the Motorcycle Battalion in February 1941, and won promotion to Unterscharführer on 1 September of that year. There followed a period of schooling and then assignment first as a platoon commander to 7./*Langemarck*, then in October 1942 to 2nd Battalion *Das Reich* Panzer Regiment of which he subsequently became adjutant. He won the Knight's Cross for combat action during November 1943, and after the death of the commander, Boska was 6th Company commander until promoted in the last weeks of the war to overall command of 2nd Battalion.

Sturmbannführer Ernst August Krag (1915–)

After joining 5./*Germania* in 1935, Krag undertook paratroop training at the Luftwaffe school at Stendal, and following his return to the division was promoted to Unterscharführer. He graduated from Bad Tolz in August 1939, and also attended the Jüterbog Artillery School. Posted as battery officer to 3. Battery, in 1940 he was then made adjutant of the 1st Battalion. During the first Russian campaigns, Krag led the 11. (schwere) Batterie, but was severely wounded in January 1942 and forced to return to Germany. Rejoining the unit, he was posted as artillery regimental adjutant and held that post until October, when he moved to the Assault Gun Battalion as commander of 2nd Battery. In August 1943 he took temporary command of the battalion and the following July he became CO of the Reconnaissance Battalion. In this post, Krag was awarded the Knight's Cross and the only Oakleaves given to a member of the Reconnaissance Battalion.

Sturmbannführer Siegfried Brosow (1918–)

Brosow joined the SS-VT in November 1937 and was assigned to the Pioneer Recruit Battalion. After graduating from Brunswick in 1940, he went to command the Bridging Section. The following February he was wounded, and spent time convalescing as an instructor at Bad Tölz, and from the autumn of 1942 at the Pioneer School. In January 1943 he returned to his battalion as 1st Company CO and held that command until he appointed to the divisional staff in October 1943. Prior to the Normandy Campaign he assumed full command of the Pioneer Battalion and led it until February 1945. Brosow ended the war as a senior officer at the Pioneer School.

Above: Emil Seibold, born in Basel, Switzerland on 26 February 1907, was the highest scoring tank ace in *Das Reich*. He is seen here as an SS-Oberscharführer, platoon leader in the 8th Company of SS Panzer Regiment 2. In June 1944 he received the German Cross in Gold and on 6 May 1945 he was awarded the Knight's Cross to commemorate his 65th tank kill, another very late war award and the last awarded in the Panzer Regiment. Emil Seibold died on 11 September 1990.

Above right: SS-Oberführer Georg Keppler. He was awarded the Knight's Cross for his part during the Western campaign and the fighting in the Netherlands (15.8.1940). At that time he was CO of SS Regiment *Der Führer*, then part of the SS-Verfügungs Division of the Eighteenth Army.

Right: SS-Brigadeführer und Generalmajor der Waffen-SS Herbert Ernst Vahl. He received his Knight's Cross on 31 March 1943 when he was an SS-Oberführer and commander of *Das Reich*.

Obersturmbannführer Hans-Albin, Freiherr von Reitzenstein (1911–43)

Reitzenstein joined the Allgemeine-SS in 1931, and served with *Leibstandarte* before moving to *Deutschland*. Wounded in Poland, he convalesced at Bad Tolz. In December 1940 he became CO of the Recce Battalion of the new SS Division *Germania*. In 1942 he was transferred to *Das Reich* and led the Recce Battalion through Russia until March 1943 when he replaced Vahl as Panzer Regiment commander. He won the Knight's Cross for actions at Belgorod, the Mius, Kharkov and Kolomak in which the regiment destroyed 839 tanks, 18 assault guns, 334 anti-tank weapons and 32 other guns. He committed suicide in November 1943.

Brigadeführer Herbert Vahl (1896–1944)

Vahl served as an Army officer with Regiment 29 in 12th Panzer Division, before he was assigned to the SS general staff in 1942. When SS Panzer Battalion 2 was expanded to Panzer Regiment 2, Vahl was made commander. When Keppler fell ill in February 1943, Vahl briefly commanded *Das Reich*, leading the division in the battles of Kharkov and near Belgorod, for which he was awarded the Knight's Cross. Subsequently wounded, he was forced to relinquish command, and was assigned to the SS training staff as Inspector of Armoured Troops. From July 1944 he was CO of 4th SS Polizei-Grenadier Division and was killed in a road accident.

Brigadeführer Georg Keppler (1894–1966)

From 1920–35 Keppler served in police units, before joining the SS-VT. As a Sturmbannführer, he took command of 1st Battalion of Standarte 1 *Deutschland* on 10 October 1935, a post he held until early 1938 when tasked with forming *Der Führer*. He led this unit through the pre-war period, and continued as regimental commander after its amalgamation into *Das Reich*. In July 1941, after leading the division in Russia, Keppler became the CO of *Totenkopf* for a brief spell then spent the remainder of 1941 recovering from a brain tumour. After convalescing, he became *Das Reich* divisional commander when it reformed as a panzergrenadier division, and led the division until February 1943, when recurrent illness forced him to relinquish his post. Following a number of admin positions within the Waffen-SS he returned to lead I SS Panzer Corps in Normandy, then from 30 October 1944 to February 1945 was CO of III SS Panzer Corps on the Eastern Front. Keppler ended the war as commander of XVIII SS Army Corps.

Sturmbannführer Dieter Kesten (1914–45)

Kesten entered the Allgemeine-SS in September 1933, serving first with the 79. and 7. Standarten before he commenced officer training at Brunswick in April 1936. Upon commissioning he was assigned to II./*Germania*, and in September 1938 became ordnance officer. Leaving *Germania* in May 1940, he held various staff positions. In May 1942 he joined *Das Reich*, first as a company CO in *Langemarck* and then divisional adjutant. Later that year he moved to the Panzer Regiment and was 6th Company commander until November 1943, at which time he became CO of 2nd Battalion. He was killed fighting for Vienna in April 1945.

Obersturmbannführer Friedrich Holzer (1912–84)

Prior to joining *Germania* in October 1936, Holzer served with SS Standarte 11. He graduated from Brunswick in 1939, was posted to Regiment *Der Führer* as a platoon commander and in May 1939 assumed the same position with 11th Company. Following a stint as an ordnance officer, Holzer was transferred to 7./*Der Führer*, attained the position of 7th Company commander in late 1941 and in January 1942 became regimental adjutant. For actions around Rzhev in February 1942 he was awarded the German Cross in Gold. In early 1943 Holzer moved to the Panzer Regiment, and later became 2nd Company OC where he won the Knight's Cross. Holzer ended the war as CO Panzer Regiment *Holzer* (SS Panzer Brigade *Westfalen*).

ASSESSMENT

Above: A hot summer's day on a Russian country road. A Waffen-SS machine gunner pauses to look at the surrounding fields without unshouldering his M 34. Note that his machine gun is in the belt-fed mode, ready for quick action, with the cartridge belt looped around his left elbow.

If we first take *Das Reich* on its purely military merits one statistic throws its achievements into bold relief. More Knight's Crosses (69) were awarded to its troops than to those of any other Waffen-SS division. But perhaps the best accolade a soldier can ever receive is from another. General Guderian said of *Das Reich*:

'I have encountered the SS Division *Leibstandarte* and the *Das Reich* in battle and later, as General-Inspector of Panzer Troops, have inspected the Waffen-SS divisions many times. They always distinguished themselves through their self-discipline, comradeship and good soldierly behaviour in battle. They fought shoulder-to-shoulder with the Army panzer divisions and became, the more so the longer the war lasted, "one of us".'

If one singles out individual actions, of particular note were the role that *Das Reich* played in the capture of Belgrade, the advance to Moscow, the Kursk action, the rescue at Falaise and the retreat from Vienna. In each of these the division made an inestimable contribution, resulting not always in victory but at least in honourable defeat. Also worthy of mention are the countless acts of selfless sacrifice by *Das Reich* troops for their brothers-in-arms, most graphically demonstrated in the rescue operations at Falaise, and finally Prague.

The darker side of the *Das Reich* history is again best quantified by someone well placed to know, Kurt 'Panzer' Meyer, former commander of 12th SS Panzer Division *Hitler Jugend*:

'In the interests of historical truth nothing must be glossed over. Things happened during the war that are unworthy of the German nation. The former soldiers of the Waffen-SS are men enough to recognise and deplore actual cases of inhuman behaviour. It would be foolish to label all the charges laid at our doorstep as the propaganda of our former enemies. Of course they made propaganda out of it... But crimes were committed. It is useless to argue about the toll of victims – the facts are burdensome enough.'

There are plenty of people who would condemn *Das Reich* soldiers for their beliefs, and actions during the war, without truly understanding or trying to understand the motivations of this unique band of fighting men. There are also many apologists, who seek to defend the acts of brutality as an inescapable and therefore, it is implied, excusable facet of warfare. The most honest appraisal lies somewhere between the two.

At the Nuremberg Trials the Waffen-SS was indicted as a criminal organisation. The leaders of the Wehrmacht who were put on trial insisted that all the atrocities in combat were committed by the Waffen-SS and not by regular Army units, and although members of the SS countered that the Nuremberg verdict was directed at the SS as a whole and did not establish individual guilt, the stigma attached to the SS because of its involvement in the Holocaust was thereafter applied to every front line soldier of the Waffen-SS

Thus, SS men were often singled out for harsh treatment by their captors, regardless of their personal complicity in acts of brutality. Those who passed into Russian captivity were rarely seen again. Many of those who did return to civilian life in Germany found it difficult to find work. A number found their way to Algeria to join the French Foreign Legion, which at the time asked no questions and offered anonymity to its soldiers, and subsequently fought in French Indo-China (now Vietnam). There they served with distinction against the Communist forces of Ho Chi Minh. It has been said by one ex-SS Foreign Legionnaire that all France's successes in the ultimately unsuccessful campaign in Indo-China were achieved by the French Paras or the German brigade of the Foreign Legion. The German brigade continued to fight as a unit until public pressure forced the French government to disband it. Even to this day, the 'Horst Wessel' marching song is sung by legionnaires, no doubt introduced by the German legionnaires in Indo-China.

Below: A lonely grave in a Russian field for a Waffen-SS machine gunner.

REFERENCE

INTERNET SITES

www.dasreich.ca
In depth look at operational history, unit designations, commanding officers, personnel, order of battle etc.

www.eliteforces.freewire.co.uk
Another comprehensive listing of facts and figures, with specific information on the SS and *Das Reich*.

www.feldgrau.com
This is probably the most comprehensive site dealing with the German Army before and during World War II currently on the web. Well-written and researched.

General

www.skalman.nu/third-reich
The Third Reich Factbook. Currently one of the most detailed sources of information on the Third Reich.

www.onwar.com/maps
Campaign maps from World War II and other wars.

www.tankclub.agava.ru/sign/sign.shtml
Russian-language site with excellent illustrations of the tactical signs of the German Army.

www.geocities.com/Pentagon/3620/
Achtung Panzer! Interesting site with very detailed information on German armour. Great colour pictures of preserved vehicles.

Re-enactment Groups

www.ssdeutschland.org/ss.htm
US-based unit of *Deutschland* Regiment re-enactors. Visit the site for more information on membership.

www.reenactor.net/ww2/units/2SS

SELECT BIBLIOGRAPHY

Knights of Steel: The Structure, Development and Personalities of the 2. SS-Panzer Division 'Das Reich', 2 vols.

With a foreword by one-time division CO Otto Baum, this covers unit composition, formation, and development. Complete biographies for each unit commander, Knight's Cross holder and all German Cross holders with data for each.

Bando, Mark, *Breakout at Normandy: The 2nd Armored Division in the Land of the Dead*.
First-hand accounts of the fighting to break out of Normandy on the part of the US 2nd Armored Division, including actions against *Das Reich*.

Hastings, Max, *Das Reich*, Michael Joseph, 1981
Brilliant retelling of the march of the division from the south of France to the D-Day beaches, June 1944.

Lucas, James, *Das Reich: The Military Role of the 2nd SS Panzer Division*, Arms and Armour, 1991.
Well written and researched history of the division from formation to destruction, based on interviews with the participants and including many personal accounts.

Moiller, N., and Restayn, J., *Operation Citadel*, Vol 1, J.J. Fedorowicz Publishing.
First volume of 2-volume photo study of the Battle of Kursk covering the southern sector of the attack culminating in the tank battle at Prokhorovka. A detailed day-by-day description of the actions of all German units involved in the attack in this sector is also included.

Nipe, George M. Jnr., *Decision in the Ukraine*, J.J. Fedorowicz Publishing.
The full story of the crucial battles on the Mius River by the Sixth Army and the successful counter-attack spearheaded by the II SS Panzer Corps, consisting of *Das Reich* and *Totenkopf*. Also covered in detail are the battles after Kursk.

Weidinger, Otto, *Das Reich*, J.J. Fedorowicz Publishing.
A 5-volume set, covering the division from its formation in 1934 to the conclusion of the war. An abundance of first-hand accounts and innumerable maps make this a first-class divisional history.

Winter, George, *Freineux and Lamormenil the Ardennes*, J.J. Fedorowicz Publishing.
Actions of elements of *Das Reich* and 'Task Force Kane' of the 3rd (US) Armored Division during the Battle of the Bulge in December 1944.

General Reference

Ailsby, C., *Images of Barbarosa*, Ian Allan Publishing 2001.

Angolia, J.R., and Schlicht, Adolf, *Uniforms & Traditions of the German Army*, Vol I.

Bender, R., and Odegard, W., *Panzertruppe – Uniforms, Organization and History*, Bender 1980.
Panzer formations 1935–45, panzer uniforms and insignia, panzer markings and camouflage are all given in detail.

Chamberlain, Peter & Ellis, Chris *Pictorial History of Tanks of the World 1915–45*, Arms and Armour, 1979.
Illustrates their technological and tactical development and examines the reasons why armoured fighting vehicles dominated the battlefield.

Culver, Bruce, & Murphy, Bill, *Panzer Colours*, Vol. 1.
170 illustrations with 69 full-colour plates provide the most detailed account of German armour during World War II.

Delaney, John, *The Blitzkrieg Campaigns: Germany's 'lightning war' strategy in action*, Arms and Armour, 1996.
Describes the origins of the strategy developed during the interwar years and studies how this technique was used during the advances into Poland, Belgium, France and Russia.

Dunnigan, James F. (ed.), *The Russian Front: Germany's War in the East, 1941–45*, Arms and Armour, 1978.

Ellis, C., & Chamberlain, P., *German Tanks and Fighting Vehicles of WWII*, Pheobus, 1976.
This tells of the secret training machines of the Weimar period, through the innovative and experimental phase, to World War II itself.

Erickson, John. *The Road to Stalingrad* & *The Road to Berlin*, Weidenfeld and Nicolson.
A definitive two-volume study of Stalin's war with Germany.

Fey, Will *Armor Battles of the Waffen-SS 1943–45*, J.J. Fedorowicz Publishing.

Fomichenko, Major Gen. *The Red Army*, Hutchinson.
Studies the development of the Soviet Army and its exploits from June 1941 when Germany launched Operation Barbarossa. Analyses how the Red Army foiled Hitler's plans for German 'living space' by victoriously pushing back the Axis forces from the Volga and the Caucasus into the Reich itself.

Fowler, W. *Blittzkrieg: 1 — Poland & Scandinavia 1939-1940*, Ian Allan Publishing 2002.

Fowler, W. *Blittzkrieg: 2 — France, Holland & Belgium 1940*, Ian Allan Publishing 2002.

Fowler, W. *Blittzkrieg: 3 — Russia 1941-1942*, Ian Allan Publishing 2002.

Fugate, B. *Operation Barbarossa: Strategy and Tactics 1941*, Spa Books, 1989.
Studies Hitler's surprise offensive against Russia and analyses his strategy and tactics on the Eastern Front during 1941.

Glantz, David, *From the Don to the Dneiper*.
Illustrations with detailed maps are included in this analysis of Red Army operations – eight vital months of struggle that finally ended Hitler's Blitzkrieg against the USSR.

Haupt, Werner, *A History of Panzer Troops 1916–1945*, Schiffer, 1990.
An illustrated study of German armour from the Battle of Cambrai in 1916 to the 1944 Ardennes offensive and the struggle to defend Berlin.

Jentz, Thomas L., *Panzertruppen*, Vol 1, 1933–42, Vol. II, 1943–45, Schiffer, 1966.
A complete guide to the creation, organization and combat employment of Germany's tank force.

Kershaw R.J., *War Without Garlands, Operation Barbarosa 1941/42*. Ian Allan Publishing, 2000.

Krawczyk, Wade, *German Army Uniforms of World War II*. Windrow and Greene, 1995.

Kurowski, Franz, *Knights of the Wehrmacht*.
A study of the Knight's Cross holders.

Lucas, James, *War on the Eastern Front, the German soldier in Russia 1941–1945*, Jane's, 1979.
An account, from the German angle, of the war against the Soviet Union.

Lucas, James, *Battle Group – German Kampfgruppen Action of WWII*, BCA, 1994.
The story of how Hitler's shock troops contributed to German military operations.

Lucas, James, *The Last Year of the German Army: May 1944 – May 45*, BCA, 1994.
A complete study of structural changes to overcome its depletion and an insight into some of its last battles.

Lucas, James, & Cooper, Matthew, *Panzer Grenadiers*, BCA, 1977.
Excellent background on the panzer-grenadier units.

Messenger, Charles, *The Art of Blitzkrieg*, Ian Allan, 1976.
Studies Blitzkrieg's evolution as a technique of war and describes how Hitler used the theory of 'lightning war' so effectively.

Meyer, Kurt, *Grenadiers*, J.J. Fedorowicz Publishing.
Meyer's autobiography offers a fascinating insight into the life at the front.

Mitcham, S.A., Jnr., *Hitler's Legions*, Leo Cooper, 1985.
The organisation and technical aspects of the German divisions are described. Every part of the Army is covered.

Perrett, Bryan: *Knights of the Black Cross*, Robert Hale, 1986.
A history of the German armoured corps and its commanders who led Hitler's conquest during 1939–42 and later formed the backbone of Germany's defence.

Piekalkiewicz, Janusz, *Operation Citadel*, Presidio, 1987.
A complete illustrated analysis of the battles of Kursk and Orel.

Restayn, Jean, *Battle for Kharkov*, J.J. Fedorowicz Publishing.
Good photo coverage of the German recapture of Kharkov in early 1943, showcasing armour, uniforms and other equipment.

Seaton, Albert, *The German Army, 1933–1945*, Weidenfeld and Nicolson, 1982.
A full length analytical study of the German Army.

Williamson, Gordon, *The SS: Hitler's Instrument of Terror*, Motorbooks International, 1994.
Well-illustrated and well-informed general history of the rise and fall of the SS.

Below: A 10.5cm LeFH 18, 1940 model with a muzzle brake fitted to the barrel to take a more powerful charge to achieve a longer range. It belongs to the 2nd Company of *Das Reich*'s Artillery Regiment.

Abbreviations

AC	Armoured car
APC	Armoured personnel carrier
Arty	Artillery
Atk	Anti-tank
BdE	Befehlshaber des Ersatzheeres (Commander of Replacement Army)
Bn	Battalion
Brig	Brigade
Bty	Battery
Coy	Company
Engr	Engineer
FBK	Führerbegleit-kommando
Hy	Heavy
leFH	leichte Feldhaubitze (light field gun)
LAH/LSSAH	Leibstandarte-SS Adolf Hitler
Lt	Lieutenant; light
MC	Motorcycle
Mor	Mortar
Mot	Motorised
NSDAP	Nationalsozialistische Deutsche Arbeiterpartei (Nazi party)
OKW	Oberkommando der Wehrmacht
OKH	Oberkommando des Heeres
Pak	Panzerabwehrkanone (anti-tank gun)
Pl	Platoon
PzBefWag	Panzerbefehls-wagen (armd comd vehicle)
PzGr	Panzergrenadier
PzJr	Panzerjäger
PzKpfw	Panzerkampfwagen tank
RHQ	Regimental HQ
SA	Sturmabteilung
Sect	Section
Sig	Signals
SP	Self-propelled
SPW	Schützen Panzer Wagen (APC)
SS	Schutzstaffel
SS-VT	SS-Verfügungstruppe (militarised troops)
Tk	Tank
WH	Wehrmacht Heer (as in car and MC numberplates)

Dates

20/7/54	20 July 1954.

INDEX

ELITE ATTACK FORCES: WAFFEN-SS

Phoney War, The, 18

Poland 1939, 14–17

Polish units: Brigades — Wielpolska Cavalry, 16; Wolwyska Cavalry, 16
Divisions — 10th Infantry, 15, 16; 17th Infantry, 16; 25th Infantry, 16

Priess, H., 49, 59

Punishment, Operation 118, 119

Reichenau, W. von, 14, 15, 16, 17, 39

Reinhardt, Hauptsturmführer Johann 139

Reinhardt, G-H., 16, 19

Reiser, Michael 152

Reitzenstein, Hans-Albin von 142, 181

Ridgway, M., 59

Röhm, Ernst 99

Rokossovsky, K., 48

Romanian units: Third Army, 43; Sixth Army, 43

Rommel, E., 19, 25, 47, 112, 128

Rosenberg, Alfred 104

Rozan 109

Rundstedt, G. von, 14, 19, 21, 23, 30, 34, 39, 42, 55, 58, 84, 108, 112, 145, 152

Russian units: 2nd Tank Army 137; 3rd Army 125; 5th Guards Tank Army 45; 32nd Siberian Division 125

Russian-Polish War 106

Seibold, Emil 180

Seyss-Inquart, Artur 105

Siegrunen (SS Runes) 158

Smigly, Rydz 110

Soviet units: Fronts — 1st Belorussian, 65; 1st Ukrainian, 52, 53, 54, 65; 2nd Ukrainian, 52, 53, 54, 64, 65; 3rd Ukrainian, 52, 54, 63, 64, 65; 4th Ukrainian, 52, 63;
Armies — First Tank, 53; Fifth Guards Tank, 49, 50, 54; Seventh Guards, 63; Ninth, 39; Thirty-seventh, 39;
Others — 1st Guards Armoured Brigade, 49; V Guards Armoured Corps, 53; VIII Guards Armoured Corps, 53; I Guard Cavalry Corps, 53

SA, 6–9, 10, 84

Sandig, R., 27, 60, 62

Smigdly-Rydz, E., Röhm, 6–9

Sonderkommandos: Berlin, 8, 9, 22; Jüterbog, 9, 22; Zossen, 8, 9, 22

Springer, H., 39

SS-VT, 10, 11, 12, 17, 18, 44, 70, 85, 86, 87, 88

Stabswache, 6, 7, 8, 22

Stadler, Sylvester 104, 140

Stalin, Josef 129

Steiner, F., 12, 101, 103, 104, 118

Stosstrupp Hitler, 6, 7

Student, K., 21, 60

Sudetenland, 13

Tiger Company 133, 172

Tolbukhin, F., 51, 63, 64

Totenkopf (Death's Head) 158

Tychsen, Christian 133, 178

US units: Armies — First , 58; Third , 59; Fifth, 51; Seventh, 62; Others — XVIII Corps, 59; 82nd Airborne Division, 62

Vahl, Herbert 181

Vatutin, F., 48, 50, 54

Wagner, Jürgen 157

Warsaw 109, 110

Weichs, M. von, 25, 43, 120, 121

Weidinger, Otto 120

Wessel, Horst 104

Wisch, T., 9, 27, 48, 85, 87

Witt, F., 27, 43, 57, 86

Wittmann, M., 56, 87

Worthmann, Karl-Heinz 132, 133

Wunsche, M., 25, 27

Yugoslavia 1941, 25

Zeitzler, K., 47, 48

Zhukov, G., 48, 53, 54, 125, 127, 133

Zimmermann, Herbert 133